James Macpherson

Morison's Edition of the Poems of Ossian, the Son of Fingal

James Macpherson

Morison's Edition of the Poems of Ossian, the Son of Fingal

ISBN/EAN: 9783741139963

Manufactured in Europe, USA, Canada, Australia, Japa

Cover: Foto ©Andreas Hilbeck / pixelio.de

Manufactured and distributed by brebook publishing software (www.brebook.com)

James Macpherson

Morison's Edition of the Poems of Ossian, the Son of Fingal

MORISON's EDITION

OF THE

POEMS

OF

OSSIAN,

THE

SON OF FINGAL.

TRANSLATED

BY JAMES MACPHERSON, Esq;

CAREFULLY CORRECTED, AND GREATLY IMPROVED,

WITH A SETT OF ELEGANT ENGRAVINGS,
FROM ORIGINAL DRAWINGS, BY STOTHARD AND ALLAN,

VOLUME FIRST.

WE MAY BOLDLY ASSIGN OSSIAN A PLACE AMONG THOSE
WHOSE WORKS ARE TO LAST FOR AGES.   BLAIR.

PERTH:

PRINTED BY R. MORISON JUNIOR,
FOR R. MORISON & SON, BOOKSELLERS, PERTH.

M,DCC,XCV.

CONTENTS

OF THE

FIRST VOLUME.

	Page.
A Dissertation concerning the Æra of Ossian's Poems	v
Fingal, Book I.	1
Book II.	23
Book III.	41
Book IV.	59
Book V.	75
Book VI.	91
Comala.	129
The War of Caros,	133
War of Inis-thona,	144
Battle of Lora,	153
Conlath and Cuthona,	165
Carthon,	172
Death of Cuchullin,	193
Dar-thula,	207
Carric-thura,	229
Songs of Selma,	250
Clathon and Colmal,	262
Lathmon,	274
Oithona,	291
Croma,	301
Berrathon,	313

A DISSERTATION

CONCERNING THE

ÆRA OF OSSIAN.

INQUIRIES into the antiquities of nations afford more pleasure than any real advantage to mankind. The ingenious may form systems of history on probabilities and a few facts; but at a great distance of time, their accounts must be vague and uncertain. The infancy of states and kingdoms is as destitute of great events, as of the means of transmitting them to posterity. The arts of polished life, by which alone facts can be preserved with certainty, are the productions of a well-formed community. It is then historians begin to write, and public transactions to be worthy remembrance. The actions of former times are left in obscurity, or magnified by uncertain traditions. Hence it is that we find so much of the marvellous in the origin of every nation; posterity being always ready to believe any thing, however fabulous, that reflects honour on their ancestors. The Greeks and Romans were remarkable for this weakness. They swallowed the most absurd fables concerning the high antiquities of their respective nations. Good historians, however, rose very early amongst them, and transmitted, with lustre, their great actions to posterity. It is to them that they owe that unrivalled fame they now enjoy, while the great actions of other nations are involved in fables, or lost in obscurity. The Celtic nations afford a striking instance of this kind. They, though once the masters of Europe from the mouth of the river Oby*, in Russia, to Cape Finistere, the western point of Gallicia in Spain, are very little mentioned in history. They trusted their fame to tradition and the songs of their bards, which, by the vicissitude of human affairs, are long since lost. Their ancient language is the only monument that remains of them: and the traces of it being found in places so widely distant of each other, serves only to shew the extent of their ancient power, but throws very little light on their history.

Of all the Celtic nations, that which possessed old Gaul is the most renowned; not perhaps on account of worth
superior

* Plin. L 6.

superior to the rest, but for their wars with a people who had historians to transmit the fame of their enemies, as well as their own, to posterity. Britain was first peopled by them, according to the testimony of the best authors *; its situation in respect to Gaul makes the opinion probable; but what puts it beyond all dispute, is, that the same customs and language prevailed among the inhabitants of both in the days of Julius Cæsar †.

The colony from Gaul possessed themselves, at first, of that part of Britain which was next to their own country; and spreading northward, by degrees, as they increased in numbers, peopled the whole island. Some adventurers passing over from those parts of Britain that are within sight of Ireland, were the founders of the Irish nation: which is a more probable story than the idle fables of Milesian and Gallician colonies. Diodorus Siculus ‡ mentions it as a thing well known in his time, that the inhabitants of Ireland were originally Britons; and his testimony is unquestionable, when we consider that, for many ages, the language and customs of both nations were the same.

Tacitus was of opinion that the ancient Caledonians were of German extract. By the language and customs which always prevailed in the north of Scotland, and which are undoubtedly Celtic, one would be tempted to differ in opinion from that celebrated writer. The Germans, properly so called, were not the same with the ancient Celtæ. The manners and customs of the two nations were similar; but their language different. The Germans ‖ are the genuine descendants of the ancient Dae, afterwards well known by the name of Daci, and passed originally into Europe by the way of the northern countries, and settled beyond the Danube, towards the vast regions of Transilvania, Wallachia, and Moldavia; and from thence advanced by degrees into Germany. The Celtæ §, it is certain, sent many colonies into that country, all of whom retained their own laws, language, and customs: and it is of them, if any colonies came from Germany into Scotland, that the ancient Caledonians were descended.

But whether the Caledonians were a colony of the Celtic Germans, or the same with the Gauls that first possessed themselves of Britain, is a matter of no moment at this distance of time. Whatever their origin was, we find them very numerous in the time of Julius Agricola, which is a presumption

* Cæf. l. 5. Tac. Agric. l. 1. c. 2.
† Cæf. Pomp. Mel. Tacitus.   ‡ Diod. Sic. l. 5.
‖ Strabo, l. 7.   § Cæf. l. 6. Liv. l. 5. Tac. de mor. Germ.

presumption that they were long before settled in the country. The form of their government was a mixture of aristocracy and monarchy, as it was in all the countries where the Druids bore the chief sway. This order of men seems to have been formed on the same system with the Dactyli Idæi and Curetes of the ancients. Their pretended intercourse with heaven, their magic and divination were the same. The knowledge of the Druids in natural causes, and the properties of certain things, the fruit of the experiments of ages gained them a mighty reputation among the people. The esteem of the populace soon increased into a veneration for the order; which a cunning and ambitious tribe of men took care to improve, to such a degree, that they, in a manner, ingrossed the management of civil, as well as religious matters. It is generally allowed that they did not abuse this extraordinary power; the preserving their character of sanctity was so essential to their influence, that they never broke out into violence or oppression. The chiefs were allowed to execute the laws, but the legislative power was entirely in the hands of the Druids*. It was by their authority that the tribes were united, in times of the greatest danger, under one head. The temporary king, or Vergobretus †, was chosen by them, and generally laid down his office at the end of the war. These priests enjoyed long this extraordinary privilege among the Celtic nations who lay beyond the pale of the Roman empire. It was in the beginning of the second century that their power among the Caledonians began to decline. The poems that celebrate Trathal and Cormac, ancestors to Fingal, are full of particulars concerning the fall of the Druids, which account for the total silence concerning their religion in the poems that are now given to the public.

The continual wars of the Caledonians against the Romans hindered the nobility from initiating themselves, as the custom formerly was, into the order of the Druids. The precepts of their religion were confined to a few, and were not much attended to by a people inured to war. The Vergobretus, or chief magistrate, was chosen without the concurrence of hierarchy, or continued in his office against their will. Continual power strengthened his interest among the tribes, and enabled him to send down, as hereditary to his posterity, the office he had only received himself by election.

On occasion of a new war against the *King of the World*, as the poems emphatically call the Roman emperor, the Druids

* Cæsl. 6.   † Fer-gubreth, *the man to judge.*

Druids, to vindicate the honour of the order, began to resume their ancient privilege of chusing the Vergobretus. Garmal, the son of Tarno, being deputed by them, came to the grandfather of the celebrated Fingal, who was then Vergobretus, and commanded him, in the name of the whole order to lay down his office. Upon his refusal, a civil war commenced, which soon ended in almost the total extinction of the religious order of the Druids. A few that remained, retired to the dark recesses of their groves, and the caves they had formerly used for their meditations. It is then we find them in *the circle of stones*, and unheeded by the world. A total disregard for the order, and utter abhorrence of the Druidical rites ensued. Under this cloud of public hate, all that had any knowledge of the religion of the Druids became extinct, and the nation fell into the last degree of ignorance of their rites and ceremonies.

It is no matter of wonder then, that Fingal and his son Ossian make so little, if any, mention of the Druids, who were the declared enemies to their succession in the supreme magistracy. It is a singular case, it must be allowed, that there are no traces of religion in the poems ascribed to Ossian; as the poetical compositions of other nations are so closely connected with their mythology. It is hard to account for it to those who are not made acquainted with the manner of the old Scottish bards. That race of men carried their notions of martial honour to an extravagant pitch. Any aid given their heroes in battle, was thought to derogate from their fame; and the bards immediately transferred the glory of the action to him who had given that aid. Had Ossian brought down gods, as often as Homer hath done, to assist his heroes, this poem had not consisted of eulogiums on his friends, but of hymns to these superior beings. To this day, those that write in the Gaelic language seldom mention religion in their profane poetry; and when they professedly write of religion, they never interlard with their compositions, the actions of their heroes. This custom alone, even though the religion of the Druids had not been previously extinguished, may, in some measure, account for Ossian's silence concerning the religion of his own times.

To say, that a nation is void of all religion, is the same thing as to say, that it does not consist of people endued with reason. The traditions of their fathers, and their own observations on the works of nature, together with that superstition which is inherent in the human frame, have, in all ages, raised in the minds of men some idea of a superior being. Hence it is, that in the darkest times, and amongst
the

THE ÆRA OF OSSIAN.

the moſt barbarous nations, the very populace themſelves had ſome faint notion, at leaſt, of a divinity. It would be doing injuſtice to Oſſian, who, upon no occaſion, ſhews a narrow mind, to think, that he had not opened his conceptions to that primitive and greateſt of all truths. But let Oſſian's religion be what it will, it is certain he had no knowledge of Chriſtianity, as there is not the leaſt alluſion to it, or any of its rites, in his poems; which abſolutely fixes him to an æra prior to the introduction of that religion. The perſecution begun by Diocleſian, in the year 303, is the moſt probable time in which the firſt dawning of Chriſtianity in the north of Britain can be fixed. The humane and mild character of Conſtantius Chlorus, who commanded them in Britain, induced the perſecuted Chriſtians to take refuge under him. Some of them, through a zeal to propagate their tenets, or through fear, went beyond the pale of the Roman empire, and ſettled among the Caledonians; who were the more ready to hearken to their doctrines, as the religion of the Druids had been exploded ſo long before.

Theſe miſſionaries, either through choice, or to give more weight to the doctrine they advanced, took poſſeſſion of the cells and groves of the Druids; and it was from this retired life they had the name of *Culdees* *, which language of the country ſignified *ſequeſtered perſons*. It was with one of the *Culdees* that Oſſian, in his extreme old age, is ſaid to have diſputed concerning the Chriſtian religion. This diſpute is ſtill extant, and is couched in verſe, according to the cuſtom of the times. The extreme ignorance on the part of Oſſian, of the Chriſtian tenets, ſhews, that that religion had only been lately introduced, as it is not eaſy to conceive, how one of the firſt rank could be totally unacquainted with a religion that had been known for any time in the country. The diſpute bears the genuine marks of antiquity. The obſolete phraſes and expreſſions peculiar to the times, prove it to be no forgery. If Oſſian then lived at the introduction of Chriſtianity, as by all appearance he did, his epoch will be the latter end of the third, and beginning of the fourth century. What puts this point beyond diſpute, is the alluſion in his poems to the hiſtory of the times.

The exploits of Fingal againſt Caracul †, the ſon of the *King of the World*, are among the firſt brave actions of his youth. A complete poem, which relates to this ſubject, is printed in this collection.

* Culdich. † Carac'huil, *terrible eye.* Carac'heallæ, *terrible look.* Carac-challamh, *a ſort of upper garment.*

A DISSERTATION CONCERNING

In the year 210 the emperor Severus, after returning from his expeditions against the Caledonians, at York fell into the tedious illness of which he afterwards died. The Caledonians and Maiatæ, resuming courage from his indisposition, took arms in order to recover the possessions they had lost. The enraged emperor commanded his army to march into their country, and to destroy it with fire and sword. His orders were but ill executed, for his son, Caracalla, was at the head of the army, and his thoughts were entirely taken up with the hopes of his father's death, and with schemes to supplant his brother Geta. He scarcely had entered the enemy's country, when news was brought him that Severus was dead. A sudden peace is patched up with the Caledonians, and, as it appears from Dion Cassius, the country they had lost to Severus was restored to them.

The Caracul of Fingal is no other than Caracalla, who, as the son of Severus, the emperor of Rome, whose dominions were extended almost over the known world, was not without reason called in the poems of Ossian, *the Son of the King of the World.* The space of time between 211, the year Severus died, and the beginning of the fourth century, is not so great, but Ossian the son of Fingal, might have seen the Christians whom the persecution under Dioclesian had driven beyond the pale of the Roman empire.

Ossian, in one of his many lamentations on the death of his beloved son Oscar, mentions among his great actions, a battle which he fought against Caros, king of ships, on the banks of the winding Carun [*]. It is more than probable, that the Caros mentioned here, is the same with that noted usurper Carausius, who assumed the purple in the year 287, and seizing on Britain, defeated the emperor Maximian Herculius, in several naval engagements, which gives propriety to his being called in Ossian's poems, *the King of Ships.* The *winding Carun* is that small river retaining still the name of Carron, and runs in the neighbourhood of Agricola's wall, which Carausius repaired to obstruct the incursions of the Caledonians. Several other passages in the poems allude to the wars of the Romans; but the two just mentioned clearly fix the epoch of Fingal in the third century; and this account agrees exactly with the Irish histories, which place the death of Fingal, the son of Comhal, in the year 283, and that of Oscar and their own celebrated Cairbre, in the year 296.

Some people may imagine, that the allusions to the Roman history might have been industriously inserted into the poems,

[*] Car-ravon, *winding river.*

THE ÆRA OF OSSIAN.

poems, to give them the appearance of antiquity. This fraud must then have been committed at least three ages ago, as the passages in which the allusions are made, are alluded to often in the compositions of those times.

Every one knows what a cloud of ignorance and barbarism overspread the north of Europe three hundred years ago. The minds of men, addicted to superstition, contracted a narrowness that destroyed genius. Accordingly we find the compositions of those times trivial and puerile to the last degree. But let it be allowed, that, amidst all the untoward circumstances of the age, a genius might arise, it is not easy to determine what could induce him to give the honour of his compositions to an age so remote. We find no fact that he has advanced, to favour any designs which could be entertained by any man who lived in the fifteenth century. But should we suppose a poet, through humour, or for reasons which cannot be seen at this distance of time, would ascribe his own compositions to Ossian, it is next to impossible, that he could impose upon his countrymen, when all of them were so well acquainted with the traditional poems of their ancestors.

The strongest objection to the authenticity of the poems now given to the public under the name of Ossian, is the improbability of their being handed down by tradition through so many centuries. Ages of barbarism, some will say, could not produce poems abounding with the disinterested and generous sentiments so conspicuous in the compositions of Ossian; and could these ages produce them, it is impossible but they must be lost, or altogether corrupted in a long succession of barbarous generations.

These objections naturally suggest themselves to men unacquainted with the ancient state of the northern parts of Britain. The bards, who were an inferior order of the Druids, did not share their bad fortune. They were spared by the victorious king, as it was through their means only he could hope for immortality to his fame. They attended him in the camp, and contributed to establish his power by their songs. His great actions were magnified, and the populace, who had no ability to examine into his character narrowly, were dazzled with his fame in the rhimes of the bards. In the mean time, men assumed sentiments that are rarely to be met with in an age of barbarism. The bards who were originally the disciples of the Druids, had their minds opened, and their ideas enlarged, by being initiated in the learning of that celebrated order. They could form a perfect hero in their own minds, and ascribe that character to their prince. The inferior chiefs made this ideal character the model of their conduct, and by degrees brought their minds to that generous spirit which breathes in all the poetry of the times. The prince, flattered by his bards, and rivalled by his own heroes, who imitated his character as described in the eulogies of his poets, endeavoured to excel his people in merit, as he was above them in station. This emulation continuing, formed at last the general character of the nation, happily compounded of what is noble in barbarity, and virtuous and generous in a polished people.

When virtue in peace, and bravery in war, are the characteristics of a nation, their actions become interesting, and their fame worthy of immortality. A generous spirit is warmed with noble actions, and becomes ambitious of perpetuating them. This is the true source of that divine inspiration, to which the poets of all ages pretended. When they found their themes inadequate to the warmth of their imaginations, they varnished them over with fables, supplied by their own fancy, or furnished by absurd traditions. These fables, however ridiculous, had their abettors; posterity either implicitly believed them, or through a vanity natural to mankind, pretended that they did. They loved to place the founders of their families in the days of fable; when poetry, without the fear of contradiction, could give what characters she pleased of her heroes. It is to this vanity that we owe the preservation of what remain of the works of Ossian. His poetical merit made his heroes famous in a country where heroism was much esteemed and admired. The posterity of these heroes, or those who pretended to be descended from them, heard with pleasure the eulogiums of their ancestors; bards were employed to repeat the poems, and to record the connection of their patrons with chiefs so renowned. Every chief in process of time had a bard in his family, and the office became at last hereditary. By the succession of these bards, the poems concerning the ancestors of the family were handed down from generation to generation; they were repeated to the whole clan on solemn occasions, and always alluded to in the new compositions of the bards. This custom came down near to our own times; and after the bards were discontinued, a great number in a clan retained by memory, or committed to writing, their compositions, and founded the antiquity of their families on the authority of their poems.

The use of letters was not known in the north of Europe till long after the institution of the bards: the records of the families of their patrons, their own, and more ancient poems

THE ÆRA OF OSSIAN.

poems were handed down by tradition. Their poetical compositions were admirably contrived for that purpose. They were adapted to mufic; and the moſt perfect harmony obſerved. Each verſe was ſo connected with thoſe which preceded or followed it, that if one line had been remembered in a ſtanza, it was almoſt impoſſible to forget the reſt. The cadences followed in ſo natural a gradation, and the words were ſo adapted to the common turn of the voice, after it is raiſed to a certain key, that it was almoſt impoſſible, from a ſimilarity of found, to ſubſtitute one word for another. This excellence is peculiar to the Celtic tongue, and is perhaps to be met with in no other language. Nor does this choice of words clog the ſenſe or weaken the expreſſion. The numerous flections of conſonants, and variation in declenſion, make the language very copious.

The deſcendants of the Celtæ, who inhabited Britain and its iſles, were not ſingular in this method of preſerving the moſt precious monuments of their nation. The ancient laws of the Greeks were couched in verſe, and handed down by tradition. The Spartans, through a long habit, became ſo fond of this cuſtom, that they would never allow their laws to be committed to writing. The actions of great men, and the eulogiums of kings and heroes were preſerved in the ſame manner. All the hiſtorical monuments of the old Germans were comprehended in their ancient ſongs;* which were either hymns to their gods, or elegies in praiſe of their heroes, and were intended to perpetuate the great events in their nation which were carefully interwoven with them. This ſpecies of compoſition was not committed to writing, but delivered by oral tradition.† The care they took to have the poems taught to their children, the uninterrupted cuſtom of repeating them upon certain occaſions, and the happy meaſure of the verſe, ſerved to preſerve them for a long time uncorrupted. This oral chronicle of the Germans was not forgot in the eighth century, and it probably would have remained to this day, had not learning, which thinks every thing, that is not committed to writing, fabulous, been introduced. It was from poetical traditions that Garcillaſſo compoſed his account of the Yncas of Peru. The Peruvians had loſt all other monuments of their hiſtory, and it was from ancient poems which his mother, a princeſs of the blood of the Yncas, taught him in his youth, that he collected the materials of his hiſtory. If other nations then, that had been often

over-run

* Tacitus de mor. Germ.
† Abbé de la Bleterie Remarques ſur la Germains.

over-run by enemies, and had sent abroad and received colonies, could, for many ages, preserve, by oral tradition, their laws and histories uncorrupted, it is much more probable that the ancient Scots, a people so free of intermixture with foreigners, and so strongly attached to the memory of their ancestors, had the works of their bards handed down with great purity.

It will seem strange to some, that poems admired for many centuries in one part of this kingdom should be hitherto unknown in the other; and that the British, who have carefully traced out the works of genius in other nations, should so long remain strangers to their own. This, in a great measure, is to be imputed to those who understood both languages and never attempted a translation. They, from being acquainted but with detached pieces, or from a modesty, which perhaps the present translator ought, in prudence, to have followed, despaired of making the compositions of their bards agreeable to an English reader. The manner of those compositions is so different from other poems, and the ideas so confined to the most early state of society, that it was thought they had not enough of variety to please a polished age.

This was long the opinion of the translator of the following collection; and though he admired the poems, in the original, very early, and gathered part of them from tradition for his own amusement, yet he never had the smallest hopes of seeing them in an English dress. He was sensible that the strength and manner of both languages were very different, and that it was next to impossible to translate the Galic poetry into any thing of tolerable English verse; a prose translation he could never think of, as it must necessarily fall short of the majesty of an original. It was a gentleman, who has himself made a figure in the poetical world that gave him the first hint concerning a literal prose translation. He tried it at his desire, and the specimen was approved. Other gentlemen were earnest in exhorting him to bring more to the light, and it is to their uncommon zeal that the world owes the Galic poems, if they have any merit.

It was at first intended to make a general collection of all the ancient pieces of genius to be found in the Galic language; but the translator had his reasons for confining himself to the remains of the works of Ossian. The action of the poem that stands the first, was not the greatest or most celebrated of the exploits of Fingal. His wars were very numerous, and each of them afforded a theme which employed the genius of his son. But, excepting the present poem,

THE ÆRA OF OSSIAN.

poem, thofe pieces are irrecoverably loft, and there only remain a few fragments in the hands of the tranflator. Tradition has ftill preferved, in many places, the ftory of the poems, and many now living have heard them, in their youth, repeated.

The complete work, now printed, would, in a fhort time, have fhared the fate of the reft. The genius of the Highlanders has fuffered a great change within thefe few years. The communication with the reft of the ifland is open, and the introduction of trade and manufactures has deftroyed that leifure which was formerly dedicated to hearing and repeating the poems of ancient times. Many have now learned to leave their mountains, and feek their fortunes in a milder climate; and though a certain *amor patriæ* may fometimes bring them back, they have, during their abfence, imbibed enough of foreign manners to defpife the cuftoms of their anceftors. Bards have been long difufed, and the fpirit of genealogy has greatly fubfided. Men begin to be lefs devoted to their chiefs, and confanguinity is not fo much regarded. When property is eftablifhed, the human mind confines its views to the pleafure it procures. It does not go back to antiquity, or look forward to fucceeding ages. The cares of life increafe, and the actions of other times no longer amufe. Hence it is, that the tafte for their ancient poetry is at a low ebb among the Highlanders. They have not, however, thrown off the good qualities of their anceftors. Hofpitality ftill fubfifts, and an uncommon civility to ftrangers. Friendfhip is inviolable, and revenge lefs blindly followed than formerly.

To fay any thing concerning the poetical merit of the poems, would be an anticipation on the judgment of the public. The poem which ftands firft in the collection is truly epic. The characters are ftrongly marked, and the fentiments breathe heroifm. The fubject of it is an invafion of Ireland by Swaran king of Lochlin, which is the name of Scandinavia in the Galic language. Cuchullin, general of the Irifh tribes in the minority of Cormac king of Ireland, upon intelligence of the invafion, affembled his forces near Tura, a caftle on the coaft of Ulfter. The poem opens with the landing of Swaran, councils are held, battles fought, and Cuchullin is, at laft, totally defeated. In the mean time, Fingal, king of Scotland, whofe aid was folicited before the enemy landed, arrived and expelled them from the country. This war, which continued but fix days and as many nights, is, including the epifodes, the whole

ftory

story of the poem. The scene is the heath of Lena near a mountain called Cromleach in Ulster.

All that can be said of the translation, is, that it is literal, and that simplicity is studied. The arrangement of the words in the original is imitated, and the inversions of the style observed. As the translator claims no merit from his version, he hopes for the indulgence of the public where he fails. He wishes that the imperfect semblance he draws, may not prejudice the world against an original, which contains what is beautiful in simplicity, and grand in the sublime.

FINGAL:

AN ANCIENT EPIC POEM.

IN SIX BOOKS.

THE ARGUMENT.

Cuchullin (general of the Irish tribes, in the minority of Cormac, king of Ireland) sitting alone beneath a tree, at the gate of Tura, a castle of Ulster (the other chiefs having gone on a hunting party to Cromla, a neighbouring hill), is informed of the landing of Swaran, king of Lochlin, by Moran, the son of Fithil, one of his scouts. He convenes the chiefs; a council is held, and disputes run high about giving battle to the enemy. Connal, the petty king of Togorma and an intimate friend of Cuchullin, was for retreating, till Fingal, king of those Caledonians who inhabited the north-west coast of Scotland, whose aid had been previously solicited, should arrive; but Calmar, the son of Matha, lord of Lara, a country in Connaught, was for engaging the enemy immediately. Cuchullin, of himself willing to fight, went into the opinion of Calmar. Marching towards the enemy, he missed three of his bravest heroes, Fergus, Duchomar, and Cathbat. Fergus

Vol. I.   A   arriving

ARGUMENT.

arriving, tells Cuchullin of the death of the two other chiefs; which introduces the affecting epifode of Morna, the daughter of Cormac. The army of Cuchullin is defcried at a diftance by Swaran, who fent the fon of Arno to obferve the motions of the enemy, while he himfelf ranged his forces in order of battle. The fon of Arno returning to Swaran, defcribes to him Cuchullin's chariot, and the terrible appearance of that hero. The armies engage, but night coming on, leaves the victory undecided. Cuchullin, according to the hofpitality of the times, fends to Swaran a formal invitation to a feaft, by his bard Carril, the fon of Kinfena. Swaran refufes to come. Carril relates to Cuchullin the ftory of Grudar and Braffolis. A party, by Connal's advice, is fent to obferve the enemy; which clofes the action of the firft day.

FINGAL:

AN ANCIENT EPIC POEM.

BOOK I.

CUCHULLIN [a] sat by Tura's wall; by the tree of the rustling leaf. His spear leaned against the mossy rock. His shield lay by him on the grass. As he thought of mighty Carbar [b], a hero whom he slew in war; the scout [c] of the ocean came, Moran [d] the son of Fithil!

"Rise," said the youth, "Cuchullin, rise; I see the ships of Swaran. Cuchullin, many are the foe: many the heroes of the dark-rolling sea."

"Moran!" replied the blue-eyed chief, "thou ever tremblest, son of Fithil: Thy fears have much increased the foe. Perhaps it is the king [e] of the lonely hills coming to aid me on green Ullin's plains.

"I saw the chief," says Moran, "tall as a rock of ice. His spear is like that blasted fir. His shield like the rising moon. He sat on a rock on the shore: his dark host rolled, like clouds around him. Many, chief of men! I said, many are our hands of war. Well art thou named, the Mighty Man, but many mighty men are seen from Tura's windy walls."

"He

"He answered, like a wave on a rock, who in this land appears like me? Heroes stand not in my presence; they fall to earth beneath my hand. None can meet Swaran in the fight, but Fingal, king of stormy hills. Once we wrestled on the heath of Malmor [f], and our heels overturned the wood. Rocks fell from their place; and rivulets, changing their course, fled murmuring from our strife. Three days we renewed our strife, and heroes stood at a distance and trembled. On the fourth, Fingal says, that the king of the ocean fell; but Swaran says, he stood. Let dark Cuchullin yield to him that is strong as the storms of Malmor."

"No!" replied the blue-eyed chief, "I will never yield to man! Dark Cuchullin shall be great or dead! Go, Fithil's son, and take my spear. Strike the sounding shield of Cabait [g]. It hangs at Tura's rustling gate; the sound of peace is not its voice. My heroes shall hear on the hill."

He went and struck the bossy shield. The hills and their rocks replied. The sound spreads along the wood: deer start by the lake of roes. Curah [h] leapt from the sounding rock; and Connal of the bloody spear. Crugal's [i] breast of snows beats high. The son of Favi leaves the dark-brown hind. It is the shield of war, said Ronar! the spear of Cuchullin, said Lugar! son of the sea put

on

on thy arms! Calmar lift thy founding steel!
Puno! dreadful hero, rife! Cairbar from thy red
tree of Cromla! Bend thy white knee, O Eth!
and defcend from the ftreams of Lena. Ca-olt
ftretch thy white fide as thou moveft along the
whiftling heath of Mora: thy fide that is white as
the foam of the troubled fea, when the dark winds
pour it on the murmuring rocks of Cuthon [k].

Now I behold the chiefs, in the pride of their
former deeds! Their fouls are kindled at the battles of old; and the actions of other times. Their
eyes are like flames of fire. And roll in fearch of
the foes of the land. Their mighty hands are on
their fwords. And lightning pours from their
fides of steel. They come like ftreams from the
mountains; each rufhes roaring from his hill.
Bright are the chiefs of battle, in the armour of
their fathers. Gloomy and dark their heroes follow, like the gathering of the rainy clouds behind
the red meteors of heaven. The founds of crafh-
ing arms afcend. The grey dogs howl between.
Unequally burfts the fong of battle. And rocking
Cromla [l] echoes round. On Lena's dufky heath
they ftand, like mift [m] that fhades the hills of autumn: when broken and dark it fettles high, and
lifts its head to heaven!

"Hail,"

"Hail," said Cuchullin, "sons of the narrow vales! hail ye hunters of the deer! Another sport is drawing near: It is like the dark rolling of that wave on the coast! Shall we fight, ye sons of war! or yield green Innisfail" to Lochlin! O Connal * speak, thou first of men! thou breaker of the shields! thou hast often fought with Lochlin: wilt thou lift thy father's spear?"

"Cuchullin!" calm the chief replied, "the spear of Connal is keen. It delights to shine in battle; and to mix with the blood of thousands. But though my hand is bent on war, my heart is for the peace of Erin ᵖ. Behold, thou first in Cormac's war, the sable fleet of Swaran. His masts are as numerous on our coast as reeds in the lake of Lego. His ships are like forests clothed with mist, when the trees yield by turns to the squally wind. Many are his chiefs in battle. Connal is for peace! Fingal would shun his arm the first of mortal men! Fingal who scatters the mighty, as stormy winds the heath; when the streams roar through echoing Cona: and night settles with all her clouds on the hill."

"Fly, thou chief of peace," said Calmar ᑫ, the son of Matha; "fly, Connal, to thy silent hills, where the spear of battle never shone! Pursue the dark-brown deer of Cromla: and stop with thine

arrows

arrows the bounding roes of Lena. But, blue-eyed son of Semo, Cuchullin, ruler of the war, scatter thou the sons of Lochlin '! and roar through the ranks of their pride. Let no vessel of the kingdom of Snow bound on the dark-rolling waves of Inis-tore '. O ye dark winds of Erin rise! roar ye whirlwinds of the heath! Amidst the tempest let me die, torn in a cloud by angry ghosts of men; amidst the tempest let Calmar die, if ever chase was sport to him, so much as the battle of shields!"

"Calmar!" slow replied the chief, "I never fled, O son of Matha! I was swift with my friends in battle; but small is the fame of Connal! The battle was won in my presence; and the valiant overcame! But, son of Semo, hear my voice, regard the ancient throne of Cormac. Give wealth and half the land for peace, till Fingal come with battle. Or, if war be thy choice, I lift the sword and spear. My joy shall be in the midst of thousands; and my soul brighten in the gloom of the fight!"

"To me," Cuchullin replies, "pleasant is the noise of arms! pleasant as the thunder of heaven before the shower of spring! But gather all the shining tribes, that I may view the sons of war! Let them move along the heath, bright as the sunshine before a storm; when the west wind collects

the

the clouds, and the oaks of Morven echo along the shore."

" But where are my friends in battle? The companions of my arm in danger? Where art thou, white-bosom'd Cathbat? Where is that cloud in war, Duchomar ᵗ? And haft thou left me, O Fergus ᵘ! in the day of the ftorm? Fergus, firft our joy at the feaft! fon of Roffa! arm of death! comeft thou like a roe ᵛ from Malmor? Like a hart from the echoing hills? Hail, thou fon of Roffa! What fhades the foul of war?"

" Four ftones ʷ " replied the chief, " rife on the grave of Cathbat. Thefe hands have laid in earth Duchomar, that cloud in war! Cathbat, fon of Torman! thou wert a fun-beam on the hill. And thou, O valiant Duchomar, like the mift of marfhy Lano; when it fails over the plains of autumn and brings death to the people. Morna, faireft of maids! calm is thy fleep in the cave of the rock. Thou haft fallen in darknefs like a ftar, that fhoots acrofs the defart, when the traveller is alone, and mourns the tranfient beam."

" Say," faid Semo's blue-eyed fon, " fay how fell the chiefs of Erin? Fell they by the fons of Lochlin, ftriving in the battle of heroes? Or what confines the chiefs of Cromla to the dark and narrow houfe ˣ."

" Cathbat,"

"Cathbat," replied the hero, " fell by the sword of Duchomar at the oak of the noisy streams. Duchomar came to Tura's cave; and spoke to the lovely Morna."

"Morna, fairest among women, lovely daughter of Cormac-cairbar. Why in the circle of stones; in the cave of the rock, alone? The stream murmurs hoarsely. The old trees groan in the wind. The lake is troubled before thee, and dark are the clouds of the sky. But thou art like snow on the heath; and thy hair like the mist of Cromla; when it curls on the rocks, and shines to the beam of the west. Thy breasts are like two smooth rocks seen from Brano of the streams; thy arms like two white pillars in the halls of the mighty Fingal."

"From whence," the white-armed maid replied, "from whence, Duchomar the most gloomy of men? Dark are thy brows and terrible. Red are thy rolling eyes. Does Swaran appear on the sea? What of the foe, Duchomar?"

"From the hill I return, O Morna, from the hill of the dark-brown hinds. Three have I slain with my bended yew. Three with my long bounding dogs of the chase. Lovely daughter of Cormac, I love thee as my soul. I have slain one stately deer for thee. High was his branchy head; and fleet his feet of wind."

"Duchomar!"

"Duchomar!" calm the maid replied, "I love thee not, thou gloomy man, hard is thy heart of rock; and dark thy terrible brow. But Cathbat, son of Torman [a], thou art the love of Morna. Thou art like a sun beam on the hill in the day of the gloomy storm. Sawest thou the son of Torman, lovely on the hill of his hinds? Here the daughter of Cormac waits the coming of Cathbat."

"And long shall Morna wait," Duchomar said, "his blood is on my sword. Long shall Morna wait for him. He fell at Branno's stream. High on Cromla I will raise his tomb, daughter of Cormac-cairbar; but fix thy love on Duchomar, his arm is strong as a storm."

"And is the son of Torman fallen?" said the maid of the tearful eye. "Is he fallen on his echoing heath; the youth with the breast of snow? he that was first in the chase of the hill; the foe of the strangers of the ocean. Duchomar thou art dark [a] indeed, and cruel is thy arm to Morna. But give me that sword, my foe! I love the blood of Cathbat."

He gave the sword to her tears. But she pierced his manly breast! He fell, like the bank of a mountain-stream; and stretching out his arm he said—

"Daughter

"Daughter of Cormac-cairbar, thou haft flain Duchomar. The fword is cold in my breaft: Morna, I feel it cold. Give me to Moina [b] the maid; Duchomar was the dream of her night. She will raife my tomb; and the hunter fhall fee it and praife me. But draw the fword from my breaft; Morna, the fteel is cold."

She came, in all her tears, fhe came, and drew it from his breaft. He pierced her white fide with fteel; and fpread her fair locks on the ground. Her burfting blood founds from her fide: and her white arm is ftained with red. Rolling in death fhe lay, and Tura's cave anfwered to her groans.

"Peace," faid Cuchullin, "to the fouls of the heroes; their deeds were great in danger. Let them ride around [c] me on clouds; and fhew their features of war; that my foul may be ftrong in danger; my arm like the thunder of heaven.—But be thou on a moon-beam, O Morna, near the window of my reft; when my thoughts are of peace; and the din of arms is over.—Gather the ftrength of the tribes, and move to the wars of Erin.—Attend the car of my battles; rejoice in the noife of my courfe. Place three fpears by my fide; follow the bounding of my fteeds; that my foul may be ftrong in my friends, when the battle darkens round the beams of my fteel."

As rushes a stream [d] of foam from the dark shady steep of Cromla; when the thunder is rolling above, and dark-brown night rests on half the hill. So fierce, so vast, so terrible, rushed on the sons of Erin. The chief, like a whale of ocean, whom all his billows follow, poured valour forth as a stream, rolling his might along the shore.

The sons of Lochlin heard the noise as the sound of a winter-stream. Swaran struck his bossy shield, and called the son of Arno. "What murmur rolls along the hill like the gathered flies of evening? The sons of Innis-fail descend, or rustling winds roar in the distant wood. Such is the noise of Gormal before the white tops of my waves arise. O son of Arno, ascend the hill and view the dark face of the heath."

He went, and trembling, swift returned. His eyes rolled wildly round. His heart beat high against his side. His words were faultering, broken, slow.

"Rise, son of ocean, rise chief of the dark-brown shields. I see the dark, the mountain-stream of the battle: the deep-moving strength of the sons of Erin.—The car, the car of battle comes, like the flame of death; the rapid car of Cuchullin, the noble son of Semo. It bends behind like a wave near a rock; like the golden mist of the heath. Its sides are embossed with stones, and sparkle like

the

the sea around the boat of night. Of polished yew is its beam, and its seat of the smoothest bone. The sides are replenished with spears; and the bottom is the footstool of heroes. Before the right side of the car is seen the snorting horse. The high-maned, broad-breasted, proud, high-leaping, strong steed of the hill. Loud and resounding is his hoof; the spreading of his mane above, is like that stream of smoke on the heath. Bright are the sides of the steed, and his name is Sulin-Sifadda.

"Before the left side of the car, is seen the snorting horse. The dark-maned, high-headed, strong-hoofed, fleet, bounding son of the hill: his name is Dusronnal among the stormy sons of the sword. A thousand thongs bind the car on high. Hard polished bits shine in a wreath of foam. Thin thongs bright-studded with gems, bend on the stately necks of the steeds. The steeds that like wreaths of mist fly over the streamy vales. The wildness of deer is in their course, the strength of the eagle descending on her prey. Their noise is like the blast of winter on the sides of the snow-headed Gormal [c].

"Within the car is seen the chief; the strong stormy son of the sword; the hero's name is Cuchullin, son of Semo king of shells. His red cheek
is

is like my polished yew. The look of his blue-rolling eye is wide beneath the dark arch of his brow. His hair flies from his head like a flame, as bending forward he wields the spear. Fly, king of ocean, fly; he comes, like a storm along the streamy vale."

"When did I fly," replied the king, "from the battle of many spears? When did I fly, son of Arno, chief of the little soul? I met the storm of Gormal when the foam of my waves was high; I met the storm of the clouds and shall I fly from a hero? Were it Fingal himself my soul should not darken before him.—Rise to the battle, my thousands; pour round me like the echoing main. Gather round the bright steel of your king; strong as the rocks of my land; that meet the storm with joy, and stretch their dark woods to the wind."

As autumn's dark storms pour from two echoing hills, towards each other approached the heroes. As two dark streams from high rocks meet, and mix and roar on the plain; loud, rough and dark in battle meet Lochlin and Innis-fail. Chief mixes his strokes with chief, and man with man; steel, clanging, sounded on steel, helmets are cleft on high. Blood bursts and smokes around.—— Strings twang on the polished yews. Darts rush
along

along the sky. Spears fall like the circles of light that gild the stormy face of night.

As the troubled noise of the ocean when roll the waves on high: as the last peal of the thunder of heaven, such is the noise of battle. Though Cormac's hundred bards were there to give the war to song; feeble were the voices of a hundred bards to send the deaths to future times. For many were the falls of the heroes; and wide poured the blood of the valiant.

Mourn, ye sons of song, the death of the noble Sith-allin [g]. Let the sighs of Fiona rise on the dark heaths of her lovely Ardan. They fell, like two hinds of the desart, by the hands of the mighty Swaran; when, in the midst of thousands he roared; like the shrill spirit of a storm, that sits dim, on the clouds of Gormal, and enjoys the death of the mariner.

Nor slept thy hand by thy side, chief of the isle of mist [h]; many were the deaths of thine arm, Cuchullin, thou son of Semo. His sword was like the beam of heaven when it pierces the sons of the vale; when the people are blasted and fall, and all the hills are burning around. Dusronnal [i] snorted over the bodies of heroes; and Sifadda [k] bathed his hoof in blood. The battle lay behind them as groves overturned on the desart of Cromla; when

the

the blast has passed the heath laden with the spirits of night.

Weep on the rocks of roaring winds, O maid of Iniftore [1], bend thy fair head over the waves, thou fairer than the fpirit of the hills; when it moves in a fun-beam at noon over the filence of Morven. He is fallen! thy youth is low; pale beneath the fword of Cuchullin. No more fhall valour raife the youth to match the blood of kings. Trenar, lovely Trenar died, thou maid of Iniftore. His gray dogs are howling at home, and fee his paffing ghoft. His bow is in the hall unftrung. No found is in the heath of his hinds.

As roll a thoufand waves on a rock, fo Swaran's hoft came on; as meets a rock a thoufand waves, fo Innis-fail met Swaran. Death raifes all his voices around, and mixes with the found of their fhields. Each hero is a pillar of darknefs, and the fword a beam of fire in his hand. The field echoes from wing to wing, as a hundred hammers that rife by turns on the red fon of the furnace.

Who are thefe on Lena's heath that are fo gloomy and dark? Who are thefe like two clouds [m] and their fwords like lightning above them? The little hills are troubled around, and the rocks tremble with all their mofs. Who is it but Ocean's fon and the car-borne chief of Erin? Many are the anxious

xious eyes of their friends, as they see them dim on the heath. Now night conceals the chiefs in her clouds, and ends the terrible fight.

It was on Cromla's shaggy side that Dorglas placed the deer; ᵃ the early fortune of the chase, before the heroes left the hill. A hundred youths collect the heath; ten heroes blow the fire; three hundred chuse the polished stones. The feast is smoking wide.

Cuchullin, chief of Erin's war, resumed his mighty soul. He stood upon his beamy spear, and spoke to the son of songs; to Carril of other times, the gray-haired son of Kinfena. ᵒ "Is this feast spread for me alone, and the king of Lochlin on Ullin's shore; far from the deer of his hills, and sounding halls of his feasts! Rise, Carril of other times, and carry my words to Swaran; tell him that came from the roaring of waters, that Cuchullin gives his feast. Here let him listen to the sound of my groves amidst the clouds of night. For cold and bleak the blustering winds rush over the foam of his seas. Here let them praise the trembling harp, and hear the songs of heroes.

Old Carril went, with softest voice, and called the king of dark-brown shields. Rise from the skins of thy chase, rise, Swaran king of groves. Cuchullin gives the joy of shells; partake the feast of Erin's blue-eyed chief." He answered like the sullen sound of Cromla before a storm. Though all thy daughters, Innis-fail! should extend their arms of snow; raise high the heavings of their breasts, and softly roll their eyes of love; yet, fixed as Lochlin's thousand rocks, here Swaran shall remain; till morn, with the young beams of my east, shall light me to the death of Cuchullin. Pleasant to my ear is Lochlin's wind. It rushes over my seas. It speaks aloft in all my shrowds, and brings my green forests to my mind; the green forests of Gormal that often echoed to my winds, when my spear was red in the chase of the boar. Let dark Cuchullin yield to me the ancient throne of Cormac, or Erin's torrents shall shew from their hills the red foam of the blood of his pride."

"Sad is the sound of Swaran's voice," said Carril of other times: "Sad to himself alone," said the blue-eyed son of Semo. "But, Carril, raise thy voice on high, and tell the deeds of other times. Send thou the night away in song; and give the joy of grief. For many heroes and maids of love have moved on Innis-fail. And lovely are the songs of woe that are heard on Albion's rocks; when the noise of the chase is over, and the streams of Cona answer to the voice of Ossian?."

"In

"In other days," Carril replies, "came the sons of Ocean to Erin." A thousand veffels bounded over the waves to Ullin's lovely plains. The sons of Innis-fail arose to meet the race of dark-brown shields. Cairbar, first of men was there, and Grudar, stately youth. Long had they strove for the spotted bull, that lowed on Golbun's echoing heath. Each claimed him as his own; and death was often at the point of their steel. Side by side the heroes fought, and the strangers of Ocean fled. Whose name was fairer on the hill than the name of Cairbar and Grudar? But ah! why ever lowed the bull on Golbun's echoing heath? They saw him leaping like the snow. The wrath of the chiefs returned.

On Lubar's graffy banks they fought, and Grudar like a sun-beam, fell. Fierce Cairbar came to the vale of the echoing Tura, where Braffolis faireft of his fifters, all alone, raised the song of grief. She sung of the actions of Grudar, the youth of her secret soul. She mourned him in the field of blood; but still she hoped for his return. Her white bosom is seen from her robe, as the moon from the clouds of night. Her voice was softer than the harp to raise the song of grief. Her soul was fixed on Grudar; the secret look of her eye was his. When shalt thou come in thine arms, thou mighty in the war?"

"Take, Braffolis," Cairbar came and said, "take, Braffolis, this shield of blood. Fix it on high within my hall, the armour of my foe." Her soft heart beat against her side. Distracted, pale, she flew. She found her youth in all his blood? she died on Cromla's heath. Here rests their dust, Cuchullin; and these two lonely yews, sprung from their tombs, wish to meet on high. Fair was Braffolis on the plain, and Grudar on the hill. The bard shall preserve their names, and repeat them to future times."

"Pleasant is thy voice, O Carril," said the blue-eyed chief of Erin. "Lovely are the words of other times. They are like the calm shower of spring, when the sun looks on the field, and the light cloud flies over the hills. Strike the harp in praise of my love, the lonely sun-beam of Dunscaich. Strike the harp in the praise of Bragela, of her that I left in the isle of Mist, the spouse of Semo's son. Dost thou raise thy fair face from the rock to find the sails of Cuchullin? The sea is rolling far distant, and its white foam shall deceive thee for my sails. Retire, for it is night, my love, and the dark winds sigh in thy hair. Retire to the halls of my feasts, and think of the times that are past; for I will not return till the storm of war

is

is ceafed. O Connal, fpeak of wars and arms, and fend her from my mind, for lovely with her raven-hair is the white bofomed daughter of Sorglan."

Connal, flow to fpeak, replied, " Guard againft the race of Ocean. Send thy troop of night abroad, and watch the ftrength of Swaran. Cuchullin! I am for peace till the race of the defart come; till Fingal come the firft of men, and beam, like the fun, on our fields."

The hero ftruck the fhield of his alarms; the warriors of the night moved on. The reft lay in the heath of the deer, and flept amidft the dufky wind. The ghofts" of the lately dead were near, and fwam on gloomy clouds. And far diftant, in the dark filence of Lena, the feeble voices were heard.

FINGAL:

AN ANCIENT EPIC POEM.

THE ARGUMENT.

The ghoſt of Crugal, one of the Iriſh heroes who was killed in battle, appearing to Connal, foretels the defeat of Cuchullin in the next battle; and earneſtly adviſes him to make peace with Swaran. Connal communicates the viſion; but Cuchullin is inflexible; from a principle of honour he would not be the firſt to ſue for peace, and he reſolved to continue the war. Morning comes; Swaran propoſes diſhonourable terms to Cuchullin, which are rejected. The battle begins, and is obſtinately fought for ſome time, until, upon the flight of Grumal, the whole Iriſh army gave way. Cuchullin and Connal cover their retreat: Carril leads them to a neighbouring hill, whither they are ſoon followed by Cuchullin himſelf, who deſcries the fleet of Fingal making towards the coaſt; but, night coming on, he loſt ſight of it again. Cuchullin, dejected after his defeat, attributes his ill ſucceſs to the death of Ferda his friend, whom he had killed ſome time before. Carril, to ſhew that ill ſucceſs did not always attend thoſe who innocently killed their friends, introduces the epiſode of Comal and Galvina.

FINGAL.

FINGAL:

AN ANCIENT EPIC POEM.

CONNAL* lay by the found of the mountain stream, beneath the aged tree. A stone, with its mofs, supported his head. Shrill through the heath of Lena, he heard the voice of night. At a distance from the heroes he lay, for the son of the sword feared no foe.

My hero saw in his rest a dark-red stream of fire coming down from the hill. Crugal sat upon the beam, a chief that lately fell. He fell by the hand of Swaran, striving in the battle of heroes. His face is like the beam of the setting moon; his robes are of the clouds of the hill: his eyes are like two decaying flames. Dark is the wound of his breast.

"Crugal," said the mighty Connal, "son of Dedgal famed on the hill of deer. Why so pale and sad, thou breaker of the shields? Thou hast never been pale for fear. What disturbs the son of the hill?"

Dim, and in tears, he stood and stretched his pale hand over the hero. Faintly he raised his feeble voice, like the gale of the reedy Lego.

"My

"My ghoft, O Connal, is on my native hills; but my corfe is on the fands of Ullin. Thou fhalt never talk with Crugal, or find his lone fteps in the heath. I am light as the blaft of Cromla, and I move like the fhadow of mift. Connal, fon of Colgar,[b] I fee the dark cloud of death: it hovers over the plains of Leno. The fons of green Erin fhall fall. Remove from the field of ghofts," Like the darkened moon [c] he retired, in the midft of the whiftling blaft.

"Stay," faid the mighty Connal, "ftay my dark-red friend. Lay by that beam of heaven, fon of the windy Cromla. What cave of the hill is thy lonely houfe? What green-headed hill is the place of thy reft? Shall we not hear thee in the ftorm? In the noife of the mountain ftream? When the feeble fons of the wind come forth, and ride on the blaft of the defart."

The foft-voiced Connal rofe in the midft of his founding arms. He ftruck his fhield above Cuchullin. The fon of battle waked.

"Why," faid the ruler of the car, "comes Connal through the night? My fpear might turn againft the found? and Cuchullin mourn the death of his friend. Speak, Connal, fon of Colgar, fpeak, thy counfel is like the fon of heaven."

"Son

"Son of Semo," replied the chief, "the ghost of Crugal came from the cave of his hill. The stars dim-twinkled through his form; and his voice was like the sound of a distant stream. He is a messenger of death. He speaks of the dark and narrow house. Sue for peace, O chief of Dunscaich; or fly over the heath of Lena."

"He spoke to Connal," replied the hero, "though stars dim-twinkled through his form. Son of Colgar, it was the wind that murmured in the caves of Lena. Or if it was the form [d] of Crugal, why didst thou not force him to my sight. Hast thou inquired where is his cave? The house of the son of the wind? My sword might find that voice, and force his knowledge from him. And small is his knowledge, Connal, for he was here to-day. He could not have gone beyond our hills, and who could tell him there of our death?"

"Ghosts fly on clouds and ride on winds," said Connal's voice of wisdom. "They rest together in their caves, and talk of mortal men."

"Then let them talk of mortal men; of every man but Erin's chief. Let me be forgot in their cave; for I will not fly from Swaran. If I must fall, my tomb shall rise amidst the fame of future times. The hunter shall shed a tear on my stone; and sorrow dwell round the high-bosomed Bragela.

I fear not death, but I fear to fly, for Fingal saw me often victorious. Thou dim phantom of the hill, shew thyself to me! come on thy beam of heaven, and shew me my death in thine hand; yet will I not fly, thou feeble son of the wind. Go, son of Colgar, strike the shield of Caithbat, it hangs between the spears. Let my heroes rise to the sound in the midst of the battles of Erin. Though Fingal delays his coming with the race of stormy hills; we shall fight, O Colgar's son, and die in the battle of heroes."

The sound spreads wide; the heroes rise, like the breaking of a blue-rolling wave. They stood on the heath, like oaks with all their branches round them ᶜ; when they echo to the stream of frost, and their withered leaves rustle to the wind.

High Cromla's head of clouds is gray; the morning trembles on the half-enlightened ocean. The blue, gray mist swims slowly by, and hides the sons of Innis-fail.

"Rise ye," said the king of the dark-brown shields, "ye that come from Lochlin's waves. The sons of Erin have fled from our arms—pursue them over the plains of Lena. And Morla, go to Cormac's hall and bid them yield to Swaran; before the people shall fall into the tomb; and the hills of Ullin be silent. They rose like a flock of
sea-fowl

sea-fowl when the waves expel them from the shore." Their sound was like a thousand streams that meet in Cona's vale, when after a stormy night, they turn their dark eddies beneath the pale light of the morning.

As the dark shades of autumn fly over the hills of grass; so gloomy, dark, successive came the chiefs of Lochlin's echoing woods. Tall as the stag of Morven moved on the king of groves. His shining shield is on his side like a flame on the heath at night, when the world is silent and dark, and the traveller sees some ghost sporting in the beam.

A blast from the troubled ocean removed the settled mist. The sons of Innis-fail appear like a ridge of rocks on the shore.

"Go, Morla, go," said Lochlin's king, "and offer peace to these. Offer the terms we give to kings when nations bow before us. When the valiant are dead in war, and the virgins weeping on the field."

Great Morla came, the son of Swart, and stately strode the king of shields. He spoke to Erin's blue-eyed son, among the lesser heroes.

"Take Swaran's peace," the warrior spoke, "the peace he gives to kings, when the nation bow before him. Leave Ullin's lovely plains to us, and give thy spouse and day. Thy spouse high-

high-bosom'd heaving fair. Thy dog that overtakes the wind. Give these to prove the weakness of thine arm, and live beneath our power."

"Tell Swaran, tell that heart of pride, that Cuchullin never yields. I give him the dark-blue rolling of ocean, or I give his people graves in Erin! Never shall a stranger have the lovely sun-beam of Dunscaich; nor ever deer fly on Lochlin's hills before the nimble-footed Luath."

"Vain ruler of the car," said Morla, "wilt thou fight the king; that king whose ships of many groves could carry off thine Isle? So little is thy green-hilled Ullin to the king of stormy waves."

"In words I yield to many, Morla; but this sword shall yield to none. Erin shall own the sway of Cormac, while Connal and Cuchullin live. O Connal, first of mighty men, thou hast heard the words of Morla; shall thy thoughts then be of peace, thou breaker of the shields? Spirit of fallen Crugal! why didst thou threaten us with death! The narrow house shall receive me in the midst of the light of renown. Exalt, ye sons of Innis-fail, exalt the spear and bend the bow; rush on the foe in darkness, as the spirits of stormy nights."

Then dismal, roaring, fierce, and deep the gloom of battle rolled along; as mist ᶠ that is pour'd on

the

the valley, when storms invade the silent sun-shine of heaven. The chief moves before in arms, like an angry ghost before a cloud; when meteors inclose him with fire; and the dark winds are in his hand. Carril, far on the heath, bids the horn of battle sound. He raises the voice of the song, and pours his soul into the minds of heroes.

"Where," said the mouth of the song, "where is the fallen Crugal? He lies forgot on earth, and the hall of shells ᵍ is silent. Sad is the spouse of Crugal, for she is a stranger ʰ in the hall of her sorrow. But who is she, that, like a sun-beam, flies before the ranks of the foe? It is Degrena ⁱ, lovely fair, the spouse of fallen Crugal. Her hair is on the wind behind. Her eye is red; her voice is shrill. Green, empty is thy Crugal now, his form is in the cave of the hill. He comes to the ear of rest, and raises his feeble voice; like the humming of the mountain-bee, or collected flies of evening. But Degrena falls like a cloud of the morn; the sword of Lochlin is in her side. Cairbar, she is fallen, the rising thought of thy youth. She is fallen, O Cairbar, the thought of thy youthful hours."

Fierce Cairbar heard the mournful sound, and rushed on like ocean's whale; he saw the death of his daughter; and roared in the midst of thousands fands [k]. His spear met a son of Lochlin, and battle spread from wing to wing. As a hundred winds in Lochlin's groves, as fire in the firs of a hundred hills; so loud, so ruinous and vast the ranks of men are hewed down. Cuchullin cut off heroes like thistles, and Swaran wasted Erin. Curach fell by his hand, and Cairbar of the bossy shield. Morglan lies in lasting rest; and Ca-olt quivers as he dies. His white breast is stained with his blood: and his yellow hair stretched in the dust of his native land. He often had spread the feast where he fell; and often raised the voice of the harp: when his dogs leapt around for joy; and the youths of the chase prepared the bow.

Still Swaran advanced, as a stream that bursts from the desart. The little hills are rolled in its course; and the rocks half-sunk by its side. But Cuchullin stood before him like a hill [l], that catches the clouds of heaven. The winds contend on its head of pines; and the hail rattles on its rocks. But, firm in its strength, it stands and shades the silent vale of Cona.

So Cuchullin shaded the sons of Erin, and stood in the midst of thousands. Blood rises like the fount of a rock, from panting heroes around him. But Erin falls on either wing like snow in the day of the sun.

O sons

"O sons of Innis-fail," said Grumal, "Lochlin conquers on the field. Why strive we as reeds against the wind! Fly to the hill of dark-brown hinds." He fled like the stag of Morven, and his spear is a trembling beam of light behind him. Few fled with Grumal, the chief of the little soul: they fell in the battle of heroes on Lena's echoing heath.

High on his car, of many gems, the chief of Erin stood; he slew a mighty son of Lochlin, and spoke, in haste, to Connal. "O Connal, first of mortal men, thou hast taught this arm of death! Though Erin's sons have fled, shall we not fight the foe? O Carril, son of other times, carry my living friends to that bushy hill. Here, Connal, let us stand like rocks, and save our flying friends."

Connal mounts the car of light. They stretch their shields like the darkened moon? the daughter of the starry skies, when she moves, a dun circle, through heaven. Sithfadda panted up the hill, and Dunfronnal haughty steed. Like waves behind a whale, behind them rushed the foe.

Now on the rising side of Cromla stood Erin's few sad sons, like a grove through which the flame had rushed, hurried on by the winds of the stormy night. Cuchullin stood beside an oak. He rolled his red eye in silence, and heard the wind in his bushy hair; when the scout of ocean came,

Moran the son of Fithil. "The ships," he cried, "the ships of the lonely isle! There Fingal comes, the first of men, the breaker of the shields. The waves foam before his black prows. His masts with sails are like groves in clouds."

"Blow," said Cuchullin, "all ye winds that rush over my isle of lovely mist. Come to the death of thousands, O chief of the hills of hinds. Thy sails, my friend, are to me like the clouds of the morning; and thy ships like the light of heaven; and thou thyself like a pillar of fire that giveth light in the night. O Connal, first of men, how pleasant are our friends! But the night is gathering around; where now are the ships of Fingal? Here let us pass the hours of darkness, and wish for the moon of heaven."

The winds came down on the woods. The torrents rushed from the rocks. Rain gathered round the head of Cromla; and the red stars trembled between the flying clouds. Sad, by the side of a stream whose sound was echoed by a tree, sad by the side of a stream the chief of Erin sat. Connal son of Colgar was there, and Carril of other times.

"Unhappy is the hand of Cuchullin," said the son of Semo, "unhappy is the hand of Cuchullin since he slew his friend. Ferda, thou son of Damman, I loved thee as myself."

"How,

"How, Cuchullin, son of Semo, fell the breaker of the shields? Well I remember," said Connal, "the noble son of Damman. Tall and fair he was like the rain-bow of the hill."

"Ferda from Albion came, the chief of a hundred hills. In Muri's[m] hall he learned the sword, and won the friendship of Cuchullin. We moved to the chase together; and one was our bed in the heath.

"Deu gala was the spouse of Cairbar, chief of the plains of Ullin. She was covered with the light of beauty, but her heart was the house of pride. She loved that sun-beam of youth, the noble son of Damman." "Cairbar," said the white armed woman, "give me half of the herd. No more I will remain in your halls. Divide the herd, dark Cairbar."

"Let Cuchullin," said Cairbar, "divide my herd on the hill. His breast is the seat of justice." Depart thou light of beauty." I went and divided the herd. One snow-white bull remained. I gave that bull to Cairbar. The wrath of Deugala rose.

"Son of Damman," begun the fair, "Cuchullin pains my soul. I must hear of his death, or Lubar's stream shall over me. My pale ghost shall wander near thee, and mourn the wound of my pride.

pride. Pour out the blood of Cuchullin or pierce this heaving breast."

"Deugala," said the fair-haired youth, "how shall I slay the son of Semo? He is the friend of my secret thoughts, and shall I lift the sword? She wept three days before him, on the fourth he consented to fight.

"I will fight my friend, Deugala! but may I fall by his sword. Could I wander on the hill and behold the grave of Cuchullin?" We fought on the hills of Muri. Our swords avoid a wound. They slide on the helmets of steel; and found on the slippery shields. Deugala was near with a smile, and said to the son of Damman: "Thine arm is feeble, thou sun-beam of youth. Thy years are not strong for steel. Yield to the son of Semo. He is like the rock of Malmor."

"The tear is in the eye of youth. He, faultering said, to me: "Cuchullin, raise thy bossy shield. Defend thee from the hand of thy friend. My soul is laden with grief: for I must slay the chief of men."

I sighed as the wind in the chink of a rock. I lifted high the edge of my steel. The sun beam of the battle fell; the first of Cuchullin's friends.

Unhappy is the hand of Cuchullin since the hero fell.

"Mournful

"Mournful is thy tale, son of the car," said Carril of other times. "It sends my soul back to the ages of old, and to the days of other years. Often have I heard of Comal who slew the friend he loved; yet victory attended his steel; and the battle was consumed in his presence.

"Comal was a son of Albion; the chief of an hundred hills. His deer drunk of a thousand streams. A thousand rocks replied to the voice of his dogs. His face was the mildness of youth. His hand the death of heroes. One was his love, and fair was she! the daughter of mighty Conloch. She appeared like a sun-beam among women. And her hair was like the wing of the raven. Her dogs were taught to the chase. Her bow-string sounded on the winds of the forest. Her soul was fixed on Comal. Often met their eyes of love. Their course in the chase was one, and happy were their words in secret. But Gormal loved the maid, the dark chief of the gloomy Ardven. He watched her lone steps in the heath; the foe of unhappy Comal.

"One day, tired of the chase, when the mist had concealed their friends, Comal and the daughter of Conloch met in the cave of Ronan [a]. It was the wonted haunt of Comal. Its sides were hung

hung with his arms. A hundred shields of thongs were there; a hundred helms of sounding steel."

"Rest here," he said, "my love Galvina; thou light of the cave of Ronan. A deer appears on Mora's brow. I go; but I will soon return." "I fear," she said, "dark Grumal my foe; he haunts the cave of Ronan. I will rest among the arms; but soon return, my love."

"He went to the deer of Mora. The daughter of Conloch would try his love. She clothed her white sides with his armour, and strode from the cave of Ronan. He thought it was his foe. His heart beat high. His colour changed, and darkness dimmed his eye. He drew the bow. The arrow flew. Galvina fell in blood. He run with wildness in his steps and called the daughter of Conloch. No answer in the lonely rock." "Where art thou, O my love!" He saw at length, her heaving heart beating around the feathered dart. "O Conloch's daughter, is it thou?"—He sunk upon her breast.

"The hunters found the hapless pair; he afterwards walked the hill. But many and silent were his steps round the dark dwelling of his love. The fleet of the ocean came. He fought; the strangers fled. He searched for his death over the field. But who could kill the mighty Comal! He threw
away

away his dark-brown shield. An arrow found his manly breast. He sleeps with his loved Galvina at the noise of the sounding surge. Their green tombs are seen by the mariner, when he bounds on the waves of the north."

FINGAL:

AN ANCIENT EPIC POEM.

THE ARGUMENT.

Cuchullin, pleafed with the ftory of Carril, infifts with that bard for more of his fongs. He relates the actions of Fingal in Lochlin, and death of Agandecca the beautiful fifter of Swaran. He had fcarce finifh.d, when Calmar the fon of Matha, who had advifed the firft battle, came wounded from the field, and told them of Swaran's defign to furprife the remains of the Irifh army. He himfelf propofes to withftand fingly the whole force of the enemy, in a narrow pafs, till the Irifh fhould make good their retreat. Cuchullin, touched with the gallant propofal of Calmar, refolves to accompany him, and orders Carril to carry off the few that remained of the Irifh. Morning comes, Calmar dies of his wounds; and, the fhips of the Caledonians appearing, Swaran gives over the purfuit of the Irifh, and returns to oppofe Fingal's landing. Cuchullin afhamed, after his defeat, to appear before Fingal, retires to the cave of Tura. Fingal engages the enemy, puts them to flight; but the coming on of night makes the victory not decifive. The king, who had obferved the gallant behaviour of his grandfon Ofcar, gives him advices concerning his conduct in peace and war. He recommends to him to place the example of his fathers before his eyes, as the beft model for his conduct; which introduces the epifode concerning Fainafollis

ARGUMENT.

lis, the daughter of the king of Craca, whom Fingal had taken under his protection, in his youth. Fillan and Oscar are difpatched to obferve the motions of the enemy by night; Gaul the fon of Morni defires the command of the army, in the next battle; which Fingal promifes to give him. Some general reflections of the poet clofe the third day.

FINGAL:
AN ANCIENT EPIC POEM.

BOOK III.[a]

"PLEASANT are the words of the song," said Cuchullin, " and lovely are the tales of other times. They are like the calm dew of the morning on the hill of roes, when the sun is faint on its side, and the lake is settled and blue in the vale. O Carril, raise again thy voice, and let me hear the song of Tura: which was sung in my halls of joy, when Fingal king of shields was there, and glowed at the deeds of his fathers."

"Fingal! thou man of battle," said Carril, " early were thy deeds in arms. Lochlin was consumed in thy wrath, when thy youth strove with the beauty of maids. They smiled at the fair-blooming face of the hero; but death was in his hands. He was strong as the waters of Lora. His followers were like the roar of a thousand streams. They took the king of Lochlin in battle, but restored him to his ships. His big heart swelled with pride; and the death of the youth was dark in his soul. For none ever, but Fingal, overcame the strength of the mighty Starno [b].

"He

"He sat in the halls of his shells in Lochlin's woody land. He called the gray-haired Snivan, that often sung round the circle [c] of Loda: when the stone of power heard his cry, and the battle turned in the field of the valiant.

"Go, gray-haired Snivan," Starno said, "go to Ardven's sea-surrounded rocks. Tell to Fingal king of the desart; he that is the fairest among his thousands, tell him I give him my daughter, the loveliest maid that ever heaved a breast of snow. Her arms are white as the foam of my waves. Her soul is generous and mild. Let him come with his bravest heroes to the daughter of the secret hall."

Snivan came to Albion's windy hills: and fair-haired Fingal went. His kindled soul flew before him as he bounded on the waves of the north.

"Welcome," said the dark-brown Starno, "welcome, king of rocky Morven; and ye his heroes of might; sons of the lonely isle! Three days within my halls shall ye feast; and three days pursue my boars, that your fame may reach the maid that dwells in the secret hall."

"The king of snow [d] designed their death, and gave the feast of shells. Fingal, who doubted the foe, kept on his arms of steel. The sons of death were afraid, and fled from the eyes of the hero.

The

The voice of fprightly mirth arofe. The trembling harps of joy are ftrung. Bards fing the battle of heroes; or the heaving breaft of love. Ullin, Fingal's bard, was there; the fweet voice of the hill of Cona. He praifed the daughter of fnow; and Morven's ᵉ high-defcended chief. The daughter of fnow overheard, and left the hall of her fecret figh. She came in all her beauty, like the moon from the cloud of the eaft. Lovelinefs was around her as light. Her fteps were like the mufic of fongs. She faw the youth and loved him. He was the ftolen figh of her foul. Her blue eye rolled on him in fecret: and fhe bleft the chief of Morven.

" The third day, with all its beams, fhone bright on the wood of boars. Forth moved the dark-browed Starno; and Fingal, king of fhields. Half the day they fpent in the chafe; and the fpear of Fingal was red in the blood of Gormal ᶠ.

" It was then the daughter of Starno, with blue eyes rolling in tears, came with her voice of love, and fpoke to the king of Morven.

" Fingal, high-defcended chief, truft not Starno's heart of pride. Within that wood he has placed his chiefs; beware of the wood of death. But, remember, fon of the hill, remember Agandecca; fave me from the wrath of my father, king of the windy Morven!"

" The

"The youth, with unconcern, went on; his heroes by his side. The sons of death fell by his hand; and Gormal echoed around.

"Before the halls of Starno the sons of the chase convened. The king's dark brows were like clouds. His eyes like meteors of night. "Bring hither," he cries, "Agandecca to her lovely king of Morven. His hand is stained with the blood of my people; and her words have not been in vain."

"She came with the red eye of tears. She came with her loose raven locks. Her white breast heaved with sighs, like the foam of the streamy Lubar. Starno pierced her side with steel. She fell like a wreath of snow that slides from the rocks of Ronan; when the woods are still, and the echo deepens in the vale.

"Then Fingal eyed his valiant chiefs, his valiant chiefs took arms. The gloom of the battle roared, and Lochlin fled or died. Pale, in his bounding ship he closed the maid of the raven hair. Her tomb ascends on Ardven, and the sea roars round the dark dwelling of Agandecca."

"Blessed be her soul," said Cuchullin, "and blessed be the mouth of the song. Strong was the youth of Fingal, and strong is his arm of age. Lochlin shall fall again before the king of echoing Morven. Shew thy face from a cloud, O moon;

light

light his white sails on the wave of the night. And if any strong spirit * of heaven sits on that low-hung cloud; turn his dark ships from the rock, thou rider of the storm!"

Such were the words of Cuchullin at the sound of the mountain-stream; when Calmar ascended the hill, the wounded son of Matha. From the field he came in his blood. He leaned on his bending spear. Feeble is the arm of battle! but strong the soul of the hero!

"Welcome! O son of Matha," said Connal, "welcome art thou to thy friends! Why bursts that broken sigh from the breast of him that never feared before?"

"And never, Connal, will he fear, chief of the pointed steel. My soul brightens in danger, and exults in the noise of battle. I am of the race of steel; my fathers never feared.

"Cormar was the first of my race. He sported through the storms of the waves. His black skiff bounded on the ocean; and travelled on the wings of the blast. A spirit once embroiled the night. Seas swell and rocks resound. Winds drive along the clouds. The lightning flies on wings of fire. He feared, and came to land; then blushed that he feared at all. He rushed again among the waves to find the son of the wind. Three youths guide

guide the bounding bark; he stood with the sword unsheathed. When the low-hung vapour passed, he took it by the curling head, aud searched its dark womb with his steel. The son of the wind forsook the air. The moon and stars returned.

"Such was the boldness of my race; and Calmar is like his fathers. Danger flies from the uplifted sword. They best succeed who dare."

"But now, ye sons of green-valley'd Erin, retire from Lena's bloody heath. Collect the sad remnant of our friends, and join the sword of Fingal. I heard the sound of Lochlin's advancing arms; but Calmar will remain and fight. My voice shall be such, my friends, as if thousands were behind me. But, son of Semo, remember me. Remember Calmar's lifeless corse. After Fingal has wasted the field, place me by some stone of remembrance, that future times may hear my fame; and the mother * of Calmar rejoice over the stone of my renown."

"No: son of Matha," said Cuchullin, "I will never leave thee. My joy is in the unequal field: my soul increases in danger. Connal, and Carril of other times, carry off the sad sons of Erin; and when the battle is over, search for our pale corses in this narrow way. For near this oak we shall stand in the stream of the battle of thousands. O
                                                      Fithil's

Fithil's fon, with feet of wind, fly over the heath of Lena. Tell to Fingal that Erin is inthralled, and bid the king of Morven haften. O let him come like the fun in a ſtorm, when he fhines on the hills of grafs."

Morning is gray on Cromla; the fons of the fea afcend. Calmar ſtood forth to meet them in the pride of his kindling foul. But pale was the face of the warrior; he leaned on his father's fpear. That fpear which he brought from Lara's hall, when the foul of his mother was fad. But ſlowly now the hero falls, like a tree on the plains of Cona. Dark Cuchullin ſtands alone like a rock! in a fandy vale. The fea comes with its waves, and roars on its hardened fides. Its head is covered with foam, and the hills are echoing around. Now from the gray miſt of the ocean, the white-failed ſhips of Fingal appear. High is the grove of their maſts as they nod, by turns, on the rolling wave.

Swaran faw them from the hill, and returned from the fons of Erin. As ebbs the refounding fea, through the hundred ifles of Iniſtore; fo loud, fo vaſt, fo immenfe returned the fons of Lochlin againſt the king of the defart hill. But bending, weeping, fad, and flow, and dragging his long fpear behind, Cuchullin funk in Cromla's wood, and

and mourned his fallen friends. He feared the face of Fingal, who was wont to greet him from the fields of renown.

"How many lie there of my heroes! the chiefs of Innis-fail! they that were cheerful in the hall, when the sound of the shells arose. No more shall I find their steps in the heath, or hear their voice in the chase of the hinds. Pale, silent, low on bloody beds are they who were my friends! O spirits of the lately dead, meet Cuchullin on his heath. Converse with him on the wind, when the rustling tree of Tura's cave resounds. There, far remote, I shall lie unknown. No bard shall hear of me. No gray stone shall rise to my renown. Mourn me with the dead, O Bragela! departed is my fame."

Such were the words of Cuchullin, when he sunk in the woods of Cromla.

Fingal, tall in his ship, stretched his bright lance before him. Terrible was the gleam of the steel: it was like the green meteor of death, setting in the heath of Malmor, when the traveller is alone, and the broad moon is darkened in heaven.

"The battle is over," said the king, "and I behold the blood of my friends. Sad is the heath of Lena! and mournful the oaks of Cromla. The hunters have fallen there in their strength; and the

the son of Semo is no more. Ryno and Fillan, my sons, found the horn of Fingal's war. Ascend that hill on the shore, and call the children of the foe. Call them from the grave of Lamdarg, the chief of other times. Be your voice like that of your father, when he enters the battles of his strength. I wait for the dark mighty man: I wait on Lena's shore for Swaran. And let him come with all his race; for strong in battle are the friends of the dead."

Fair Ryno flew like lightning; dark Fillan as the shade of autumn. On Lena's heath their voice is heard; the sons of ocean heard the horn of Fingal's war. As the roaring eddy of ocean returning from the kingdom of snows; so strong, so dark, so sudden came down the sons of Lochlin. The king in their front appears in the dismal pride of his arms. Wrath burns in his dark-brown face: and his eyes roll in the fire of his valour.

Fingal beheld the son of Starno; and he remembered Agandecca. For Swaran with the tears of youth had mourned his white-bosomed sister. He sent Ullin of the songs to bid him to the feast of shells. For pleasant on Fingal's soul returned the remembrance of the first of his loves.

Ullin came with aged steps, and spoke to Starno's son. " O thou that dwellest afar, surrounded, like a rock, with thy waves, come to the feast of the king, and pafs the day in reft. To-morrow, let us fight, O Swaran, and break the echoing shields."

"To-day," faid Starno's wrathful fon, "we break the echoing fhields: to-morrow my feaft will be fpread; and Fingal lie on earth."

"And, to-morrow, let his feaft be fpread," faid Fingal with a fmile; "for, to-day, O my fons, we fhall break the echoing fhields. Offian, ftand thou near my arm. Gaul, lift thy terrible fword. Fergus, bend thy crooked yew. Throw, Fillan, thy lance through heaven.—Lift your fhields like the the darkened moon. Be your fpears the meteors of death. Follow me in the path of my fame; and equal my deeds in battle."

As a hundred winds on Morven; as the ftreams of a hundred hills; as clouds fly fucceffive over heaven; or, as the dark ocean affaults the fhore of the defart: fo roaring, fo vaft, fo terrible the armies mixed on Lena's echoing heath. The groan of the people fpread over the hills; it was like the thunder of night, when the cloud burfts on Cona; and a thoufand ghofts fhriek at once on the hollow wind.

Fingal rufhed on in his ftrength, terrible as the fpirit of Trenmor; when, in a whirlwind, he comes to Morven to fee the children of his pride. The oaks refound on their hills, and the rocks fall down before him. Bloody was the hand of my father when he whirled the lightning of his fword. He remembers the battles of his youth, and the field is wafted in his courfe.

Ryno went on like a pillar of fire. Dark is the brow of Gaul. Fergus rufhed forward with feet of wind; and Fillan like the mift of the hill. Myfelf [k], like a rock, came down, I exulted in the ftrength of the king. Many were the deaths of my arm; and difmal was the gleam of my fword. My locks were not then fo gray; nor trembled my hands of age. My eyes were not clofed in darknefs; nor failed my feet in the race.

Who can relate the deaths of the people; or the deeds of mighty heroes; when Fingal, burning in his wrath, confumed the fons of Lochlin? Groans fwelled on groans, from hill to hill, till night had covered all. Pale, ftaring like a herd of deer, the fons of Lochlin convene on Lena.

We fat and heard the fprightly harp at Lubar's gentle ftream. Fingal himfelf was next to the foe; and liftened to the tales of bards. His godlike race were in the fong, the chiefs of other times. Attentive, leaning on his fhield, the king of Morven fat. The wind whiftled through his aged locks,

and

and his thoughts are of the days of other years. Near him, on his bending spear, my young, my lovely Oscar stood. He admired the king of Morven: and his actions were swelling in his soul.

"Son of my son," begun the king, "O Oscar, pride of youth, I saw the shining of thy sword and gloried in my race. Pursue the glory of our fathers, and be what they have been; when Trenmor lived, the first of men, and Trathal the father of heroes. They fought the battle in their youth, and are the song of bards. O Oscar! bend the strong in arms: but spare the feeble hand. Be thou a stream of many tides against the foes of thy people; but like the gale that moves the grass to those who ask thine aid. So Trenmor lived; such Trathal was; and such has Fingal been. My arm was the support of the injured; and the weak rested behind the lightning of my steel.

"Oscar! I was young like thee, when lovely Fainasollis came: that sun-beam! that mild light of love! the daughter of Craca's king! I then returned from Cona's heath, and few were in my train. A white-sailed boat appeared far off; we saw it like a mist that rode on ocean's blast. It soon approached; we saw the fair. Her white breast heaved with sighs. The wind was in her loose dark hair; her rosy cheek had tears. "Daughter

ter of beauty," calm I faid, " what figh is in that
breaſt? Can I, young as I am, defend thee, daughter of the fea? My fword is not unmatched in war,
but dauntlefs is my heart."

" To thee I fly," with fighs fhe replied, " O
chief of mighty men! To thee I fly, chief of fhells,
fupporter of the feeble hand! The King of Craca's
echoing iſle owned me the fun-beam of his race.
And often did the hills of Cromla reply to the fighs
of love for the unhappy Fainafollis. Sora's chief
beheld me fair; and loved the daughter of Craca.
His fword is like a beam of light upon the warrior's fide. But dark is his brow; and tempefts
are in his foul. I fhun him on the rolling fea; but
Sora's chief purfues."

" Reft thou," I faid, " behind my fhield; reft
in peace, thou beam of light! The gloomy chief
of Sora will fly, if Fingal's arm is like his foul. In
fome lone cave I might conceal thee, daughter of
the fea! But Fingal never flies; for where the danger threatens, I rejoice in the ſtorm of fpears." I
faw the tears upon her cheek. I pitied Craca's fair.

Now, like a dreadful wave afar, appeared the
fhip of ftormy Borbar. His mafts high-bended
over the fea behind their fheets of fnow. White
roll the waters on either fide. The ftrength of o-
ccan

cean founds. "Come thou," I faid, "from the roar of ocean, thou rider of their ftorm. Partake the feaft within my hall. It is the houfe of ftrangers." "The maid ftood trembling by my fide; he drew the bow: fhe fell. "Unerring is thy hand,' I faid, "but feeble was the foe." We fought, nor weak was the ftrife of death: He funk beneath my fword. We laid them in two tombs of ftones; the unhappy children of youth.

Such have I been in my youth, O Ofcar; be thou like the age of Fingal. Never feek the battle, nor fhun it when it comes. "Fillan and Ofcar of the dark-brown hair; ye children of the race; fly over the heath of roaring winds; and view the fons of Lochlin. Far off I hear the noife of their fear, like the ftorms of echoing Cona. Go; that they may not fly my fword along the waves of the north. For many chiefs of Erin's race lie here on the dark bed of death. The children of the ftorm are low; the fons of echoing Cromla."

The heroes flew like two dark clouds; two dark clouds that are the chariots of ghofts; when air's dark children come to frighten haplefs men.

It was then that Gaul [m], the fon of Morni, ftood like a rock in the night. His fpear is glittering to the ftars; his voice like many ftreams. "Son of battle," cried the chief, "O Fingal, king of fhells!

let

let the bards of many fongs footh Erin's friends to reft. And, Fingal, fheath thy fword of death; and let thy people fight. We wither away without our fame; for our king is the only breaker of fhields. When morning rifes on our hills, behold at a diftance our deeds. Let Lochlin feel the fword of Morni's fon, that bards may fing of me. Such was the cuftom heretofore of Fingal's noble race. Such was thine own, thou king of fwords, in battles of the fpear."

"O fon of Morni," Fingal replied, "I glory in thy fame. Fight; but my fpear fhall be near to aid thee in the midft of danger. Raife, raife the voice, fons of the fong, and lull me into reft. Here will Fingal lie amidft the wind of night. And if thou, Agandecca, art near, among the children of thy land; if thou fitteft on a blaft of wind among the high fhrowded mafts of Lochlin; come to my dreams", my fair one, and fhew thy bright face to my foul."

Many a voice and many a harp in tuneful founds arofe. Of Fingal's noble deeds they fung, and of the noble race of the hero. And fometimes on the lovely found was heard the name of the now mournful Offian.

Often have I fought, and often won in battles of the fpear. But blind, and tearful, and forlorn I now

I now walk with little men. O Fingal, with thy race of battle I now behold thee not. The wild roes feed upon the green tomb of the mighty king of Morven. Bleſt be thy ſoul, thou king of ſwords, thou moſt renowned on the hills of Cona!

FINGAL:

FINGAL:

AN ANCIENT EPIC POEM.

THE ARGUMENT.

The action of the poem being suspended by night, Ossian takes that opportunity to relate his own actions at the lake of Lego, and his courtship of Everallin, who was the mother of Oscar, and had died some time before the expedition of Fingal into Ireland. Her ghost appears to him, and tells him that Oscar, who had been sent, the beginning of the night, to observe the enemy, was engaged with an advanced party, and almost overpowered. Ossian relieves his son; and an alarm is given to Fingal of the approach of Swaran. The king rises, calls his army together, and, as he had promised the preceding night, devolves the command on Gaul the son of Morni, while he himself, after charging his sons to behave gallantly and defend his people, retires to a hill, from whence he could have a view of the battle. The battle joins; the poet relates Oscar's great actions. But when Oscar, in conjunction with his father, conquered in one wing, Gaul, who was attacked by Swaran in person, was on the point of retreating in the other. Fingal sends Ullin his bard to encourage him with a war song, but notwithstanding Swaran prevails; and Gaul and his army are obliged to give way. Fingal, descending from the hill, rallies them again; Swaran desists from the pursuit, possesses himself of a rising ground, restores the ranks, and waits the approach

ARGUMENT.

proach of Fingal. The king, having encouraged his men, gives the necessary orders, and renews the battle. Cuchullin, who, with his friend Connal, and Carril his bard, had retired to the cave of Tura, hearing the noise, came to the brow of the hill, which overlooked the field of battle, where he saw Fingal engaged with the enemy. He, being hindered by Connal from joining Fingal, who was himself upon the point of obtaining a complete victory, sends Carril to congratulate that hero on his success.

FINGAL:

AN ANCIENT EPIC POEM.

BOOK IV.^a

WHO comes with her songs from the mountain, like the bow of the showery Lena? It is the maid of the voice of love. The white-armed daughter of Toscar. Often hast thou heard my song, often given the tear of beauty. Dost thou come to the battles of thy people? and to hear the actions of Oscar? When shall I cease to mourn, by the streams of the echoing Cona? My years have passed away in battle, and my age is darkened with sorrow.

Daughter of the hand of snow! I was not so mournful and blind; I was not so dark and forlorn, when Everallin loved me! Everallin with the dark-brown hair, the white-bosomed love of Cormac. A thousand heroes sought the maid, she denied her love to a thousand; the sons of the sword were despised: for graceful in her eyes was Ossian.

I went, in suit of the maid, to Lego's sable surge; twelve of my people were there, the sons of the streamy Morven. We came to Branno, friend of strangers: Branno of the sounding mail. "From whence,".

whence," he said, "are the arms of steel? Not easy to win is the maid, that has denied the blue-eyed sons of Erin. But blest be thou, O son of Fingal. Happy is the maid that waits thee. Tho' twelve daughters of beauty were mine, thine were the choice, thou son of fame!" Then he opened the hall of the maid, the dark haired Everallin. Joy kindled in our breasts of steel and blest the maid of Branno.

Above us on the hill appeared the people of stately Cormac. Eight were the heroes of the chief; and the heath flamed with their arms. There Colla, Durra of the wounds, there mighty Toscar and Tago, there Frestal the victorious stood; Dairo of the happy deeds, and Dala the battle's bulwark in the narrow way. The sword flamed in the hand of Cormac, and graceful was the look of the hero.

Eight were the heroes of Ossian; Ullin stormy son of war; Mullo of the generous deeds; the noble, the graceful Scelacha; Olgan, and Cerdal the wrathful, and Dumariccan's brows of death. And why should Ogar be the last; so wide renowned on the hills of Ardven?

Ogar met Dala the strong, face to face, on the field of heroes. The battle of the chiefs was like the wind on ocean's foamy waves. The dagger is remembered by Ogar; the weapon which he loved;

nine

nine times he drowned it in Dala's side. The stormy battle turned. Three times I pierced Cormac's shield: three times he broke his spear. But, unhappy youth of love! I cut his head away. Five times I shook it by the lock. The friends of Cormac fled.

Whoever would have told me, lovely maid *b* when then I strove in battle; that blind, forsaken, and forlorn I now should pass the night; firm ought his mail to have been, and unmatched his arm in battle.

Now *c* on Lena's gloomy heath the voice of music died away. The inconstant blast blew hard, and the high oak shook its leaves around me; of Everallin were my thoughts, when she, in all the light of beauty, and her blue eyes rolling in tears, stood on a cloud before my sight, and spoke with feeble voice.

"O Ossian, rise and save my son; save Oscar chief of men, near the red oak of Lubar's stream, he fights with Lochlin's sons." She sunk into her cloud again. I clothed me with my steel. My spear supported my steps, and my rattling armour rung. I hummed, as I was wont in danger, the songs of heroes of old. Like distant thunder *d* Lochlin heard; they fled; my son pursued.

I called

I called him like a diſtant ſtream. "My ſon return over Lena. No further purſue the foe," I ſaid, "though Oſſian is behind thee." He came; and lovely in my ear was Oſcar's ſounding ſteel. "Why didſt thou ſtop my hand," he ſaid, "till death had covered all? For dark and dreadful by the ſtream they met thy ſon and Fillan. They watched the terrors of the night. Our ſwords have conquered ſome. But as the winds of night pour the ocean over the white ſands of Mora, ſo dark advance the ſons of Lochlin over Lena's ruſtling heath. The ghoſts of night ſhriek afar; and I have ſeen the meteors of death. Let me awake the king of Morven, he that ſmiles in danger; for he is like the ſon of heaven that riſes in a ſtorm."

Fingal had ſtarted from a dream, and leaned on Trenmor's ſhield; the dark-brown ſhield of his fathers; which they had lifted of old in the battles of their race. The hero had ſeen in his reſt the mournful form of Agandecca; ſhe came from the way of the ocean, and ſlowly, lonely, moved over Lena. Her face was pale like the miſt of Cromla; and dark were the tears of her cheek. She often raiſed her dim hand from her robe; her robe which was of the clouds of the deſart: ſhe raiſed

raised her dim hand over Fingal, and turned away her silent eyes.

"Why weeps the daughter of Starno," said Fingal, with a sigh? "Why is thy face so pale, thou daughter of the clouds?" She departed on the wind of Lena; and left him in the midst of the night. She mourned the sons of her people that were to fall by Fingal's hand.

The hero started from rest, and still beheld her in his soul. The sound of Oscar's steps approached. The king saw the gray shield on his side. For the faint beam of the morning came over the waters of Ullin.

"What do the foes in their fear!" said the rising king of Morven. "Or fly they through ocean's foam, or wait they the battle of steel? But why should Fingal ask? I hear their voice on the early wind. Fly over Lena's heath, O Oscar, and awake our friends to battle."

The king stood by the stone of Lubar; and thrice raised his terrible voice. The deer started from the fountains of Cromla; and all the rocks shook on their hills. Like the noise of a hundred mountain-streams, that burst, and roar, and foam; like the clouds that gather to a tempest on the blue face of the sky; so met the sons of the desart, round the terrible voice of Fingal. For pleasant

I   was

was the voice of the king of Morven to the warriors of his land : often had he led them to battle, and returned with the spoils of the foe.

"Come to battle," said the king, " ye children of the storm, Come to the death of thousands. Comhal's son will see the fight. My sword shall wave on that hill, and be the shield of my people. But never may you need it, warriors; while the son of Morni fights, the chief of mighty men. He shall lead my battle; that his fame may rise in the song. O ye ghosts of heroes dead! ye riders of the storm of Cromla! receive my falling people with joy, and bring them to your hills. And may the blast of Lena carry them over my seas, that they may come to my silent dreams, and delight my soul in rest.

" Fillan and Oscar, of the dark-brown hair, fair Ryno, with the pointed steel! advance with valour to the fight; and behold the son of Morni, Let your swords be like his in the strife! and behold the deeds of his hands. Protect the friends of your father : and remember the chiefs of old. My children, I shall see you yet, though here ye should fall in Erin. Soon shall our cold, pale ghosts meet in a cloud, and fly over the hills of Cona."

Now

Now like a dark and stormy cloud, edged round with the red lightning of heaven, and flying westward from the morning's beam, the king of hills removed. Terrible is the light of his armour, and two spears are in his hand. His gray hair falls on the wind. He often looks back on the war. Three bards attend the son of fame, to carry his words to the heroes. High on Cromla's side he sat, waving the lightning of his sword, and as he waved we moved.

Joy rose in Oscar's face. His cheek is red. His eye sheds tears. The sword is a beam of fire in his hand. He came, and smiling, spoke to Ossian " O ruler of the fight of steel! my father, hear thy son. Retire with Morven's mighty chief; and give me Ossian's fame. And if here I fall; my king, remember that breast of snow, that lonely sun-beam of my love, the white-handed daughter of Toscar. For, with red cheek from the rock, and bending over the stream, her soft hair flies about her bosom, as she pours the sigh for Oscar. Tell her I am on my hills a lightly-bounding son of the wind; that hereafter, in a cloud, I may meet the lovely maid of Toscar."

" Raise, Oscar, rather raise my tomb. I will not yield the fight to thee. For first and bloodiest in the war my arm shall teach thee how to fight. But, remember,

remember, my son, to place this sword, this bow, and the horn of my deer, within that dark and narrow house, whose mark is one gray stone. Oscar, I have no love to leave to the care of my son; for graceful Everallin is no more, the lovely daughter of Branno."

Such were our words, when Gaul's loud voice came growing on the wind. He waved on high the sword of his father, and rushed to death and wounds.

As waves white-bubbling over the deep come swelling, roaring on; as rocks of ooze meet roaring waves: so foes attacked and fought. Man met with man, and steel with steel. Shields sound; men fall. As a hundred hammers on the son of the furnace, so rose, so rung their swords.

Gaul rushed on like a whirlwind in Ardven. The destruction of heroes is on his sword. Swaran was like the fire of the desart in the echoing heath of Gormal. How can I give to the song the death of many spears? My sword rose high, and flamed in the strife of blood. And, Oscar, terrible wert thou, my best, my greatest son! I rejoiced in my secret soul, when his sword flamed over the slain. They fled amain through Lena's heath: and we pursued and flew. As stones that bound from rock to rock; as axes in echoing woods; as thunder

rolls

rolls from hill to hill in difmal broken peals; fo blow fucceeded to blow, and death to death, from the hand of Ofcar ᶜ and mine.

But Swaran clofed round Morni's fon, as the ftrength of the tide of Iniftore. The king half-rofe from his hill at the fight, and half-affumed the fpear. " Go, Ullin, go, my aged bard," begun the king of Morven. " Remind the mighty Gaul of battle; remind him of his fathers. Support the yielding fight with fong; for fong enlivens war." Tall Ullin went, with fteps of age, and fpoke to the king of fwords.

" Son ᶠ of the chief of generous fteeds! high-bounding king of fpears. Strong arm in every perilous toil. Hard heart that never yields. Chief of the pointed arms of death. Cut down the foe; let no white fail bound round dark Iniftore. Be thine arm like thunder. Thine eyes like fire, thy heart of folid rock. Whirl round thy fword as a meteor at night, and lift thy fhield like the flame of death. Son of the chief of generous fteeds, cut down the foe. Deftroy." The hero's heart beat high. But Swaran came with battle. He cleft the fhield of Gaul in twain; and the fons of the defart fled.

Now Fingal arofe in his might, and thrice he reared his voice. Cromla anfwered around, and the

the sons of the desart stood still. They bent their red faces to the earth, ashamed at the presence of Fingal. He came like a cloud of rain in the days of the sun, when slow it rolls on the hill, and fields expect the shower. Swaran beheld the terrible king of Morven, and stopped in the midst of his course. Dark he leaned on his spear, rolling his red eyes around. Silent and tall he seemed as an oak on the banks of Lubar, which had its branches blasted of old by the lightning of heaven. It bends over the stream, and the gray moss whistles in the wind: so stood the king. Then slowly he retired to the rising heath of Lena. His thousands pour around the hero, and the darkness of battle gathers on the hill.

Fingal, like a beam from heaven, shone in the midst of his people. His heroes gather around him, and he sends forth the voice of his power. "Raise my standards [5] on high. Spread them on Lena's wind, like the flames of an hundred hills. Let them sound on the winds of Erin, and remind us of the fight. Ye sons of the roaring streams, that pour from a thousand hills, be near the king of Morven: attend to the words of his power. Gaul, strongest arm of death! O Oscar, of the future fights; Connal, son of the blue steel of Sora; Dermid

mid of the dark-brown hair, Ossian king of many songs, be near your father's arm."

We reared the sun-beam * of battle; the standard of the king. Each hero's soul exulted with joy, as, waving, it flew on the wind. It was studded with gold above, as the blue wide shell of the nightly sky. Each hero had his standard too; and each his gloomy men.

"Behold," said the king of generous shells, "how Lochlin divides on Lena. They stand like broken clouds on the hill, or an half consumed grove of oaks; when we see the sky through its branches, and the meteor passing behind. Let every chief among the friends of Fingal take a dark troop of those that frown so high; nor let a son of the echoing groves bound on the waves of Iniftore."

"Mine," said Gaul, "be the seven chiefs that came from Lano's lake." "Let Iniftore's dark king," said Ofcar, "come to the sword of Ossian's son." "To mine the king of Inifcon," said Connal, "heart of steel!" "Or Mudan's chief or I," said brown-haired Dermid, "shall sleep on clay-cold earth." My choice, though now so weak and dark, was Torman's battling king; I promised with my hand to win the hero's dark-brown shield.

"Blest and victorious be my chiefs," said Fingal

of the mildeſt look; "Swaran, king of roaring waves, thou art the choice of Fingal."

Now, like an hundred different winds that pour through many vales; divided, dark, the ſons of the hill advanced, and Cromla echoed around.

How can I relate the deaths when we cloſed in the ſtrife of our ſteel? O daughter of Toſcar! bloody were our hands! The gloomy ranks of Lochlin fell like the banks of the roaring Cona. Our arms were victorious on Lena; each chief fulfilled his promiſe. Beſide the murmur of Branno thou didſt often ſit, O maid; when thy white boſom roſe frequent, like the down of the ſwan when ſlow ſhe ſails the lake, and ſidelong winds are blowing. Thou haſt ſeen the ſun ᵇ red and ſlow behind his cloud; night gathering round on the mountain, while the unfrequent blaſt ᶦ roared in narrow vales. At length the rain beats hard: and thunder rolls in peals. Lightning glances on the rocks. Spirits ride on beams of fire. And the ſtrength of the mountain-ſtreams roaring down the hills. Such was the noiſe of battle, maid of the arms of ſnow. Why, daughter of the hill, that tear? the maids of Lochlin have cauſe to weep. The people of their country fell, for bloody was the blue ſteel of the race of my heroes. But I am ſad, forlorn, and blind; and no more the companion

nion of heroes. Give, lovely maid, to me thy tears, for I have feen the tombs of all my friends.

It was then by Fingal's hand a hero fell, to his grief. Gray-haired he rolled in the duft, and lifted his faint eyes to the king. " And is it by me thou haft fallen," faid the fon of Connal, " thou friend of Agandecca! I faw thy tears for the maid of my love in the halls of the bloody Starno. Thou haft been the foe of the foes of my love, and haft thou fallen by my hand? Raife, Ullin, raife the grave of the fon of Mathron; and give his name to the fong of Agandecca; for dear to my foul haft thou been, thou darkly-dwelling maid of Ardven.

Cuchullin from the cave of Cromla, heard the noife of the troubled war. He called to Connal chief of fwords, and Carril of other times. The gray-haired heroes heard his voice, and took their afpen fpears. They came, and faw the tide of battle, like the crowded waves of the ocean, when the dark wind blows from the deep, and rolls the billows through the fandy vale.

Cuchullin kindled at the fight, and darknefs gathered on his brow. His hand is on the fword of his fathers: his red-rolling eyes on the foe. He thrice attempted to rufh to battle, and thrice did Connal ftop him. " Chief of the ifle of mift," he

K

he said, "Fingal subdues the foe. Seek not a part of the fame of the king; himself is like a storm."

"Then, Carril, go," replied the chief, "and greet the king of Morven. When Lochlin falls away like a stream after rain, and the noise of the battle is over, then be thy voice sweet in his ear to praise the king of swords. Give him the sword of Caithbat; for Cuchullin is worthy no more to lift the arms of his fathers.

"But, O ye ghosts of the lonely Cromla! ye souls of chiefs that are no more! be ye the companions of Cuchullin, and talk to him in the cave of his sorrow. For never more shall I be renowned among the mighty in the land. I am like a beam that has shone; like a mist that fled away, when the blast of the morning came, and brightened the shaggy side of the hill. Connal, talk of arms no more: departed is my fame. My sighs shall be on Cromla's wind, till my footsteps cease to be seen. And thou, white-bosom'd Bragela, mourn over the fall of my fame; for, vanquished, I will never return to thee, thou sun-beam of Dunscaich."

FINGAL;

FINGAL:

AN ANCIENT EPIC POEM.

THE ARGUMENT.

Cuchullin and Connal still remain on the hill. Fingal and Swaran meet; the combat is described. Swaran is overcome, bound and delivered over as a prisoner to the care of Ossian, and Gaul the son of Morni; Fingal, his younger sons, and Oscar, still pursue the enemy. The episode of Orla, a chief of Lochlin, who was mortally wounded in the battle, is introduced. Fingal, touched with the death of Orla, orders the pursuit to be discontinued; and calling his sons together, he is informed that Ryno, the youngest of them, was killed. He laments his death, hears the story of Lamdarg and Gelchossa, and returns towards the place where he had left Swaran. Carril, who had been sent by Cuchullin to congratulate Fingal on his victory, comes in the mean time to Ossian. The conversation of the two poets closes the action of the fourth day.

FINGAL:

AN ANCIENT EPIC POEM.

BOOK V.ª

NOW Connal, on Cromla's windy side, spoke to the chief of the noble car. "Why that gloom, son of Semo? Our friends are the mighty in battle. And renowned art thou, O warrior! many were the deaths of thy steel. Often has Bragela met with blue-rolling eyes of joy, often has she met her hero, returning in the midst of the valiant when his sword was red with slaughter, and his foes silent in the fields of the tomb. Pleasant to her ears were thy bards, when thine actions rose in the song.

"But behold the king of Morven; he moves below like a pillar of fire. His strength is like the stream of Lubar, or the wind of the echoing Cromla; when the branchy forests of night are overturned.

"Happy are thy people, O Fingal, thine arm shall fight their battles: thou art the first in their dangers; the wisest in the days of their peace. Thou speakest and thy thousands obey; and armies

tremble

tremble at the found of thy fteel. Happy are thy people, Fingal, chief of the lonely hills.

"Who is that so dark and terrible, coming in the thunder of his courfe? who is but Starno's fon to meet the king of Morven? Behold the battle of the chiefs: it is like the ftorm of the ocean, when two fpirits meet far diftant, and contend for the rolling of the wave. The hunter hears the noife on his hill; and fees the high billows advancing to Ardven's fhore."

Such were the words of Connal, when the heroes met in the midft of their falling people. There was the clang of arms! there every blow, like the hundred hammers of the furnace! Terrible is the battle of the kings, and horrid the look of their eyes. Their dark-brown fhields are cleft in twain; and their fteel flies, broken, from their helmets. They fling their weapons down. Each rufhes [b] to the grafp of his foe. Their finewy arms bend round each other: they turn from fide to fide, and ftrain and ftretch their large fpreading limbs below. But when the pride of their ftrength arofe, they fhook the hill with their heels; rocks tumble from their places on high; the green-headed bufhes are overturned. At length the ftrength of Swaran fell; and the king of the groves is bound.

Thus

Thus have I seen on Cona; (but Cona I behold no more) thus have I seen two dark hills removed from their place by the strength of the bursting stream. They turn from side to side, and their tall oaks meet one another on high. Then they fall together with all their rocks and trees. The streams are turned by their sides, and the red ruin is seen afar.

"Sons of the king of Morven," said the noble Fingal, "guard the king of Lochlin; for he is strong as his thousand waves. His hand is taught to the battle, and his race of the times of old. Gaul, thou first of my heroes, and Ossian king of songs, attend the friend of Agandecca, and raise to joy his grief. But, Oscar, Fillan, and Ryno, ye children of the Race! pursue the rest of Lochlin over the heath of Lena; that no vessel may hereafter bound on the dark-rolling waves of Inistore."

They flew like lightning over the heath. He slowly moved as a cloud of thunder when the sultry plain of summer is silent. His sword is before him as a sun-beam, terrible as the streaming meteor of night. He came toward a chief of Lochlin, and spoke to the son of the wave.

"Who is that like a cloud at the rock of the roaring stream? He cannot bound over its course,

yet

yet stately is the chief! his bossy shield is on his side; and his spear like the tree of the desart. Youth of the dark-brown hair, art thou of Fingal's foes?"

"I am a son of Lochlin," he cries, "and strong is my arm in war. My spouse is weeping at home, but Orla ᶜ will never return."

"Or fights or yields the hero," said Fingal of the noble deeds? "foes do not conquer in my presence: but my friends are renowned in the hall. Son of the wave, follow me; partake the feast of my shells; pursue the deer of my desart; and be the friend of Fingal."

"No," said the hero, I assist the feeble: my strength shall remain with the weak in arms. My sword has been always unmatched, O warrior: let the king of Morven yield."

"I never yielded, Orla, Fingal never yielded to man. Draw thy sword and chuse thy foe. Many are my heroes."

"And does the king refuse the combat," said Orla of the dark-brown hair? "Fingal is a match for Orla: and he alone of all his race. But, king of Morven, if I shall fall; (as one time the warrior must die;) raise my tomb in the midst, and let it be the greatest on Lena. And send, over the dark-blue wave, the sword of Orla to the spouse of his love;

love; that she may shew it to her son, with tears, to kindle his soul to war."

"Son of the mournful tale," said Fingal, "why doft thou awaken my tears? One day the warriors muft die, and the children fee their uſeleſs arms in the hall. But, Orla, thy tomb ſhall riſe, and thy white-boſomed ſpouſe weep over thy ſword."

They fought on the heath of Lena, but feeble was the arm of Orla. The ſword of Fingal deſ‑ cended, and cleft his ſhield in twain. It fell and glittered on the ground, as the moon on the ſtream of night.

"King of Morven," ſaid the hero, "lift thy ſword, and pierce my breaſt. Wounded and faint from battle my friends have left me here. The mournful tale ſhall come to my love on the banks of the ſtreamy Loda; when ſhe is alone in the wood; and the ruſtling blaſt in the leaves."

"No;" ſaid the king of Morven, "I will never wound thee, Orla. On the banks of Loda let her ſee thee eſcaped from the hands of war. Let thy gray-haired father, who, perhaps, is blind with age, hear the ſound of thy voice in his hall. With joy let the hero riſe, and ſearch for his ſon with his hands."

"But never will he find him, Fingal;" ſaid the youth of the ſtreamy Loda. "On Lena's

L   heath

heath I shall die; and foreign bards will talk of me. My broad belt covers my wound of death. And now I give it to the wind."

The dark blood poured from his side, he fell pale on the heath of Lena. Fingal bends over him as he dies, and calls his younger heroes.

"Oscar and Fillan, my sons, raise high the memory of Orla. Here let the dark-haired hero rest far from the spouse of his love. Here let him rest in his narrow house far from the sound of Loda. The sons of the feeble will find his bow at home, but will not be able to bend it. His faithful dogs howl on his hills, and his boars, which he used to pursue, rejoice. Fallen is the arm of battle; the mighty among the valiant is low!

"Exalt the voice, and blow the horn, ye sons of the king of Morven: let us go back to Swaran, and send the night away on song. Fillin, Oscar, and Ryno, fly, over the heath of Lena. Where, Ryno, art thou, young son of fame? Thou art not wont to be the last to answer thy father."

"Ryno," said Ullin first of bards, "is with the awful forms of his fathers. With Trathal king of shields, and Trenmor of the mighty deeds. The youth is low, the youth is pale, he lies on Lena's heath."

"And

"And fell the swiftest in the race," said the king, "the first to bend the bow? Thou scarce hast been known to me: why did young Ryno fall? But sleep thou softly on Lena, Fingal shall soon behold thee. Soon shall my voice be heard no more, and my footsteps cease to be seen. The bards will tell of Fingal's name; the stones will talk of me. But, Ryno, thou art low indeed, thou hast not received thy fame. Ullin, strike the harp for Ryno; tell what the chief would have been. Farewell, thou first in every field. No more shall I direct thy dart. Thou that hast been so fair; I behold thee not. Farewell."

The tear is on the cheek of the king; for terrible was his son in war. His son! that was like a beam of fire by night on the hill; when the forests sink down in its course, and the traveller trembles at the sound.

"Whose fame is in that dark-green tomb," begun the king of generous shells? "four stones with their heads of moss stand there; and mark the narrow house of death. Near it let my Ryno rest, and be the neighbour of the valiant. Perhaps some chief of fame is here to fly with my son on clouds. O Ullin, raise the songs of other times. Bring to memory the dark dwellers of the tomb. If in the field of the valiant they never fled from danger, my son shall rest with them, far from his friends, on the heath of Lena."

"Here," said the mouth of the song, "here rest the first of heroes. Silent is Lamderg ᵈ in this tomb, and Ullin king of swords. And who, soft smiling from her cloud, shews me her face of love? Why, daughter, why so pale art thou, first of the maids of Cromla? Dost thou sleep with the foes in battle, Gelchossa, white-bosomed daughter of Tuathal? Thou hast been the love of thousands, but Lamderg was thy love." He came to Selma's mossy towers, and, striking his dark buckler, spoke.—

"Where is Gelchossa, my love, the daughter of the noble Tuathal? I left her in the hall of Selma, when I fought with the gloomy Ulfadda. Return soon, O Lamderg, she said, for here I am in in the midst of sorrow. Her white breast rose with sighs. Her cheek was wet with tears. But I see her not coming to meet me; and to sooth my soul after battle. Silent is the hall of my joy; I hear not the voice of the bard. Bran ᵉ does not shake his chains at the gate, glad at the coming of Lamderg. Where is Gelchossa, my love, the mild daughter of the generous Tuathal?"

"Lamderg!" says Ferchios the son of Aidon, "Gelchossa may be on Cromla; she and the maids of the bow pursuing the flying deer!"

"Ferchios!"

"Ferchios!" replied the chief of Cromla, "no noise meets the ear of Lamderg. No sound is in the woods of Lena. No deer fly in my sight. No panting dog pursues. I see not Gelchossa my love, fair as the full moon setting on the hills of Cromla. Go, Ferchios, go to Allad ‡ the gray-haired son of the rock. His dwelling is in the circle of stones. He may know of Gelchossa."

The son of Aidon went; and spoke to the ear of age. "Allad! thou that dwellest in the rock, thou that tremblest alone, what saw thine eyes of age?"

"I saw" answered Allad the old, "Ullin the son of Cairbar. He came like a cloud from Cromla; and he hummed a surly song like a blast in a leafless wood. He entered the hall of Selma. "Lamderg," he said, "most dreadful of men, fight or yield to Ullin." "Lamderg," replied Gelchossa, "the son of battle, is not here. He fights Ulfadda mighty chief. He is not here, thou first of men. But Lamderg never yielded. He will fight the son of Cairbar."

"Lovely art thou," said terrible Ullin, "daughter of the generous Tuathal. I carry thee to Cairbar's halls. The valiant shall have Gelchossa. Three days I remain on Cromla, to wait that son

of

of battle, Lamderg. On the fourth Gelchoſſa is mine, if the mighty Lamderg flies."

"Allad! ſaid the chief of Cromla, "peace to thy dreams in the cave. Ferchios, found the horn of Lamderg that Ullin may hear on Cromla. Lamderg [6], like a roaring ſtorm, aſcended the hill from Selma. He hummed a ſurly ſong as he went, like the noiſe of a falling ſtream. He ſtood like a cloud on the hill, that varies its form to the wind. He rolled a ſtone, the ſign of war. Ullin heard in Cairbar's hall. The hero heard, with joy, his foe, and took his father's ſpear. A ſmile brightens his dark-brown cheek, as he places his ſword by his ſide. The dagger glittered in his hand. He whiſtled as he went.

Gelchoſſa ſaw the ſilent chief, as a wreath of miſt aſcending the hill. She ſtruck her white and heaving breaſt; and ſilent, tearful, feared for Lamderg.

"Cairbar, hoary chief of ſhells," ſaid the maid of the tender hand; "I muſt bend the bow on Cromla; for I ſee the dark-brown hinds."

"She haſted up the hill. In vain! the gloomy heroes fought. Why ſhould I tell the king of Morven how wrathful heroes fight! Fierce Ullin fell. Young Lamderg came all pale to the daughter of generous Tuathal."

"What

"What blood, my love," the soft-haired woman said, "what blood runs down my warrior's side?" "It is Ullin's blood," the chief replied, "thou fairer than the snow of Cromla! Gelchossa, let me rest here a little while." The mighty Lamderg died.

"And sleepest thou so soon on earth, O chief of shady Cromla? three days she mourned beside her love. The hunters found her dead. They raised this tomb above the three. Thy son, O king of Morven, may rest here with heroes."

"And here my son shall rest," said Fingal, "the noise of their fame has reached my ears. Fillan and Fergus! bring hither Orla; the pale youth of the stream of Loda. Not unequalled shall Ryno lie in earth when Orla is by his side. Weep, ye daughters of Morven; and ye maids of the streamy Loda. Like a tree they grew on the hills; and they have fallen like the oak * of the desart; when it lies across a stream, and withers in the wind of the mountain.

"Oscar! chief of every youth! thou seest how they have fallen. Be thou, like them, on earth renowned. Like them the song of bards. Terrible were their forms in battle; but calm was Ryno in the days of peace. He was like the bow of the shower seen far distant on the stream; when the sun is setting on Mora, and silence on the hill of deer.

deer. Rest, youngest of my sons, rest, O Ryno, on Lena. We two shall be no more; for the warrior one day must fall."

Such was thy grief, thou king of hills, when Ryno lay on earth. What must the grief of Ossian be, for thou thyself art gone. I hear not thy distant voice on Cona. My eyes perceive thee not. Often forlorn and dark I sit at thy tomb; and feel it with my hands. When I think I hear thy voice; it is but the blast of the desart. Fingal has long since fallen asleep, the ruler of the war.

Then Gaul and Ossian sat with Swaran on the soft green banks of Lubar. I touched the harp to please the king. But gloomy was his brow. He rolled his red eyes towards Lena. The hero mourned his people."

I lifted my eyes to Cromla, and I saw the son of generous Semo. Sad and slow he retired from his hill towards the lonely cave of Tura. He saw Fingal victorious, and mixed his joy with grief. The sun is bright on his armour, and Connal slowly followed. They sunk behind the hill like two pillars of the fire of night: when winds pursue them over the mountain, and the flaming heath resounds. Beside a stream of roaring foam his cave is in a rock. One tree bends above it; and the rushing winds echo against its sides. Here rests the chief

of

of Dunſcaich, the ſon of generous Semo. His thoughts are on the battle he loſt; and the tear is on his cheek. He mourned the departure of his fame that fled like the miſt of Cona. O Bragela, thou art too far remote to cheer the ſoul of the hero. But let him, ſee thy bright form in his ſoul; that his thoughts may return to the lonely ſunbeam of Dunſcaich.

Who comes with the locks of age? It is the ſon of ſongs. Hail, Carril of other times, thy voice is like the harp in the halls of Tura. Thy words are pleaſant as the ſhower that falls on the fields of the ſun. Carril of the times of old, why comeſt thou from the ſon of the generous Semo?"

"Oſſian king of ſwords," replied the bard, "thou beſt raiſeſt the ſong. Long haſt thou been known to Carril, thou ruler of battles. Often have I touched the harp to lovely Everallin. Thou too haſt often accompanied my voice in Branno's hall of generous ſhells. And often, amidſt our voices, was heard the mildeſt Everallin. One day ſhe ſung of Cormac's fall, the youth that died for her love. I ſaw the tears on her cheek, and on thine, thou chief of men. Her ſoul was touched for the unhappy, though ſhe loved him not. How fair among a thouſand maids was the daughter of the generous Branno!"

M "Bring

"Bring not, Carril," I replied, "bring not her memory to my mind. My soul muft melt at the remembrance. My eyes muft have their tears. Pale in the earth is fhe the foftly-blufhing fair of my love. But fit thou on the heath, O bard, and let us hear thy voice. It is pleafant as the gale of fpring that fighs on the hunter's ear; when he wakens from dreams of joy, and has heard the mufic of the fpirits of the hill."

FINGAL:

FINGAL:

AN ANCIENT EPIC POEM.

THE ARGUMENT.

Night comes on. Fingal gives a feast to his army, at which Swaran is present. The king commands Ullin his bard to give the song of peace; a custom always observed at the end of a war. Ullin relates the actions of Trenmor great grandfather to Fingal, in Scandinavia, and his marriage with Inibacca, the daughter of a king of Lochlin who was ancestor to Swaran; which consideration, together with his being brother to Agandecca, with whom Fingal was in love in his youth, induced the king to releafe him, and permit him to return, with the remains of his army, into Lochlin, upon his promife of never returning to Ireland in a hostile manner. The night is spent in settling Swaran's departure, in songs of bards, and in a conversation in which the story of Grumal is introduced by Fingal. Morning comes. Swaran departs; Fingal goes on a hunting party, and finding Cuchullin in the cave of Tura, comforts him, and sets sail, the next day, for Scotland; which concludes the poem.

FINGAL:

AN ANCIENT EPIC POEM.

BOOK VI.[a]

THE clouds of night come rolling down, and reſt on Cromla's dark-brown ſteep. The ſtars of the north ariſe over the rolling of the waves of Ullin; they ſhew their heads of fire thro' the flying miſt of heaven. A diſtant wind roars in the wood; but ſilent and dark is the plain of death.

Still on the darkening Lena aroſe in my ears the tuneful voice of Carril. He ſung of the companions of our youth, and the days of former years; when we met on the banks of Lego, and ſent round the joy of the ſhell. Cromla, with its cloudy ſteeps anſwered to his voice. The ghoſts of thoſe he ſung came in the ruſtling blaſts. They were ſeen to bend with joy towards the ſound of their praiſe.

Be thy ſoul bleſt, O Carril, in the midſt of thy eddying winds. O that thou would come to my hall when I am alone by night! And thou doſt come, my friend, I hear often thy light hand on my harp: when it hangs on the diſtant wall, and the feeble ſound touches my ear. Why doſt thou not speak to me in my grief, and tell when I shall behold my friends? But thou passest away in thy murmuring blast: and thy wind whistles through the gray hair of Ossian.

Now on the side of Mora the heroes gathered to the feast. A thousand aged oaks are burning to the wind. The strength ᵇ of the shells goes round. And the souls of warriors brighten with joy. But the king of Lochlin is silent, and sorrow reddens in the eyes of his pride. He often turned toward Lena and remembered that he fell.

Fingal leaned on the shield of his father. His gray locks slowly waved on the wind, and glittered to the beam of night. He saw the grief of Swaran, and spoke to the first of bards.

" Raise, Ullin, raise the song of peace, and sooth my soul after battle, that my ear may forget the noise of arms. And let a hundred harps be near to gladden the king of Lochlin. He must depart from us with joy.——None ever went sad from Fingal. Oscar! the lightning of my sword is against the strong in battle; but peaceful it lies by my side when warriors yield in war."

" Trenmor ᶜ," said the mouth of the songs, " lived in the days of other years. He bounded over the waves of the north: companion of the storm. The high rocks of the land of Lochlin,

and

and its groves of murmuring founds appeared to
the hero through the mift; he bound his white-
bofomed fails. Trenmor purfued the boar that
roared along the woods of Gormal. Many had
fled from its prefence; but the fpear of Trenmor
flew it.

" Three chiefs, that beheld the deed, told of
the mighty ftranger. They told that he ftood like
a pillar of fire in the bright arms of his valour.
The king of Lochlin prepared the feaft, and called
the blooming Trenmor. Three days he feafted at
Gormal's windy towers; and got his choice in the
combat.

" The land of Lochlin had no hero that yielded
not to Trenmor. The fhell of joy went round
with fongs in praife of the king of Morven; he that
came over the waves, the firft of mighty men.

" Now when the fourth gray morn arofe, the
hero launched his fhip; and walking along the filent fhore waited for the rufhing wind. For loud
and diftant he heard the blaft murmuring in the
grove.

" Covered over with arms of fteel a fon of the
woody Gormal appeared. Red was his cheek and
fair his hair. His fkin like the fnow of Morven.
Mild rolled his blue and fmiling eye when he fpoke
to the king of fwords.

" Stay,

"Stay, Trenmor, stay thou first of men, thou hast not conquered Lonval's son. My sword has often met the brave. And the wife shun the strength of my bow."

"Thou fair-haired youth," Trenmor replied, "I will not fight with Lonval's son. Thine arm is feeble, sun-beam of beauty. Retire to Gormal's dark-brown hinds."

"But I will retire," replied the youth, "with the sword of Trenmor; and exult in the sound of my fame. The virgins shall gather with smiles around him who conquered Trenmor. They shall sigh with the sighs of love, and admire the length of thy spear; when I shall carry it among thousands, and lift the glittering point to the sun."

"Thou shalt never carry my spear," said the angry king of Morven. "Thy mother shall find thee pale on the shore of the echoing Gormal; and looking over the dark-blue deep, see the sails of him that slew her son."

"I will not lift the spear," replied the youth, "my arm is not strong with years. But with the feathered dart I have learned to pierce a distant foe. Throw down that heavy mail of steel; for Trenmor is covered all over. I first will lay my mail on earth. Throw now thy dart, thou king of Morven."

He

He saw the heaving of her breast. It was the sister of the king. She had seen him in the halls of Gormal; and loved his face of youth. The spear dropt from the hand of Trenmor! he bent his red cheek to the ground, for he had seen her like a beam of light that meets the sons of the cave, when they revisit the fields of the sun, and bend their aching eyes.

"Chief of the windy Morven," begun the maid of the arms of snow; "let me rest in thy bounding ship, far from the love of Corla. For he, like the thunder of the desart, is terrible to Inabaca. He loves me in the gloom of his pride, and shakes ten thousand spears!"

"Rest thou in peace," said the mighty Trenmor, "behind the shield of my fathers. I will not fly from the chief, though he shakes ten thousand spears."

"Three days he waited on the shore; and sent his horn abroad. He called Corla to battle from all his echoing hills. But Corla came not to battle. The king of Lochlin descended. He feasted on the roaring shore; and gave the maid to Trenmor."

"King of Lochlin," said Fingal, "thy blood flows in the veins of thy foe. Our families met in battle, because they loved the strife of spears. But often did they feast in the hall; and send round the joy of the shell. Let thy face brighten with gladness, and thine ear delight in the harp. Dreadful as the storm of thine ocean thou haft poured thy valour forth; thy voice has been like the voice of thousands when they engage in battle. Raise, to-morrow, thy white sails to the wind, thou brother of Agandecca. Bright as the beam of noon she comes on my mournful soul. I saw thy tears for the fair one, and spared thee in the halls of Starno; when my sword was red with slaughter, and my eye full of tears for the maid. Or dost thou chuse the fight? The combat which thy fathers gave to Trenmor is thine; that thou mayest depart renowned like the sun setting in the west."

"King of the race of Morven," said the chief of the waves of Lochlin; "never will Swaran fight with thee, first of a thousand heroes! I saw thee in the halls of Starno, and few were thy years beyond my own. When shall I, said I to my soul, lift the spear like the noble Fingal? We have fought heretofore, O warrior, on the side of the shaggy Malmor; after my waves had carried me to thy halls, and the feast of a thousand shells was spread. Let the bards send his fame who overcame to future years, for noble was the strife of Malmor.

"But

"But many of the ships of Lochlin have lost their youths on Lena. Take these, thou king of Morven, and be the friend of Swaran: And when thy sons shall come to the mossy towers of Gormal, the feast of shells shall be spread, and the combat offered on the vale.

"Nor ship," replied the king, "shall Fingal take, nor land of many hills. The desart is enough to me with all its deer and woods. Rise on thy waves again, thou noble friend of Agandecca. Spread thy white sails to the beam of the morning, and return to the echoing hills of Gormal."

"Blest be thy soul, thou king of shells," said Swaran of the dark-brown shield. "In peace thou art the gale of spring. In war the mountain-storm. Take now my hand in friendship, thou noble king of Morven. Let thy bards mourn those who fell. Let Erin give the sons of Lochlin to earth; and raise the mossy stones of their fame. That the children of the north hereafter may behold the place where their fathers fought. And some hunter may say, when he leans on a mossy tomb, here Fingal and Swaran fought, the heroes of other years. Thus hereafter shall he say, and our fame shall last for ever!"

"Swaran," said the king of the hills, "to-day our fame is greatest. We shall pass away like a
dream.

dream. No found will be in the fields of our battles. Our tombs will beloft in the heath. The hunter fhall not know the place of our reft. Our names may be heard in fong, but the ftrength of our arms will ceafe. O Offian, Carril, and Ullin, you know of heroes that are no more. Give us the fong of other years. Let the night pafs away on the found, and morning return with joy."

We gave the fong to the kings, and a hundred harps accompanied our voice. The face of Swaran brightened like the full moon of heaven, when the clouds vanifh away, and leave her calm and broad in the midft of the fky.

It was then that Fingal fpoke to Carril the chief of other times. "Where is the fon of Semo; the king of the ifle of mift? has he retired, like the meteor of death, to the dreary cave of Tura?"

"Cuchullin," faid Carril of other times, lies in the dreary cave of Tura. His hand is on the fword of his ftrength. His thoughts on the battle which he loft. Mournful is the king of fpears; for he has often been victorious. He fends the fword of his war to reft on the fide of Fingal. For like the ftorm of the defart, thou has fcattered all his foes. Take, O Fingal, the fword of the hero; for his fame is departed like mift when it flies before the ruftling wind of the vale.

"No:"

"No:" replied the king, "Fingal shall never take his sword. His arm is mighty in war; his fame shall never fail. Many have been overcome in battle, that have shone afterwards like the sun of heaven.

"O Swaran, king of the resounding woods, give all thy grief away. The vanquished, if brave are renowned; they are like the sun in a cloud when he hides his face in the south, but looks again on the hills of grass.

"Grumal was a chief of Cona. He sought the battle on every coast. His soul rejoiced in blood; his ear in the din of arms. He poured his warriors on the sounding Craca; and Craca's king met him from his grove; for then within the circle of Brumo [d] he spoke to the stone of power.

"Fierce was the battle of the heroes, for the maid of the breast of snow. The fame of the daughter of Craca had reached Grumal at the streams of Cona; he vowed to have the white-bosomed maid, or die on the echoing Craca. Three days they strove together, and Grumal on the fourth was bound.

"Far from his friend they placed him in the horrid circle of Brumo; where often, they said, the ghosts of the dead howled round the stone of the fear. But afterwards he shone like a pillar of

the

the light of heaven. They fell by his mighty hand, and Grumal had his fame.

"Raise, ye bards of other times, raise high the praise of heroes; that my soul may settle on their fame; and the mind of Swaran cease to be sad."

They lay in the heath of Mora; the dark winds rustled over the heroes. A hundred voices at once arose, a hundred harps were strung; they sung of other times, and the mighty chiefs of former years.

When now shall I hear the bard; or rejoice at the fame of my fathers? The harp is not strung on Morven; nor the voice of music raised on Cona. Dead with the mighty is the bard; and fame is in the desart no more.

Morning trembles with the beam of the east, and glimmers on gray-headed Cromla. Over Lena is heard the horn of Swaran, and the sons of the ocean gather around. Silent and sad they mount the wave, and the blast of Ullin is behind their sails. White, as the mist of Morven, they float along the sea.

"Call," said Fingal, "call my dogs, the long-bounding sons of the chase. Call white-breasted Bran; and the surly strength of Luath. Fillan, and Ryno, but he is not here! My son rests on the bed of death. Fillan and Fergus, blow my horn,

horn, that the joy of the chase may arise; that the deer of Cromla may hear and start at the lake of roes."

The shrill sound spreads along the wood. The sons of heathy Cromla arise. A thousand dogs fly off at once, gray-bounding through the heath. A deer fell by every dog, and three by the white-breasted Bran. He brought them, in their flight, to Fingal, that the joy of the king might be great.

One deer fell at the tomb of Ryno; and the grief of Fingal returned. He saw how peaceful lay the stone of him who was the first at the chase. "No more shalt thou rise, O my son, to partake of the feast of Cromla. Soon will thy tomb be hid, and the grass grow rank on thy grave. The sons of the feeble shall pass over it, and shall not know that the mighty lie there.

"Ossian and Fillan, sons of my strength, and Gaul king of the blue swords of war, let us ascend the hill to the cave of Tura, and find the chief of the battles of Erin. Are these the walls of Tura? gray and lonely they rise on the heath. The king of shells is sad, and the halls are desolate. Come let us find the king of swords, and give him all our joy. But is that Cuchullin, O Fillan, or a pillar of smoke on the heath? The wind of Cromla is on my eyes, and I distinguished not my friend."

"Fingal!"

"Fingal!" replied the youth, "it is the son of Semo. Gloomy and sad is the hero; his hand is on his sword. Hail to the son of battle, breaker of the shields?"

"Hail to thee," replied Cuchullin, "hail to all the sons of Morven. Delightful is thy presence, O Fingal, it is like the sun on Cromla; when the hunter mourns his absence for a season, and sees him between the clouds. Thy sons are like stars that attend thy course, and give light in the night. It is not thus thou hast seen me, O Fingal, returning from the wars of the desart; when the kings of the world ʻ had fled, and joy returned to the hill of hinds."

"Many are thy words, Cuchullin," said Connan ʻ of small renown. "Thy words are many, son of Semo, but where are thy deeds in arms? Why did we come over the ocean to aid thy feeble sword? Thou flyest to thy cave of sorrow, and Connan fights thy battles: Resign to me these arms of light; yield them, thou son of Erin."

"No hero," replied the chief, "ever fought the arms of Cuchullin; and had a thousand heroes fought them it were in vain, thou gloomy youth. I fled not to the cave of sorrow, as long as Erin's warriors lived."

"Youth

"Youth of the feeble arm," said Fingal, "Connan, say no more. Cuchullin is renowned in battle, and terrible over the desart. Often have I heard thy fame, thou stormy chief of Innis-fail. Spread now they white sails for the isle of mist, and see Bragela leaning on her rock. Her tender eye is in tears, and the winds lift her long hair from her heaving breast. She listens to the winds of night to hear the voice of thy rowers [5]; to hear the song of the sea, and the sound of thy distant harp."

"And long shall she listen in vain; Cuchullin shall never return. How can I behold Bragela to raise the sigh of her breast? Fingal, I was always victorious in the battles of other spears!"

"And hereafter thou shalt be victorious," said Fingal king of shells. "The fame of Cuchullin shall grow like the branchy tree of Cromla. Many battles await thee, O chief, and many shall be the wounds of thy hand. Bring hither, Oscar, the deer, and prepare the feast of shells; that our souls may rejoice after danger, and our friends delight in our presence."

We sat, we feasted, and we sung. The soul of Cuchullin rose. The strength of his arm returned and gladness brightened on his face. Ullin gave the song, and Carril raised the voice. I often joined

joined the bards, and sung of battles of the spear. Battles! where I often fought; but now I fight no more. The fame of my former actions is ceased; and I sit forlorn at the tombs of my friends.

Thus they passed the night in the song; and brought back the morning with joy. Fingal arose on the heath, and shook his glittering spear. He moved first toward the plains of Lena, and we followed like a ridge of fire. "Spread the sail," said the king of Morven, "and catch the winds that pour from Lena." We rose on the wave with songs, and rushed, with joy, through the foam of the ocean.

NOTES
ON
FINGAL.

BOOK I.

[a] Cuchullin, or rather Cuth-Ullin, *the voice of Ullin*, a poetical name given the son of Semo, grandson to Caithbat, a druid celebrated by the bards for his wisdom and valour, from his commanding the forces of the Province of Ulster against the Ferbolg or Belgæ, who were in possession of Connaught. Cuchullin when very young married Bragela the daughter of Sorglan, and passing over into Ireland, lived for some time with Connal, grandson by a daughter to Congal the petty king of Ulster. His wisdom and valour in a short time gained him such reputation, that in the minority of Cormac the supreme king of Ireland, he was chosen guardian to the young king, and sole manager of the war against Swaran king of Lochlin. After a series of great actions he was killed in battle somewhere in Connaught, in the twenty-seventh year of his age. He was so remarkable for his strength, that to describe a strong man it has passed into a proverb, "He has the strength of Cuchullin." They shew the remains of his palace at Dunscaich in the isle of Sky; and a stone to which he bound his dog Luath, goes still by his name.

[b] Cairbar or Cairbre, signifies *a strong man*.

¹ Crom-leach signified a place of worship among the Druids. It is here the proper name of a hill on the coast of Ullin or Ulster.

> ᵐ So when th' embattled clouds in dark array,
> Along the skies their gloomy lines display;
> The low-hung vapours motionless and still
> Rest on the summits of the shaded hill. *Pope.*

ⁿ Ireland, so called from a colony that settled there called Falans. Innis-fail, *i. e.* the island of the Fail or Falans.

º Connal, the friend of Cuchullin, was the son of Cathbait prince of Tongorma or the *island of blue waves*, probably one of the Hebrides. His mother was Fioncoma the daughter of Congal. He had a son by Foba of Conachar-nessar, who was afterwards king of Ulster. For his services in the war against Swaran, he had lands conferred on him, which, from his name, were called Tir-chonnuil or Tir-connel, *i. e.* the land of Connal.

ᵖ Erin, a name of Ireland; from *ear* or *iar* West, and *in* an island. This name was not always confined to Ireland, for there is the highest probability that the *Ierne* of the ancients was Britain to the North of the Forth. For Ierne is said to be to the North of Britain, which could not be meant of Ireland.
     Strabo, lib. 2. et 4. *Casaub.* lib. 1.

ᵠ Calm-er, *a strong man.*

ʳ The Gaelic name of Scandinavia in general; in a more confined sense that of the peninsula of Jutland.

ˢ Innis-tore, *the island of whales*, the ancient name of the Orkney islands.

ᵗ Dubhchomar, *a black well-shaped man.*

ᵘ Fear-guth, *the man of the word;* or a commander of an army.

ᵛ Be

ᵛ Be thou like a roe or young hart on the mountains of Bether.   *Solomon's Song.*

ʷ This paſſage alludes to the manner of burial among the ancient Scots. They opened a grave ſix or eight feet deep: the bottom was lined with fine clay; and on this they laid the body of the deceaſed, and, if a warrior, his ſword, and the heads of twelve arrows by his ſide. Above they laid another ſtratum of clay, in which they placed the horn of a deer, the ſymbol of hunting. The whole was covered with a fine mold, and four ſtones placed on end to mark the extent of the grave. Theſe are the four ſtones alluded to here.

ˣ The grave. The houſe appointed for all living. *Job.*

ʸ Muirne, or Morna, *a woman beloved by all.*

ᶻ Torman, *thunder.* This is the true origin of the Jupiter Taramis of the ancients.

ᵃ She alludes to his name, *the dark man.*

ᵇ Moina, *ſoft in temper and perſon.*

ᶜ It was the opinion then, as indeed it is to this day, of ſome of the Highlanders, that the ſouls of the deceaſed hovered round their living friends; and ſometimes appeared to them when they were about to enter on any great undertaking.

ᵈ As torrents roll encreaſ'd by numerous rills
With rage impetuous down the echoing hills;
Ruſh to the vales, and pour'd along the plain,
Roar thro' a thouſand channels to the main.   *Pope*

ᵉ A hill of Locblin.

ᶠ The reader may compare this paſſage with a ſimilar one in Homer. Iliad. 4. v. 446.

Now ſhield with ſhield, with helmet helmet cloſ'd,
To armour armour, lance to lance oppos'd.

Hoſt

Host against host, with shadowy squadrons drew,
The sounding darts in iron tempests flew;
With streaming blood the slipp'ry fields are dy'd,
And slaughter'd heroes swell the dreadful tide. *Pope.*

   Arms on armour crashing, bray'd
Horrible discord, and the madding wheels
Of brazen chariots rag'd, &c.   *Milton.*

⁸ Sithallin signifies *a handsome man;* Fiona, *a fair maid;* and Ardan, *pride.*

ʰ The Isle of Sky; not improperly called the *Isle of Mist,* as its high hills, which catch the clouds from the western ocean, occasion almost continual rains.

ⁱ One of Cuchullin's horses. Dubhstron-gheal.

ᵏ Sith-fadda, *i. e. a long stride.*

ˡ *The maid of Iniftore* was the daughter of Gorlo king of Iniftore or Orkney islands. Trenar was brother to the king of Iniscon, supposed to be one of the islands of Shetland. The Orkneys and Shetland were at that time subject to the king of Lochlin. We find that the dogs of Trenar are sensible at home of the death of their master, the very instant he is killed. It was the opinion of the times, that the souls of heroes went immediately after death to the hills of their country, and the scenes they frequented the most happy time of their life. It was thought too that dogs and horses saw the ghosts of the deceased.

ᵐ ———As when two black clouds
 With heaven's artillery fraught, come rattling on
 Over the Caspian. *Milton.*

ⁿ The ancient manner of preparing feasts after hunting, is handed down by tradition. A pit lined with smooth stones was made; and near it stood a heap of smooth flat stones

NOTES ON FINGAL.

king of Ireland, paſſed over into Ireland, probably by Fingal's order, to take upon him the adminiſtration of affairs in that kingdom during the minority of Cormac the ſon of Artho. He left his wife Bragela in Dunſcaich, the ſeat of the family in the iſle of Sky.

*** It was long the opinion of the ancient Scots, that a ghoſt was heard ſhrieking near the place where a death was to happen ſoon after. The accounts given to this day, among the vulgar, of this extraordinary matter, are very poetical. The ghoſt comes mounted on a meteor, and ſurrounds twice or thrice the place deſtined for the perſon to die; and then goes along the road through which the funeral is to paſs, ſhrieking at intervals; at laſt, the meteor and ghoſt diſappear above the burial place.

BOOK II.

* The ſcene of Connal's repoſe is familiar to thoſe who have been in the Highlands of Scotland. The poet removes him to a diſtance from the army, to add more horror to the deſcription of Crugal's ghoſt by the lonelineſs of the place. It perhaps will not be diſagreeable to the reader, to ſee how two other ancient poets handled a ſimilar ſubject.

>   When lo! the ſhade, before his cloſing eyes,
>   Of ſad Patroclus roſe, or ſeem'd to riſe,
>   In the ſame robe he living wore, he came,
>   In ſtature, voice, and pleaſing look the ſame.
>   The form familiar hover'd o'er his head,
>   And ſleeps Achilles thus? the phantom ſaid. *Pope.*

Vol. I.   P   When

When Hector's ghost before my sight appears:
A bloody shroud he seem'd, and bath'd in tears.
Such as he was, when, by Pelides slain,
Thessalian coursers dragg'd him o'er the plain.
Swoln were his feet, as when the thongs were thrust
Through the bor'd holes; his body black with dust.
Unlike that Hector, who return'd from toils
Of war triumphant, in Æacian spoils:
Or him, who made the fainting Greeks retire,
And launch'd against their navy Phrygian fire.
His hair and beard stood stiffen'd with his gore;
And all the wounds he for his country bore. *Dryden.*

ᵇ Connal the son of Caithbat, the friend of Cuchullin, is sometimes, as here, called the son of Colgar; from one of that name who was the founder of his family.

ᶜ Like a thin smoke he sees the spirit fly,
And hears a feeble, lamentable cry. *Pope.*

ᵈ The poet teaches us the opinions that prevailed in his time concerning the state of separate souls. From Connal's expression, "That the stars dim-twinkled through the form of Crugal," and Cuchullin's reply, we may gather that they both thought the soul was material: something like the εἴδωλον of the ancient Greeks.

ᵉ ————As when heaven's fire
Hath scath'd the forest oaks, or mountain pines
With singed tops, their stately growth though bare
Stand on the blasted heath. *Milton.*

ᶠ ————As evening mist
Ris'n from a river o'er the marish glides
And gathers ground fast at the lab'rers heel
Homeward returning. *Milton.*

ᶠ The ancient Scots, as well as the present Highlanders, drunk in shells; hence it is that we so often meet; in the old poetry, with *the chief of shells*, and *the halls of shells*.

ᵍ Crugal had married Degrena but a little time before the battle, consequently she may with propriety be called a stranger in the hall of her sorrow.

ʰ Deo-grena signifies *a sun beam*.

ᵏ *Mediisque in millibus ardet.* Virg.

ˡ Virgil and Milton have made use of a comparison similar to this; I shall lay both before the reader, and let him judge for himself which of these two great poets have best succeeded.

 Like Eryx or like Athos great he shows
 Or father Appenine when white with snows;
 His head divine obscure in clouds he hides,
 And shakes the sounding forest on his sides. *Dryden.*

 On th' other side Satan alarm'd,
 Collecting all his might, dilated stood
 Like Teneriff or Atlas unremov'd:
 His stature reach'd the sky. *Milton.*

ᵐ Muri, say the Irish bards, was an academy in Ulster for teaching the use of arms. The signification of the word is a *cluster of people;* which renders the opinion probable. Cuchullin is said to have been the first who introduced into Ireland complete armour of steel. He is famous among the Senachies, for teaching horsemanship to the Irish, and for being the first who used a chariot in that kingdom; which last circumstance was the occasion of Ossian's being so circumstantial in his description of Cuchullin's car, in the first book.

ⁿ The unfortunate death of this Roman is the subject of the sixth fragment of Ancient Poetry, published in 1764;

it is not the work of Ossian though it is writ in his manner, and bears the genuine marks of antiquity. The concise expressions of Ossian are imitated, but the thoughts are too jejune and confined to be the production of that poet. Many poems go under his name that have been evidently composed since his time; they are very numerous in Ireland, and some have come to the translator's hands. They are trivial and dull to the last degree; swelling into ridiculous bombast, or sinking into the lowest kind of prosaic style.

BOOK III.

ᵃ The second night, since the opening of the poem, continues; and Cuchullin, Connal, and Carril still sit in the place described in the preceding book. The story of Agandecca is introduced here with propriety, as great use is made of it in the course of the poem, and as it, in some measure, brings about the catastrophe.

ᵇ Starno was the father of Swaran as well as Agandecca. His fierce and cruel character is well marked in other poems concerning the times.

ᶜ This passage most certainly alludes to the religion of Lochlin, and *the stone of power* here mentioned is the image of one of the deities of Scandinavia.

ᵈ Starno is here poetically called the king of snow, from the great quantities of snow that fall in his dominions.

ᵉ All the north-west coast of Scotland probably went of old under the name of Morven, which signifies a ridge of very high hills.

ᶠ Gormal

f Gormal is the name of a hill in Lochlin, in the neighbourhood of Starno's palace.

g This is the only paſſage in the poem that has the appearance of religion. But Cuchullin's apoſtrophe to this ſpirit is accompanied with a doubt, ſo that it is not eaſy to determine whether the hero meant a ſuperior being, or the ghoſts of deceaſed warriors, who were ſuppoſed in thoſe times to rule the ſtorms, and to tranſport themſelves in a guſt of wind from one country to another.

h Aleletha, her lamentation over her ſon is introduced in the poem concerning the death of Cuchullin, printed in this collection.

i So ſome tall rock o'erhangs the hoary main,
By winds aſſail'd, by billows beat in vain,
Unmov'd it hears, above, the tempeſts blow,
And ſees the wat'ry mountains break below. *Pope.*

k Here the poet celebrates his own actions, but he does it in ſuch a manner that we are not diſpleaſed. The mention of the great actions of his youth immediately ſuggeſts to him the helpleſs ſituation of his age. We do not deſpiſe him for ſelfiſh praiſe, but feel his misfortunes.

l What the Craca here mentioned was, is not, at this diſtance of time, eaſy to determine. The moſt probable opinion is, that it was one of the Shetland iſles. There is a ſtory concerning a daughter of the king of Craca in the ſixth book.

m Gaul, the ſon of Morni, was chief of a tribe that diſputed long the pre-eminence with Fingal himſelf. They were reduced at laſt to obedience, and Gaul, from an enemy, turned Fingal's beſt friend and greateſt hero. His character is ſomething like that of Ajax in the Iliad; a hero of more ſtrength than conduct in battle. He was very fond

of

of military fame, and here he demands the next battle to himself. The poet, by an artifice, removes Fingal, that his return may be the more magnificent.

a The poet prepares us for the dream of Fingal in the next book.

BOOK IV.

a Fingal being asleep, and the action suspended by night, the poet introduces the story of his courtship of Everallin the daughter of Branno. The episode is necessary to clear up several passages that follow in the poem; at the same time that it naturally brings on the action of the book, which may be supposed to begin about the middle of the third night from the opening of the poem. The book, as many of Ossian's other compositions, is addressed to the beautiful Malvina the daughter of Toscar. She appears to have been in love with Oscar, and to have affected the company of the father after the death of the son.

b The poet addresses himself to Malvina the daughter of Toscar.

c The poet returns to his subject. If one could fix the time of the year in which the action of the poem happened, from the scene described here, I should be tempted to place it in autumn. The trees shed their leaves, and the winds are variable, both which circumstances agree with that season of the year.

d Ossian gives the reader a high idea of himself. His very song frightens the enemy. This passage resembles one in the eighteenth Iliad, where the voice of Achilles frightens the Trojans from the body of Patroclus.

Forth

Forth march'd the chief, and diflant from the crowd
High on the rampart rais'd his voice aloud.
So high his brazen voice the hero rear'd
Hofts drop their arms and trembled as they fear'd. *Pope.*

ᵉ Offian never fails to give a fine character to his beloved fon. His fpeech to his father is that of a hero; it contains the fubmiffion due to a parent, and the warmth that becomes a young warriour. There is a propriety in dwelling here on the actions of Ofcar, as the beautiful Malvina, to whom the book is addreffed, was in love with that hero.

ᶠ The war-fong of Ullin varies from the reft of the poem, in the verfification. It runs down like a torrent; and confifts almoft entirely of epithets. The cuftom of encouraging men in battle with extempore rhymes, has been carried down almoft to our own times. Several of thefe warfongs are extant, but the moft of them are only a group of epithets, without beauty or harmony, utterly deftitute of poetical merit.

ᵍ Th' imperial enfign, which full high advanc'd
Shone like a meteor ftreaming to the wind. *Milton.*

ʰ Fingal's ftandard was diftinguifhed by the name of *fun-beam*; probably on account of its bright colour, and its being ftudded with gold. To begin a battle is expreffed, in old compofition, by *lifting of the fun-beam.*

ⁱ Above the reft, the fun, who never lies,
Foretells the change of weather in the fkies.
For if he rife, unwilling to his race,
Clouds on his brow, and fpots upon his face;
Or if through mifts he fhoots his fullen beams,
Frugal of light, in loofe and ftraggling ftreams,
Sufpect a drifling day. *Dryden.*

 ᵏ For ere the rising winds begin to roar,
  The working seas advance to wash the shore;
  Soft whispers run along the leafy wood,
  And mountains whistle to the murm'ring flood. *Dryden.*
 ˡ The rapid rains, descending from the hills,
  To rolling torrents swell the creeping rills. *Dryden.*

BOOK V.

 ᵃ The fourth day still continues. The poet by putting the narration in the mouth of Connal, who still remained with Cuchullin on the side of Cromla, gives propriety to the praises of Fingal. The beginning of this book, in the original, is one of the most beautiful parts of the poem. The versification is regular and full, and agrees very well with the sedate character of Connal. No poet has adapted the cadence of his verse more to the temper of the speaker, than Ossian has done. It is more than probable that the whole poem was originally designed to be sung to the harp, as the versification is so various, and so much suited to the different passions of the human mind.

 ᵇ This passage resembles one in the twenty-third Iliad.
  Close lock'd above, their heads and arms are mixt;
  Below their planted feet at distance fixt;
  Now to the grasp each manly body bends;
  The humid sweat from ev'ry pore descends;
  Their bones resound with blows: sides, shoulders, thighs;
  Swell to each gripe, and bloody tumours rise. *Pope.*

 ᶜ The story of Orla is so beautiful and affecting in the original, that many are in possession of it in the north of Scotland, who never heard a syllable more of the poem. It va-
                ries

ries the action, and awakes the attention of the reader when he expected nothing but languor in the conduct of the poem, as the great action was over in the conquest of Swaran.

ᵈ Lamh-dhearg, signifies *bloody hand*. Gelchossa, *white legged*. Tuathal, *surly*. Ulfadda, *long-beard*. Ferchios, *the conqueror of men*.

ᵉ Bran is a common name of gray-hounds to this day. It is a custom in the north of Scotland, to give the names of the heroes mentioned in this poem to their dogs; a proof that they are familiar to the ear, and their fame generally known.

ᶠ Allad is plainly a druid: he is called the son of the rock, from his dwelling in a cave; and the circle of stones here mentioned is the pale of the druidical temple. He is here consulted as one who had a supernatural knowledge of things; from the druids, no doubt, came the ridiculous notion of the second sight, which prevailed in the Highlands and isles.

ᵍ The reader will find this passage altered from what it was in ancient poetry. It is delivered down very differently by tradition, and the translator has chosen that reading which favours least of bombast.

ʰ ———as the mountain oak
Nods to the ax, till with a groaning sound
It sinks and spreads its honours on the ground. *Pope.*

BOOK VI.

ᵃ This book opens with the fourth night, and ends on the morning of the sixth day. The time of five days, five nights, and a part of the sixth day is taken up in the poem.

VOL. I.   Q   The

The scene lies in the heath of Lena, and the mountain Cromla on the coast of Ulster.

ᵇ By the strength of the shell is meant the liquor the heroes drunk; of what kind it was, cannot be ascertained at this distance of time. The translator has met with several ancient poems that mention wax-lights and wine as common in the halls of Fingal. The names of both are borrowed from the Latin, which plainly shews that our ancestors had them from the Romans, if they had them at all. The Caledonians in their frequent incursions to the province, might become acquainted with those conveniencies of life, and introduce them into their own country, among the booty which they carried from South Britain.

ᶜ Trenmor was great grandfather to Fingal. The story is introduced to facilitate the dismission of Swaran.

ᵈ This passage alludes to the religion of the king of Craca. See a note on a similar subject in the third book.

ᵉ This is the only passage in the poem, wherein the wars of Fingal against the Romans are alluded to: the Roman emperor is distinguished in old compositions by the title of *king of the world.*

ᶠ Connan was of the family of Morni. He is mentioned in several other poems, and always appears with the same character. The poet passed him over in silence till now, and his behaviour here deserves no better usage.

ᵍ The practice of singing when they row is universal among the inhabitants of the north-west coast of Scotland and the isles. It deceives time, and inspirits the rowers.

COMALA:

A DRAMATIC POEM.

THE ARGUMENT.

This poem is valuable on account of the light it throws on the antiquity of Ossian's compositions. The Caracul mentioned here, is the same with Caracalla the son of Severus, who in the year 211 commanded an expedition against the Caledonians. The variety of the measure shews that the poem was originally set to music, and perhaps presented before the chiefs upon solemn occasions. Tradition has handed down the story more complete than it is in the poem. "Comala, the daughter of Sarno king of Inistore or Orkney islands, fell in love with Fingal the son of Comhal at a feast, to which her father had invited him, (Fingal, B. III.) upon his return from Lochlin, after the death of Agandecca. Her passion was so violent, that she followed him, disguised like a youth, who wanted to be employed in his wars. She was soon discovered by Hidallan the son of Lamor, one of Fingal's heroes, whose love she had slighted some time before. Her romantic passion and beauty recommended her so much to the king, that he had resolved to make her his wife; when news was brought him of Caracul's expedition. He marched to stop the progress of the enemy, and Comala attended him. He left her on a hill, within sight of Caracul's army, when he himself went to battle, having previously promised, if he survived, to return that night." The sequel of the story may be gathered from the poem itself.

COMALA:

A DRAMATIC POEM.

THE PERSONS.

FINGAL. MELILCOMA.
HIDALLAN. DERSAGRENA. } Daughters of MORNI.
COMALA. BARDS.

Derſagrena.

THE chaſe is over. No noiſe on Ardven but the torrent's roar! Daughter of Morni, come from Crona's banks. Lay down the bow and take the harp. Let the night come on with ſongs, and our joy be great on Ardven.

[a] *Melil.* And night comes on, thou blue-eyed maid, gray night grows dim along the plain. I ſaw a deer at Crona's ſtream; a moſſy bank he ſeemed through the gloom, but ſoon he bounded away. A meteor played round his branchy horns; and the awful faces of other times looked from the clouds of Crona.

[b] *Derſa.* Theſe are the ſigns of Fingal's death. The king of ſhields is fallen! and Caracul prevails. Riſe Comala,[c] from thy rocks; daughter of Sarno,
riſe

rife in tears. The youth of thy love is low, and his ghost is already on our hills.

Melil. There Comala sits forlorn; two gray dogs near shake their rough ears, and catch the flying breeze. Her red cheek rests on her arm, and the mountain wind is in her hair. She turns her blue-rolling eyes towards the fields of his promise. Where art thou, O Fingal, for the night is gathering around?

Comala. O Carun [d] of the streams! why do I behold thy waters rolling in blood? Has the noise of the battle been heard on thy banks; and sleeps the king of Morven? Rise, moon, thou daughter of the sky! look from between thy clouds, that I may behold the light of his steel, on the field of his promise. Or rather let the meteor, that lights our departed fathers through the night, come, with its red light, to shew me the way to my fallen hero. Who will defend me from sorrow? Who from the love of Hidallan? Long shall Comala look before she can behold Fingal in the midst of his host; bright as the beam of the morning in the cloud of an early shower.

Hidal. Roll, thou mist of gloomy Crona, roll on the path of the hunter. Hide his steps from mine eyes, and let me remember my friend no more. The bands of battle are scattered, and no

crowding

crowding steps are round the noise of his steel.
O Carun, roll thy streams of blood, for the chief
of the people fell.

Comala. Who fell on Carun's grassy banks, son
of the cloudy night? Was he white as the snow of
Ardven? Blooming as the bow of the shower?
Was his hair like the mist of the hill, soft and curling in the day of the sun? Was he like the thunder of heaven in battle? Fleet as the roe of the desart?

Hidal. O that I might behold his love, fair-leaning from her rock! Her red eye dim in tears, and her blushing cheek half hid in her locks! Blow, thou gentle breeze, and lift the heavy locks of the maid, that I may behold her white arm, and lovely cheek of her sorrow!

Comala. And is the son of Comhal fallen, chief of the mournful tale? The thunder rolls on the hill! The lightning flies on wings of fire! But they frighten not Comala; for her Fingal fell. Say, chief of the mournful tale, fell the breaker of shields?

Hidal. The nations are scattered on their hills; for they shall hear the voice of the chief no more.

Comala. Confusion pursue thee over thy plains; and destruction overtake thee, thou king of the world. Few be thy steps to the grave; and let one
virgin

virgin mourn thee. 'Let her be, like Comala, tearful in the days of her youth. Why haſt thou told me, Hidallan, that my hero fell? I might have hoped a little while his return, and have thought I ſaw him on the diſtant rock; a tree might have deceived me with his appearance; and the wind of the hill been the ſound of his horn in mine ear. O that I were on the banks of Carun! that my tears might be warm on his cheek!

Hidal. He lies on the banks of Carun: on Ardven, heroes raiſe his tomb. Look on them, O moon, from thy clouds; be thy beam bright on his breaſt, that Comala may behold him in the light of his armour.

Comala. Stop, ye ſons of the grave, till I behold my love. He left me at the chace alone. I knew not that he went to war. He ſaid he would return with the night; and the king of Morven is returned. Why didſt thou not tell me that he would fall, O trembling ſon of the rock! Thou haſt ſeen him in the blood of his youth, but thou didſt not tell Comala.

Melil. What ſound is that on Ardven! Who is that bright in the vale? Who comes like the ſtrength of rivers, when their crowded waters glitter to the moon?

Comala.

Comala. Who is it but the foe of Comala, the son of the king of the world! Ghost of Fingal! do thou, from thy cloud, direct Comala's bow. Let him fall like the hart of the desart. It is Fingal in the crowd of his ghosts. Why dost thou come, my love, to frighten and please my soul?

Fingal. Raise, ye bards of the song, the wars of the streamy Carun. Caracul has fled from my arms along the fields of his pride. He sets far distant like a meteor that incloses a spirit of night, when the winds drive it over the heath, and the dark woods are gleaming around. I heard a voice like the breeze of my hills. Is it the huntress of Galmal, the white-handed daughter of Sarno? Look from thy rocks, my love; and let me hear the voice of Comala.

Comala. Take me to the cave of thy rest, O lovely son of death!

Fingal. Come to the cave of my rest. The storm is over, and the sun is on our fields. Come to the cave of my rest, huntress of echoing Cona.

Comala. He is returned with his fame; I feel the right hand of his battles. But I must rest beside the rock till my soul settle from fear. Let the harp be near; and raise the song, ye daughters of Morni.

Dersa. Comala has slain three deer on Ardven, and the fire ascends on the rock; go to the feast of Comala, king of the woody Morven!

Fingal. Raise ye sons of song, the wars of the streamy Caran; that my white-handed maid may rejoice: while I behold the feast of my love.

Bards. Roll, streamy Carun, roll in joy, the sons of battle fled. The steed is not seen on our fields; and the wings [5] of their pride spread in other lands. The sun will now rise in peace, and the shadows descend in joy. The voice of the chase will be heard; and the shields hang in the hall. Our delight will be in the war of the ocean, and our hands be red in the blood of Lochlin. Roll, streamy Carun, roll in joy, the sons of battle fled.

Melil. Descend, ye light mists from high; ye moon-beams, lift her soul. Pale lies the maid at the rock! Comala is no more!

Fingal. Is the daughter of Sarno dead; the white bosomed maid of my love? Meet me Comala, on my heaths, when I sit alone at the streams of my hills.

Hidal. Ceased the voice of the huntress of Galmal? Why did I trouble the soul of the maid? When shall I see thee, with joy, in the chase of the dark-brown hinds?

Fingal.

Fingal. Youth of the gloomy brow! no more shalt thou feast in my halls. Thou shalt not pursue my chase, and my foes shall not fall by thy sword [h]. Lead me to the place of her rest that I may behold her beauty. Pale she lies at the rock, and the cold winds lift her hair. Her bow-string sounds in the blast, and her arrow was broken in her fall. Raise the praise of the daughter of Sarno, and give her name to the wind of hills.

Bards. See meteors roll around the maid; and moon beams lift her soul! Around her, from their clouds, bend the awful faces of her fathers; Sarno [i] of the gloomy brow; and the red-rolling eyes of Fidallan. When shall thy white-hand arise, and thy voice be heard on our rocks? The maids shall seek thee on the heath, but they will not find thee. Thou shalt come, at times, to their dreams, and settle peace in their soul. Thy voice shall remain in their ears, and they shall think with joy on the dreams of their rest. Meteors roll around the maid, and moon-beams lift her soul!

R 2   NOTES

NOTES

ON

COMALA.

---

^a Melilcoma, *soft-rolling eye.*

^b Dersagrena, *the brightness of a sun-beam.*

^c Comala, *the maid of the pleasant brow.*

^d Caran or Cra'on, *a winding river.* This river retains still the name of Carron, and falls into the Forth some miles to the north of Falkirk.

^e Hidallan was sent by Fingal to give notice to Comala of his return; he, to revenge himself on her for slighting his love some time before, told her that the king was killed in battle. He even pretended that he carried his body from the field to be buried in her presence; and this circumstance makes it probable that the poem was presented of old.

^f By *the son of the rock* she means a druid. It is probable that some of the order of the druids remained as late as the beginning of the reign of Fingal; and that Comala had consulted one of them concerning the event of the war with Caracul.

^g Perhaps the poet alludes to the Roman eagle.

^h The sequel of the story of Hidallan is introduced, as an episode, in the poem which immediately follows in this collection.

ⁱ Sarno the father of Comala died soon after the flight of his daughter. Fidallan was the first king that reigned in Iniftore.

THE
WAR OF CAROS:
A POEM.

THE ARGUMENT.

Caros is probably the noted usurper Carausius, by birth a Menapian, who assumed the purple in the year 284; and, seizing on Britain, defeated the emperor Maximian Herculius in several naval engagements, which gives propriety to his being called in this poem *the king of ships*. He repaired Agricola's wall, in order to obstruct the incursions of the Caledonians; and when he was employed in that work, it appears he was attacked by a party under the command of Oscar the son of Ossian. This battle is the foundation of the present poem, which is addressed to Malvina the daughter of Toscar.

BRING, daughter of Toscar, bring the harp; the light of the song rises in Ossian's soul. It is like the field, when darkness covers the hills around, and the shadow grows slowly on the plain of the sun.

I behold my son, O Malvina, near the mossy rock of Crona but it is the mist of the desart tinged with the beam of the west: Lovely is the mist that assumes the form of Oscar! turn from it, ye winds, when ye roar on the side of Ardven.

Who comes towards my son, with the murmur of a song? His staff is in his hand, his gray hair loose on the wind. Surely joy lightens his face; and he often looks back to Caros. It is Ryno [b] of the song, he that went to view the foe.

"What does Caros king of ships," said the son of the now mournful Ossian? "spreads he the wings [c] of his pride, bard of the times of old?"

"He spreads them, Oscar," replied the bard, "but it is behind his gathered heap [d]. He looks over his stones with fear, and beholds thee, terrible, as the ghost of night that rolls the wave to his ships."

"Go, thou first of my bards," says Oscar, "and take the spear of Fingal. Fix a flame on its point, and shake it to the winds of heaven. Bid him in songs to advance, and leave the rolling of his wave. Tell to Caros that I long for battle; and that my bow is weary of the chase of Cona. Tell him the mighty are not here; and that my arm is young."

He went with the sound of his song. Oscar reared his voice on high. It reached his heroes on Ardven, like the noise of a cave; when the sea of Togorma rolls before it; and its trees meet the roaring winds. They gather around my son like the streams of the hill; when, after rain, they roll in the pride of their course.

Ryno

Ryno came to the mighty Caros, and ſtruck his flaming ſpear. "Come to the battle of Oſcar, O thou that ſitteſt on the rolling of waters. Fingal is diſtant far; he hears the ſongs of his bards in Morven: and the wind of his hall is in his hair. His terrible ſpear is at his ſide; and his ſhield that is like that darkened moon. Come to the battle of Oſcar, the hero is alone."

He came not over the ſtreamy Carun; the bard returned with his ſong. Gray night grows dim on Crona. The feaſt of ſhells is ſpread. A hundred oaks burn to the wind, and faint light gleams over the heath. The ghoſts of Ardven paſs through the beam, and ſhew their dim and diſtant forms. Comala is half unſeen on her meteor; and Hidallan is ſullen and dim, like the darkened moon behind the miſt of night.

"Why art thou ſad?" ſaid Ryno; for he alone beheld the chief. "Why art thou ſad, Hidallan, haſt thou not received thy fame? The ſongs of Oſſian have been heard, and thy ghoſt has brightened in the wind, when thou didſt bend from thy cloud to hear the ſong of Morven's bard."

"And do thine eyes behold the hero," ſaid Oſcar, "like the dim meteor of night? Say, Ryno, ſay, how fell the chief that was ſo renowned in the days of our fathers? His name remains on the rocks

rocks of Cona; and I have often seen the streams of his hills."

Fingal, replied the bard, had driven Hidallan from his wars. The king's soul was sad for Comala, and his eyes could not behold Hidallan. Lonely, sad, along the heath, he slowly moved with silent steps. His arms hang disordered on his side. His hair flies loose from his helmet. The tear is in his down-cast eyes; and the sigh half silent in his breast. Three days he strayed unseen, alone, before he came to Lamor's halls: the mossy halls of his fathers, at the stream of Balva.⁶ There Lamor sat alone beneath a tree; for he had sent his people with Hidallan to war. The stream ran at his feet, and his grey hairs rested on his staff. Sightless are his aged eyes. He hums the song of other times. The noise of Hidallan's feet came to his ear: he knew the tread of his son.

"Is the son of Lamor returned; or is it the sound of his ghost? Hast thou fallen on the banks of Carun, son of the aged Lamor? Or, if I hear the sound of Hidallan's feet; where are the mighty in war? where are my people, Hidallan, that were wont to return with their echoing shields? Have they fallen on the banks of Carun?"

"No:" replied the sighing youth, "the people of Lamor live. They are renowned in battle, my father;

ther; but Hidallan is renowned no more. I muſt ſit alone on the banks of Balva, when the roar of the battle grows."

"But thy fathers never ſat alone," replied the riſing pride of Lamor. "They never ſat alone on the banks of Balva, when the roar of battle roſe. Doſt thou not behold that tomb? Mine eyes diſcern it not: there reſts the noble Garmallon who never fled from war. Come, thou renowned in battle, he ſays, come to thy father's tomb. How am I renowned, Garmallon? my ſon has fled from war!"

"King of the ſtreamy Balva!" ſaid Hidallan with a ſigh, "why doſt thou torment my ſoul? Lamor, I never feared. Fingal was ſad for Comala, and denied his wars to Hidallan: Go to the gray ſtreams of thy land, he ſaid, and moulder like a leafleſs oak, which the winds have bent over Balva, never more to grow!"

"And muſt I hear," Lamor replied, "the lonely tread of Hidallan's feet? When thouſands are renowned in battle, ſhall he bend over my gray ſtreams? Spirit of the noble Garmallon! carry Lamor to his place; his eyes are dark; his ſoul is ſad: and his ſon has loſt his fame!"

"Where," ſaid the youth, "ſhall I ſearch for fame to gladden the ſoul of Lamor? From whence

VOL. I.   S   ſhall

shall I return with renown, that the sound of my arms may be pleasant in his ear? If I go to the chase of hinds, my name will not be heard. Lamor will not feel my dogs, with his hands, glad at my arrival from the hill. He will not inquire of his mountains, or of the dark-brown deer of his deserts.

"I must fall," said Lamor, "like a leafless oak: it grew on a rock, but the winds have overturned it. My ghost will be seen on my hills, mournful for my young Hidallan. Will not ye, ye mists, as ye rise, hide him from my sight? My son! go to Lamor's hall: there the arms of our fathers hang. Bring the sword of Garmallon; he took it from a foe."

He went and brought the sword with all its studded thongs. He gave it to his father. The gray-haired hero felt the point with his hand.

"My son! lead me to Garmallon's tomb: it rises beside that rustling tree. The long grass is withered; I heard the breeze whistling there. A little fountain murmurs near, and sends its water to Balva. There let me rest; it is noon: and the sun is on our fields."

He led him to Garmallon's tomb. Lamor pierced the side of his son. They sleep together; and their ancient halls moulder on Balva's banks.

Ghosts

Ghosts are seen there at noon: the valley is silent, and the people shun the place of Lamor.

"Mournful is thy tale," said Oscar, "son of the times of old! My soul sighs for Hidallan; he fell in the days of his youth. He flies on the blast of the desart, and his wandering is in a foreign land. Sons of the echoing Morven! draw near to the foes of Fingal. Send the night away in songs; and watch the strength of Caros. Oscar goes to the people of other times; to the shades of silent Ardven; where his fathers sit dim in their clouds, and behold the future war. And art thou there, Hidallan, like a half-extinguished meteor? Come to my sight, in thy sorrow, chief of the roaring Balva!"

The heroes move with their songs. Oscar slowly ascends the hill. The meteors of night are setting on the heath before him. A distant torrent faintly roars. Unfrequent blasts rush through aged oaks. The half enlightened moon sinks dim and red behind her hill. Feeble voices are heard on the heath. Oscar drew his sword.

"Come," said the hero, "O ye ghosts of my fathers! ye that fought against the kings of the world! Tell me the deeds of future times; and your discourse in your caves: when you talk together and behold your sons in the fields of the valiant."

Trenmor came, from his hill, at the voice of his mighty son. A cloud, like the steed of the stranger, supported his airy limbs. His robe is of the mist of Lano, that brings death to the people. His sword is a meteor half-extinguished. His face is without form, and dark. He sighed thrice over the hero; and thrice the winds of the night roared around. Many were his words to Oscar: but they only came by halves to our ears: they were dark as the tales of other times, before the light of the song arose. He slowly vanished like a mist that melts on the sunny hill. It was then, O daughter of Toscar, my son began first to be sad. He foresaw the fall of his race; and, at times, he was thoughtful and dark; like the sun when he carries a cloud on his face: but he looks afterwards on the hills of Cona.

Oscar passed the night among his fathers, gray morning met him on the banks of Carun. A green vale surrounded a tomb which arose in the times of old. Little hills lift their heads at a distance; and stretch their old trees to the wind. The warriors of Caros sat there, for they had passed the stream by night. They appeared, like the trunks of aged pines, to the pale light of the morning. Oscar stood at the tomb, and raised thrice his terrible voice. The rocking hills echoed around: the starting

ing roes bounded away. And the trembling ghosts of the dead fled, shrieking on their clouds. So terrible was the voice of my son, when he called his friends.

A thousand spears rose around; the people of Caros rose. Why, daughter of Tofcar, why that tear? My son, though alone, is brave. Oscar is like a beam of the sky; he turns around and the people fall. His hand is like the arm of a ghost, when he stretches it from a cloud; the rest of his thin form is unseen: but the people die in the vale! My son beheld the approach of the foe; and he stood in the silent darkness of his strength. "Am I alone, said Oscar, in the midst of a thousand foes? Many a spear is there! many a darkly-rolling eye! Shall I fly to Ardven? But did my fathers ever fly! The mark of their arm is in a thousand battles. Oscar too will be renowned. Come, ye dim ghosts of my fathers, and behold my deeds in war! I may fall; but I will be renowned like the race of the echoing Morven." He stood dilated in his place, like a flood swelling in a narrow vale. The battle came, but they fell: bloody was the sword of Oscar.

The noise reached his people at Crona; they came like a hundred streams. The warriors of Caros fled, and Oscar remained like a rock left by the ebbing sea.

Now

Now dark and deep, with all his steeds, Caros rolled his might along: the little streams are lost in his course; and the earth is rocking round. Battle spreads from wing to wing: ten thousand swords gleam at once in the sky. But why should Ossian sing of battles? For never more shall my steel shine in war. I remember the days of my youth with sorrow; when I feel the weakness of my arm. Happy are they who fell in their youth, in the midst of their renown! They have not beheld the tombs of their friends: or failed to bend the bow of their strength. Happy art thou, O Oscar, in the midst of thy rushing blast. Thou often goest to the fields of thy fame, where Caros fled from thy lifted sword.

Darkness comes on my soul, O fair daughter of Toscar, I behold not the form of my son at Carun; nor the figure of Oscar on Crona. The rustling winds have carried him far away; and the heart of his father is sad.

But lead me, O Malvina, to the sound of my woods, and the roar of my mountain streams. Let the chace be heard on Cona; that I may think on the days of other years. And bring me the harp, O maid, that I may touch it when the light of my soul shall arise. Be thou near, to learn the song; and future times shall hear of Ossian.

The

The sons of the feeble hereafter will lift the voice on Cona; and, looking up to the rocks, say, "Here Ossian dwelt." They shall admire the chiefs of old, and the race that are no more: while we ride on our clouds, Malvina, on the wings of the roaring winds. Our voices shall be heard, at times, in the desart; and we shall sing on the winds of the rock.

NOTES ON
THE WAR OF CAROS:

ᵃ Crona is the name of a small stream which runs into the Carron. On its banks is the scene of the preceding dramatic poem.

ᵇ Ryno is often mentioned in the ancient poetry. He seems to have been a bard, of the first rank, in the days of Fingal.

ᶜ The Roman eagle.

ᵈ Agricola's wall, which Carausius repaired.

ᵉ The river Carron..

ᶠ This is the scene of Comala's death, which is the subject of the dramatic poem. The poet mentions her in this place, in order to introduce the sequel of Hidallan's story, who, on account of her death, had been expelled from the wars of Fingal.

ᵍ This is perhaps that small stream, still retaining the name of Balva, which runs through the romantic valley of Glentivar in Stirlingshire. Balva signifies *a silent stream;* and Glentivar, *the sequestered vale.*

THE WAR OF INIS-THONA:
A POEM.

THE ARGUMENT.

This poem is an episode introduced in a great work composed by Ossian, in which the actions of his friends, and his beloved son Oscar, were interwoven. The work itself is lost, but some episodes, and the story of the poem, are handed down by tradition. Inis-thona was an island of Scandinavia, subject to its own king, but depending upon the kingdom of Lochlin.

OUR youth is like the dream of the hunter on the hill of heath. He sleeps in the mild beams of the sun; but he awakes amidst a storm; the red lightning flies around: and the trees shake their heads to the wind. He looks back with joy on the day of the sun, and the pleasant dreams of his rest!

When shall Ossian's youth return, or his ear delight in the sound of arms? When shall I, like Oscar, travel in the light of my steel? Come, with your streams, ye hills of Cona, and listen to the voice of Ossian? The song rises, like the sun, in my soul; and my heart feels the joys of other times.

I behold

I behold my towers, O Selma! and the oaks of thy shaded wall: thy streams sound in my ear; thy heroes gather round. Fingal sits in the midst; and leans on the shield of Trenmor: his spear stands against the wall; he listens to the song of his bards. The deeds of his arm are heard; and the actions of the king in his youth.

Oscar had returned from the chase, and heard the hero's praise. He took the shield of Branno [a] from the wall; his eyes were filled with tears. Red was the cheek of youth. His voice was trembling, low. My spear shook its bright head in his hand: he spoke to Morvén's king.

"Fingal! thou king of heroes! Ossian, next to him in war! ye have fought the battle in your youth; your names are renowned in song. Oscar is like the mist of Cona: I appear and vanish. The bard will not know my name. The hunter will not search in the heath for my tomb. Let me fight, O heroes, in the battles of Inis-thona. Distant is the land of my war! ye shall not hear of Oscar's fall. Some bard may find me there, and give my name to the song. The daughter of the stranger shall see my tomb, and weep over the youth that came from afar. The bard shall say, at the feast, hear the song of Oscar from the distant land."

"Oscar,"

"Oscar," replied the king of Morven; "thou shalt fight, son of my fame! Prepare my dark-bosomed ship to carry my hero to Inis-thona. Son of my son, regard our fame: for thou art of the race of renown. Let not the children of strangers say, feeble are the sons of Morven! Be thou, in battle, like the roaring storm: mild as the evening sun in peace. Tell, Oscar, to Inis-thona's king, that Fingal remembers his youth; when we strove in the combat together in the days of Agandecca."

They lifted up the sounding sail; the wind whistled through the thongs [b] of their masts. Waves lashed the oozy rocks: the strength of ocean roared. My son beheld, from the wave, the land of groves. He rushed into the echoing bay of Runa; and sent his sword to Annir king of spears. The gray-haired hero rose, when he saw the sword of Fingal. His eyes were full of tears; and he remembered the battles of their youth. Twice they lifted the spear before the lovely Agandecca: heroes stood far distant, as if two ghosts contended.

"But now," begun the king, "I am old; the sword lies useless in my hall. Thou who art of Morven's race! Annir has been in the strife of spears; but he is pale and withered now, like the oak of Lano. I have no son to meet thee with joy, or to carry thee to the halls of his fathers. Argon

Argon is pale in the tomb, and Ruro is no more. My daughter is in the hall of strangers, and longs to behold my tomb. Her spouse shakes ten thousand spears; and comes ᶜ like a cloud of death from Lano. Come thou to share the feast of Annir, son of echoing Morven."

Three days they feasted together; on the fourth Annir heard the name of Oscar.ᵈ They rejoiced in the shell;ᵉ and pursued the boars of Runa. Beside the fount of mossy stones, the weary heroes rest. The tear steals in secret from Annir: and he broke the rising sigh. "Here darkly rest," the hero said, "the children of my youth. This stone is the tomb of Ruro: that tree sounds over the grave of Argon. Do ye hear my voice, O my sons, within your narrow house? Or do ye speak in these rustling leaves, when the winds of the desart rise?"

"King of Inis-thona," said Oscar, "how fell the children of youth? The wild-boar often rushes over their tombs, but he does not disturb the hunters. They pursue deer ᶠ formed of clouds, and bend their airy-bow. They still love the sport of their youth; and mount the wind with joy."

"Cormalo," replied the king, "is chief of ten thousand spears; he dwells at the dark-rolling waters of Lano;ᵍ which send forth the cloud of death. He came to Runa's echoing halls, and sought the honour

honour of the spear.[a] The youth was lovely as the first beam of the sun; and few were they who could meet him in fight! My heroes yielded to Cormalo: and my daughter loved the son of Lano. Argon and Ruro returned from the chase; the tears of their pride descended: They rolled their silent eyes on Runa's heroes, because they yielded to a stranger: three days they feasted with Cormalo: on the fourth my Argon fought. But who could fight with Argon! Lano's chief was overcome. His heart swelled with the grief of pride, and he resolved in secret to behold the death of my sons. They went to the hills of Runa, and pursued the dark-brown hinds. The arrow of Cormalo flew in secret; and my children fell. He came to the maid of his love; to Inis-thona's dark-haired maid. They fled over the desart, and Annir remained alone. Night came on and day appeared; nor Argon's voice, nor Ruro's came. At length their much loved dog is seen; the fleet and bounding Runar. He came into the hall and howled; and seemed to look towards the place of their fall. We followed him: we found them there: and laid them by this mossy stream. This is the haunt of Annir, when the chase of the hinds is over. I bend like the trunk of an aged oak above them: and my tears for ever flow."

"O Ronnan!"

"O Ronnan!" said the rising Oscar, "Ogar king of spears! call my heroes to my side, the sons of streamy Morven. To-day we go to Lano's water, that sends forth the cloud of death. Cormalo will not long rejoice: death is often at the point of our swords."

They came over the desart like stormy clouds, when the winds roll them over the heath: their edges are tinged with lightning: and the echoing groves foresee the storm. The horn of Oscar's battle was heard; and Lano shook in all its waves. The children of the lake convened around the sounding shield of Cormalo. Oscar fought, as he was wont in battle. Cormalo fell beneath his sword: and the sons of the dismal Lano fled to their secret vales. Oscar brought the daughter of Inis-thona to Annir's echoing halls. The face of age was bright with joy; he blest the king of swords.

How great was the joy of Ossian, when he beheld the distant sail of his son! it was like a cloud of light that rises in the east, when the traveller is sad in a land unknown; and dismal night, with her ghosts, is sitting around him. We brought him, with songs, to Selma's halls. Fingal ordered the feast of shells to be spread. A thousand bards raised the name of Oscar: and Morven answered to the noise. The daughter of Toscar was there,

and

and her voice was like the harp; when the distant
sound comes, in the evening, on the soft rustling
breeze of the vale.

O lay me, ye that see the light, near some rock
of my hills: let the thick hazels be around, let the
rustling oak be near. Green be the place of my
rest; and let the sound of the distant torrent be
heard. Daughter of Toscar, take the harp, and
raise the lovely song of Selma; that sleep may o-
vertake my soul in the midst of joy; that the
dreams of my youth may return, and the days of
the mighty Fingal. Selma! I behold thy towers,
thy trees, and shaded wall. I see the heroes of
Morven; and hear the song of bards. Oscar lifts
the sword of Cormalo; and a thousand youths admire its studded thongs. They look with wonder
on my son; and admire the strength of his arm.
They mark the joy of his father's eyes; they long
for an equal fame. And ye shall have your fame,
O sons of streamy Morven. My soul is often
brightened with the song; and I remember the
companions of my youth. But sleep descends with
the sound of the harp; and pleasant dreams begin
to rise. Ye sons of the chase stand far distant, nor
disturb my rest. The bard of other times conver-
ses now with his fathers, the chiefs of the days of
old.

old. Sons of the chase stand far distant; disturb not the dreams of Ossian.

NOTES ON

THE WAR OF INIS-THONA.

ᵃ This is Branno, the father of Everallin, and grandfather to Oscar; he was of Irish extraction, and lord of the country round the lake of Lego. His great actions are handed down by tradition, and his hospitality has passed into a proverb.

ᵇ Leather thongs were used in Ossian's time, instead of ropes.

ᶜ Cormalo had resolved on a war against his father-in-law Annir king of Inis-thona, in order to deprive him of his kingdom; the injustice of his designs was so much resented by Fingal, that he sent his grandson, Oscar, to the assistance of Annir. Both armies came soon to a battle, in which the conduct and valour of Oscar obtained a complete victory. An end was put to the war by the death of Cormalo, who fell in a single combat, by Oscar's hand. Thus is the story delivered down by tradition; though the poet, to raise the character of his son, makes Oscar himself propose the expedition.

ᵈ It was thought, in those days of heroism, an infringement upon the laws of hospitality, to ask the name of a stranger, before he had feasted three days in the great hall of the family. *He that asks the name of the stranger*, is, to

this

this day, an opprobrious term applied, in the north, to the inhospitable.

 ᵉ *To rejoice in the shell* is a phrase for feasting sumptuously, and drinking freely.

 ᶠ The notion of Ossian concerning the state of the deceased, was the same with that of the ancient Greeks and Romans. They imagined that the souls pursued, in their separate state, the employments and pleasures of their former life.

 ᵍ Lano was a lake of Scandinavia, remarkable, in the days of Ossian, for emitting a pestilential vapour in autumn. *And thou, O valiant Duchômar, like the mist of marshy Lano; when it sails over the plains of autumn, and brings death to the people.* Fingal, B. I.

 ʰ By *the honour of the spear* is meant a kind of tournament practised among the ancient northern nations.

BATTLE OF LORA.

She followed over the heath.

THE

BATTLE OF LORA:

A POEM.

THE ARGUMENT.

Fingal, on his return from Ireland, after he had expelled Swaran from that kingdom, made a feast to all his heroes: he forgot to invite Ma-ronnan and Aldo, two chiefs, who had not been along with him on his expedition. They resented his neglect: and went over to Erragon king of Sora, a country of Scandinavia, the declared enemy of Fingal. The valour of Aldo soon gained him a great reputation in Sora; and Lorma the beautiful wife of Erragon fell in love with him. He found means to escape with her, and to come to Fingal, who resided then in Selma on the western coast. Erragon invaded Scotland, and was slain in battle by Gaul the son of Morni, after he had rejected terms of peace offered him by Fingal. In this war Aldo fell, in a single combat, by the hands of his rival Erragon; and the unfortunate Lorma afterwards died of grief.

SON of the distant land, who dwellest in the secret cell! do I hear the sounds of thy grove? or is it the voice of thy songs? The torrent was loud in my ear, but I heard a tuneful voice; dost thou

thou praise the chiefs of thy land; or the spirits [a] of the wind? But, lonely dweller of the rocks! look over that heathy plain: thou seest green tombs, with their rank, whistling grass; with their stones of mossy heads: thou seest them, son of the rock; but Ossian's eyes have failed.

A mountain stream comes roaring down and sends its waters round a green hill: four mossy stones, in the midst of withered grass, rear their heads on the top: two trees which the storms have bent, spread their whistling branches around. This is thy dwelling, Erragon [b]; this thy narrow house: the sound of thy shells has been long forgot in Sora: and thy shield is become dark in thy hall. Erragon, king of ships! chief of distant Sora: how hast thou fallen on our mountains? How is the mighty low? Son of the secret cell! dost thou delight in songs? Hear the battle of Lora: the sound of its steel is long since past. So thunder on the darkened hill roars and is no more. The sun returns with his silent beams: the glittering rocks, and the green heads of the mountains smile.

The bay of Cona received our ships [c], from Ullin's rolling waves: our white sheets hung loose to the masts: and the boisterous winds roared behind the groves of Morven. The horn of the king

is

is founded, and the deer start from the rocks. Our arrows flew in the woods; and the feast of the hill was spread. Our joy was great on our rocks, for the fall of the terrible Swaran. Two heroes were forgot at our feast; and the rage of their bosoms burned. They rolled their red eyes in secret: the sigh burst from their breasts. They are seen to talk together, and to throw their spears on earth. They were two dark clouds, in the mist of our joy; like pillars of mist on the settled sea: it glitters to the sun, but the mariners fear a storm.

"Raise my white sails," said Ma-ronna, "raise them to the winds of the west; let us rush, O Aldo, through the foam of the northern wave. We are forgot at the feast: but our arms have been red in blood. Let us leave the hills of Fingal, and serve the king of Sora. His countenance is fierce, and the war darkens round his spear. Let us be renowned, O Aldo, in the battles of echoing Sora."

They took their swords and shields of thongs; and rushed to Lumar's sounding bay. They came to Sora's haughty king, the chief of bounding steeds. Erragon had returned from the chase: his spear was red in blood. He bent his dark face to the ground: and whistled as he went. He took strangers

strangers to his feasts: they fought and conquered in his wars.

Aldo returned with his fame towards Sora's lofty walls. From her tower looked the spouse of Erragon, the humid, rolling eyes of Lorma. Her dark-brown hair flies on the wind of ocean: her white breast heaves, like snow on the heath; when the gentle winds arise, and slowly move it in the light. She saw young Aldo, like the beam of Sora's setting sun. Her soft heart sighed: tears filled her eyes; and her white arm supported her head. Three days she sat within the hall, and covered grief with joy. On the fourth she fled with the hero, along the rolling sea. They came to Cona's mossy towers, to Fingal king of spears.

"Aldo of the heart of pride!" said the rising king of Morven, "shall I defend thee from the wrath of Sora's injured king? who will now receive my people into their halls, or give the feast of strangers, since Aldo of the little soul, has carried away the fair of Sora? Go to thy hills, thou feeble hand, and hide thee in thy caves; mournful is the battle we must fight, with Sora's gloomy king. Spirit of the noble Trenmor! when will Fingal cease to fight? I was born in the midst of battles [d], and my steps must move in blood to my tomb. But my hand did not injure the weak, my steel

steel did not touch the feeble in arms. I behold thy tempests, O Morven, which will overturn my halls; when my children are dead in battle, and none remain to dwell in Selma. Then will the feeble come, but they will not know my tomb: my renown is in the song: and my actions shall be as a dream to future times."

His people gathered around Erragon, as the storms round the ghost of night; when he calls them from the top of Morven, and prepares to pour them on the land of the stranger. He came to the shore of Cona, and sent his bard to the king; to demand the combat of thousands; or the land of many hills. Fingal sat in his hall with the companions of his youth around him. The young heroes were at the chase, and far distant in the desart. The gray-haired chiefs talked of other times, and of the actions of their youth; when the aged Narthmor[e] came, the king of streamy Lora.

"This is no time," begun the chief, "to hear the songs of other years: Erragon frowns on the coast, and lifts ten thousand swords. Gloomy is the king among his chiefs! he is like the darkened moon, amidst the meteors of night."

"Come," said Fingal, "from thy hall, thou daughter of my love; come from thy hall, Bosmina[f], maid of streamy Morven! Narthmor, take the

the steeds [g] of the strangers, and attend the daughter of Fingal: let her bid the king of Sora to our feast, to Selma's shaded wall. Offer him, O Bosmina, the peace of heroes, and the wealth of generous Aldo: our youths are far distant, and age is on our trembling hands."

She came to the host Erragon, like a beam of light to a cloud. In her right hand shone an arrow of gold; and in her left a sparkling shell, the sign of Morven's peace. Erragon brightened in her presence as a rock, before the sudden beams of the sun; when they issue from a broken cloud, divided by the roaring wind.

"Son of the distant Sora," begun the mildly blushing maid, "come to the feast of Morven's king, to Selma's shaded walls. Take the peace of heroes, O warriour, and let the dark sword rest by thy side. And if thou chusest the wealth of kings, hear the words of the generous Aldo. He gives to Erragon an hundred steeds, the children of the rein; an hundred maids from distant lands; an hundred hawks with fluttering wing, that fly across the sky. An hundred girdles [h] shall also be thine, to bind high-bosomed women; the friends of the births of heroes, and the cure of the sons of toil. Ten shells studded with gems shall shine in Sora's towers; the blue water trembles on their stars,

stars, and seems to be sparkling wine. They gladdened once the kings of the world [1], in the midst of their echoing halls. These, O hero, shall be thine; or thy white-bosomed spouse. Lorma shall roll her bright eyes in thy halls; though Fingal loves the generous Aldo: Fingal! who never injured a hero, though his arm is strong."

"Soft voice of Cona!" replied the king, "tell him, that he spreads his feast in vain. Let Fingal pour his spoils around me; and bend beneath my power. Let him give me the swords of his fathers, and the shields of other times: that my children may behold them in my halls, and say, *These are the arms of Fingal.*"

"Never shall they behold them in thy halls," said the rising pride of the maid. "They are in the mighty hands of heroes who never yielded in war. King of the echoing Sora! the storm is gathering on our hills. Dost thou not foresee the fall of thy people, son of the distant land?"

She came to Selma's silent halls; the king beheld her down-cast eyes. He rose from his place, in his strength, and shook his aged locks. He took the sounding mail of Trenmor, and the dark-brown shield of his fathers. Darkness filled Selma's hall, when he stretched his hand to his spear: the ghosts of thousands were near, and foresaw

the

the death of the people. Terrible joy rose in the face of the aged heroes: they rushed to meet the foe; their thoughts are on the actions of other years; and on the fame of the tomb.

Now the dogs of the chase appeared at Trathal's tomb: Fingal knew that his young heroes followed them, and he stopt in the midst of his course. Oscar appeared the first; then Morni's son, and Nemi's race: Fercuth * shewed his gloomy form: Dermid spread his dark-hair on the wind. Ossian came the last. I hummed the song of other times: my spear supported my steps over the little streams, and my thoughts were of mighty men. Fingal struck his bossy shield; and gave the dismal sign of war; a thousand swords, at once unsheathed, gleam on the waving heath. Three gray-haired sons of song raise the tuneful, mournful voice. Deep and dark with sounding steps, we rush, a gloomy ridge, along: like the shower of a storm when it pours on the narrow vale.

The king of Morven sat on his hill: the sunbeam of the battle flew on the wind: the companions of his youth are near, with all their waving locks of his age. Joy rose in the hero's eyes when he beheld his sons in war; when he saw them amidst the lightning of swords, and mindful of the deeds of their fathers. Erragon came on, in his ſtrength, like the roar of a winter ſtream: the battle falls in his courſe, and death is at his ſide.

"Who comes," ſaid Fingal, "like the bounding roe, like the hart of echoing Cona? His ſhield glitters on his ſide; and the clang of his armour is mournful. He meets with Erragon in the ſtrife! Behold the battle of the chiefs! it is like the contending of ghoſts in a gloomy ſtorm. But falleſt thou, ſon of the hill, and is thy white boſom ſtained with blood? Weep, unhappy Lorma, Aldo is no more."

The king took the ſpear of his ſtrength; for he was ſad for the fall of Aldo: he bent his deathful eyes on the foe; but Gaul met the king of Sora. Who can relate the fight of the chiefs? The mighty ſtranger fell.

"Sons of Cona!" Fingal cried aloud, "ſtop the hand of death. Mighty was he that is now ſo low! and much is he mourned in Sora! The ſtranger will come towards his hall, and wonder why it is ſilent. The king is fallen, O ſtranger, and the joy of his houſe is ceaſed. Liſten to the ſound of his woods: perhaps his ghoſt is there; but he is far diſtant, on Morven, beneath the ſword of a foreign foe." Such were the words of Fingal, when the bard raiſed the ſong of peace; we ſtopped our uplifted ſwords, and ſpared the feeble foe. We laid

laid Erragon in that tomb; and I raifed the voice of grief: the clouds of night came rolling down, and the ghoft of Erragon appeared to fome. His face was cloudy and dark; and an half-formed figh is in his breaft. Bleft be thy foul, O king of Sora! thine arm was terrible in war!

Lorma fat, in Aldo's hall, at the light of a flaming oak: the night came, but he did not return: and the foul of Lorma is fad. "What detains thee, hunter of Cona? for thou didft promife to return. Has the deer been diftant far; and do the dark winds figh, round thee, on the heath? I am in the land of ftrangers, where is my friend, but Aldo? Come from thy echoing hills, O my beft beloved!"

Her eyes are turned toward the gate, and fhe liftens to the ruftling blaft. She thinks it is Aldo's tread, and joy rifes in her face: but forrow returns again, like a thin cloud on the moon. "And wilt thou not return, my love? Let me behold the face of the hill. The moon is in the caft. Calm and bright is the breaft of the lake! When fhall I behold his dogs returning from the chafe? When fhall I hear his voice, loud and diftant on the wind? Come from thy echoing hills, hunter of woody Cona?"

His

His thin ghost appeared, on a rock, like the watry beam of the moon, when it rushes from between two clouds, and the midnight shower is on the field. She followed the empty form over the heath, for she knew that her hero fell. I heard her approaching cries on the wind, like the mournful voice of the breeze, when it sighs on the grass of the cave.

She came, she found her hero: her voice was heard no more: silent she rolled her sad eyes; she was pale as a watry cloud, that rises from the lake, to the beam of the moon. Few were her days on Cona: she sunk into the tomb: Fingal commanded his bards; and they sung over the death of Lorma. The daughters of Morven mourned her for one day in the year, when the dark winds of autumn returned.

Son of the distant land * thou dwellest in the field of fame: O let thy song rise, at times, in the praise of those that fell: that their thin ghosts may rejoice around thee; and the soul of Lorma come on a moon-beam,¹ when thou liest down to rest, and the moon looks into thy cave. Then shalt thou see her lovely; but the tear is still on her cheek.

NOTES ON
THE BATTLE OF LORA.

ᵃ The poet alludes to the religious hymns of the Culdees.

ᵇ Erragon, or Ferg-thonn, signifies *the rage of the waves;* probably a poetical name given him by Ossian himself; he goes by the name of Annir in tradition.

ᶜ This was at Fingal's return *from* his war against Swaran.

ᵈ Comhal the father of Fingal was slain in battle, against the tribe of Morni, the very day that Fingal was born; so that he may, with propriety, be said to have been *born in the midst of battles.*

ᵉ Neart-mor, *great strength.* Lora, *noisy.*

ᶠ Bos-mhina, *soft and tender hand.* She was the youngest of Fingal's children.

ᵍ These were probably horses taken in the incursions of the Caledonians into the Roman province, which seems to be intimated in the phrase of the *steeds of strangers.*

ʰ Sanctified girdles, till very lately, were kept in many families in the north of Scotland; they were bound about women in labour, and were supposed to alleviate their pains, and to accelerate the birth. They were impressed with several mystical figures, and the ceremony of binding them about the woman's waist, was accompanied with words and gestures which shewed the custom to have come originally from the druids.

ⁱ The Roman emperors. These shells were some of the spoils of the province.

ᵏ Fear-cuth, the same with Fergus, *the man of the word,* or a commander of an army.

ˡ The poet addresses himself to the Culdee.

ᵐ Be thou on a moon-beam, O Morna, near the window of my rest; when my thoughts are of peace; and the din of arms is over.   *Fingal,* B. I.

CONLATH AND CUTHONA:
A POEM.

THE ARGUMENT.

Conlath was the youngest of Morni's sons, and brother to the celebrated Gaul, who is so often mentioned in Ossian's poems. He was in love with Cuthona the daughter of Rumar, when Toscar the son of Kinfena, accompanied by Fercuth his friend, arrived, from Ireland, at Mora where Conlath dwelt. He was hospitably received, and according to the custom of the times, feasted, three days, with Conlath. On the fourth he set sail, and coasting the *island of waves*, probably, one of the Hebrides, he saw Cuthona hunting, fell in love with her, and carried her away, by force, in his ship. He was forced, by stress of weather, into I-thona a desert isle. In the mean time Conlath, hearing of the rape, sailed after him, and found him on the point of sailing for the coast of Ireland. They fought; and they and their followers fell by mutual wounds. Cuthona did not long survive; for she died of grief the third day after. Fingal, hearing of their unfortunate death, sent Stormal the son of Moran to bury them, but forgot to send a bard to sing the funeral song over their tombs. The ghost of Conlath came, long after, to Ossian, to entreat him to transmit, to posterity, his and Cuthona's fame. For it was the opinion of the times, that the souls of the deceased were not happy, till their elegies were composed by a bard.

DID not Ossian hear a voice? or is it the sound of days that are no more? Often does the memory

memory of former times come, like the evening sun, on my soul. The noise of the chase is renewed; and, in thought, I lift the spear. But Ossian did hear a voice: Who art thou, son of the night? The sons of little men are asleep, and the midnight wind is in my hall. Perhaps it is. the shield of Fingal that echoes to the blast, it hangs in Ossian's hall, and he feels it sometimes with his hands. Yes! I hear thee, my friend: long has thy voice been absent from mine ear! What brings thee, on thy cloud, to Ossian, son of the generous Morni? Are the friends of the aged near thee? Where is Oscar, son of fame? He was often near thee, O Conlath, when the din of battle rose.

Ghost of Conlath. Sleeps the sweet voice of Cona, in the midst of his rustling hall? Sleeps Ossian in his hall, and his friends without their fame? The sea rolls round the dark I-thona, and our tombs are not seen by the stranger. How long shall our fame be unheard, son of the echoing Morven?

Ossian. O that mine eyes could behold thee, as thou sittest, dim, on thy cloud! Art thou like the mist of Lano; or an half-extinguished meteor? Of what are the skirts of thy robe? Of what is thine airy bow? But he is gone on his blast like the shadow of mist. Come from thy wall, my harp, and let me hear thy sound. Let the light of memory

rise

rife on I-thona; that I may behold my friends. And Ossian does behold his friends on the dark-blue isle. The cave of Thona appears, with its mossy rocks and bending trees. A stream roars at its mouth, and Toscar bends over its course. Fer-cuth is sad by his side: and the maid [b] of his love sits at a distance and weeps. Does the wind of the waves deceive me? Or do I hear them speak?

Toscar. The night was stormy. From their hills the groaning oaks came down. The sea darkly tumbled beneath the blast, and the roaring waves were climbing against our rocks. The lightning came often and shewed the blasted fern. Ferçuth! I saw the ghost of night.[c] Silent he stood, on that bank; his robe of mist flew on the wind. I could behold his tears: an aged man he seemed, and full of thought.

Ferçuth. It was thy father, O Toscar; and he foresees some death among his race. Such was his appearance on Cromla, before the great Ma-ronnan[d] fell. Ullin![e] with thy hills of grass, how pleasant are thy vales! Silence is near thy blue streams, and the sun is on thy fields. Soft is the sound of the harp in Selama,[f] and pleasant the cry of the hunter on Cromla. But we are in the dark I-thona, sur-rounded by the storm. The billows lift their white
heads

heads above our rocks: and we tremble amidst the night.

Toscar. Whither is the soul of battle fled, Fercuth with the locks of age? I have seen thee undaunted in danger, and thine eyes burning with joy in the fight. Whither is the soul of battle fled? Our fathers never feared. Go: view the settling sea: the stormy wind is laid. The billows still tremble on the deep, and seem to fear the blast. But view the settling sea: morning is gray on our rocks. The sun will look soon from his east; in all his pride of light. I lifted up my sails, with joy, before the halls of generous Conlath. My course was by the isle of waves, where his love pursued the deer. I saw her, like that beam of the sun that issues from the cloud. Her hair was on her heaving breast; she, bending forward, drew the bow: her white arm seemed, behind her, like the snow of Cromla: Come to my soul, I said, thou huntress of the isle of waves! But she spends her time in tears, and thinks of the generous Conlath. Where can I find thy peace, Cuthona, lovely maid?

Cuthona. ⁱ A distant steep bends over the sea, with aged trees and mossy rocks: the billows roll at its feet: on its side is the dwelling of roes. The people call it Ardven. There the towers of Mora rise. There Conlath looks over the sea for his only love.

love. The daughters of the chafe returned, and he beheld their downcaft eyes. Where is the daughter of Rumar? But they anfwered not. My peace dwells on Ardven, fon of the diftant land!

Tofcar. And Cuthona fhall return to her peace; to the halls of generous Conlath. He is the friend of Tofcar: I have feafted in his halls. Rife, ye gentle breezes of Ullin, and ftretch my fails towards Ardven's fhores. Cuthona fhall reft on Ardven: but the days of Tofcar will be fad. I fhall fit in my cave in the field of the fun. The blaft will ruftle in my trees, and I fhall think it is Cuthona's voice. But fhe is diftant far, in the halls of the mighty Conlath.

Cuthona. Oh! what cloud is that? It carries the ghofts of my fathers. I fee the fkirts of their robes, like gray and watry mift. When fhall I fall, O Rumar? Sad Cuthona fees her death. Will not Conlath behold me, before I enter the narrow houfe?

Offian. And he will behold thee, O maid: he comes along the rolling fea. The death of Tofcar is dark on his fpear, and a wound is in his fide. He is pale at the cave of Thona, and fhews his ghaftly wound. Where art thou with thy tears, Cuthona? the chief of Mora dies. The vifion grows dim on my mind: I behold the chiefs no more

more. But, O ye bards of future times, remember the fall of Conlath with tears: he fell before his day; and sadness darkened in his hall. His mother looked to his shield on the wall, and it was bloody [1]. She knew that her hero died, and her sorrow was heard on Mora. Art thou pale on thy rock, Cuthona, beside the fallen chiefs? Night comes, and day returns, but none appears to raise their tomb. Thou frightnest the screaming fowls away, and thy tears for ever flow. Thou art pale as a watry cloud, that rises from a lake.

The sons of the desart came, and they found her dead. They raise a tomb over the heroes; and she rests at the side of Conlath. Come not to my dreams, O Conlath; for thou hast received thy fame. Be thy voice far distant from my hall; that sleep may descend at night. O·that I could forget my friends: till my footsteps cease to be seen! till I come among them with joy! and lay my limbs in the narrow aged house!

NOTES

NOTES ON

CONLATH AND CUTHONA:

ᵃ I-thona, *island of waves*, one of the uninhabited western isles.

ᵇ Cuthona the daughter of Rumar, whom Tofcar had carried away by force.

ᶜ It was long thought, in the north of Scotland, that ftorms were raifed by the ghofts of the deceafed. This notion is ftill entertained by the vulgar; for they think that whirlwinds, and fudden fqualls of wind are occafioned by fpirits, who tranfport themfelves, in that manner, from one place to another.

ᵈ Ma-ronnan was the brother of Tofcar.

ᵉ Ulfter in Ireland.

ᶠ Selamath—*beautiful to behold*, the name of Tofcar's palace, on the coaft of Ulfter, near the mountain Cromla, the fcene of the epic poem.

ᵍ Cuthona, *the mournful found of the waves;* a poetical name given her by Offian, on account of her mourning to the found of the waves; her name, in tradition, is Gormbuil, *the blue-eyed maid*.

ʰ The grave.

ⁱ It was the opinion of the times, that the arms left by the heroes at home, became bloody the very inftant their owners were killed, though at ever fo great a diftance.

CARTHON:
A POEM.

THE ARGUMENT.

This poem is complete, and the subject of it, as of most of Ossian's compositions, tragical. In the time of Comhal the son of Trathal, and father of the celebrated Fingal, Clessammor the son of Thaddu and brother of Morna, Fingal's mother, was driven by a storm into the river Clyde, on the banks of which stood Balclutha, a town belonging to the Britons between the walls. He was hospitably received by Reuthamir, the principal man in the place, who gave him Moina his only daughter in marriage. Reuda, the son of Cormo, a Briton who was in love with Moina, came to Reuthamir's house, and behaved haughtily towards Clessammor. A quarrel ensued, in which Reuda was killed; the Britons, who attended him pressed so hard on Clessammor, that he was obliged to throw himself into the Clyde, and swim to his ship. He hoisted sail, and the wind being favourable, bore him out to sea. He often endeavoured to return, and carry off his beloved Moina by night; but the wind continuing contrary, he was forced to desist.

Moina, who had been left with child by her husband, brought forth a son, and died soon after. Reuthamir named the child Carthon, *i. e. the murmur of waves,* from the storm which carried off Clessammor his father, who was supposed to have been cast away. When Carthon

ARGUMENT.

thon was three years old, Combal the father of Fingal, in one of his expeditions against the Britons, took and burnt Balclutha. Ruthamir was killed in the attack: and Carthon was carried safe away by his nurse, who fled farther into the country of the Britons. Carthon, coming to man's estate, was resolved to revenge the fall of Balclutha on Comhal's posterity. He set sail from the Clyde, and, falling on the coast of Morven, defeated two of Fingal's heroes, who came to oppose his progress. He was, at last, unwittingly killed by his father Cleſſammor, in a single combat. This story is the foundation of the present poem, which opens on the night preceding the death of Carthon, so that what passed before is introduced by way of episode. The poem is addressed to Malvina the daughter of Toscar.

A TALE of the times of old! The deeds of days of other years!

The murmur of thy streams, O Lora, brings back the memory of the past. The sound of thy woods Garmallar, is lovely in mine ear. Dost thou not behold, Malvina, a rock with its head of heath? Three aged firs bend from its face; green is the narrow plain at its feet; there the flower of the mountain grows, and shakes its white head in the breeze. The thistle is there alone, and sheds its aged beard. Two stones, half sunk in the ground, shew their heads of moss. The deer of the mountain avoids the place, for he be-

holds

holds the gray ghost that guards it [a], for the mighty lie, O Malvina, in the narrow plain of the rock.

A tale of the times of old! the deeds of days of other years.

Who comes from the land of strangers, with his thousands around him? the sun-beam pours its bright stream before him; and his hair meets the wind of his hills. His face is settled from war. He is calm as the evening beam that looks, from the cloud of the west, on Cona's silent vale. Who is it but Comhal's son [b], the king of mighty deeds! He beholds his hills with joy, and bids a thousand voices raise. Ye have fled over your fields, ye sons of the distant lands! The king of the world sits in his hall, and hears of his people's flight. He lifts his red eye of pride, and takes his father's sword. "Ye have fled over your fields, sons of the distant land!"

Such were the words of the bards, when they came to Selma's halls. A thousand lights [c] from the stranger's land rose, in the midst of the people. The feast is spread around; and the night passed away in joy. Where is the noble Clessammor [d] said the fair haired Fingal! Where is the companion of my father, in the days of my joy? Sullen and dark he passes his days in the vale of
echoing

echoing Lora: but, behold, he comes from the hill, like a steed in his strength, who finds his companions in the breeze; and tosses his bright mane in the wind. Blest be the soul of Clessammor, why so long from Selma?

"Returns the chief" said Clessammor, "in the midst of his fame? Such was the renown of Comhal in the battles of his youth. Often did we pass over Carun to the land of the strangers: our swords returned, not unstained with blood: nor did the kings of the world rejoice. Why do I remember the battles of my youth? My hair is mixed with gray. My hand forgets to bend the bow; and I lift a lighter spear. O that my joy would return, as when I first beheld the maid; the white bosomed daughter of strangers, Moina [e] with the darkblue eyes!"

"Tell," said the mighty Fingal, "the tale of thy youthful days. Sorrow like a cloud on the sun, shades the soul of Clessammor. Mournful are thy thoughts, alone, on the banks of the roaring Lora. Let us hear the sorrow of thy youth, and the darkness of thy days.

"It was in the days of peace," replied the great Clessammor, "I came, in my bounding ship, to Balclutha's [f] walls of towers. The winds had roared behind my sails, and Clutha's [g] streams received

my

my dark-bosomed vessel. Three days I remained in
Reuthamir's halls, and saw that beam of light, his
daughter. The joy of the shell went round, and
the aged hero gave the fair. Her breasts were like
foam on the wave, and her eyes like stars of light:
her hair was dark as the raven's wing: her soul was
generous and mild. My love for Moina was great:
and my heart poured forth in joy.

"The son of a stranger came; a chief who loved
the white bosomed Moina. His words were mighty
in the hall, and he often half unsheathed his sword.
Where, he said, is the mighty Comhal, the restless
wanderer* of the heath? Comes he, with his host,
to Balclutha, since Clessammor is so bold? My
soul, I replied, O warrior! burns in a light of its
own. I stand without fear in the midst of thousands, though the valiant are distant far. Stranger! thy words are mighty, for Clessammor is a-
lone. But my sword trembles by my side, and
longs to glitter in my hand. Speak no more of
Comhal, son of the winding Clutha!"

"The strength of his pride arose. We fought;
he fell beneath my sword. The banks of Clutha
heard his fall, and a thousand spears glittered
around. I fought: the strangers prevailed: I
plunged into the stream of Clutha. My white
sails rose over the waves, and I bounded on the

dark-blue sea. Moina came to the shore, and rolled the red eye of her tears: her dark hair flew on the wind; and I heard her cries. Often did I turn my ship! but the winds of the east prevailed. Nor Clutha ever since have I seen: nor Moina of the dark-brown hair. She fell on Balclutha; for I have seen her ghost. I knew her as she came through the dusky night, along the murmur of Lora: she was like the new moon seen through the gathered mist: when the sky pours down its flaky snow, and the world is silent and dark."

"Raise, ye bards," said the mighty Fingal, "the praise of unhappy Moina. Call her ghost, with your songs, to our hills; that she may rest with the fair of Morven, the sun-beams of other days; and the delight of heroes of old. I have seen the walls of Balclutha, but they were desolate. The fire had resounded in the halls: and the voice of the people is heard no more. The stream of Clutha was removed from its place, by the fall of the walls. The thistle shook, there, its lonely head: the moss whistled to the wind. The fox looked out, from the windows, the rank grass of the wall waved round his head. Desolate is the dwelling of Moina, silence is in the house of her fathers. Raise the song of mourning, O bards, over the land of strangers. They have but fallen before us: for, one day, we muſt fall. Why doſt thou build the hall, ſon of the winged days? Thou lookeſt from thy towers to-day; yet a few years, and the blaſt of the deſart comes; it howls in thy empty court, and whiſtles round thy half-worn ſhield. And let the blaſt of the deſart come! we ſhall be renowned in our day. The mark of my arm ſhall be in the battle, and my name in the ſong of bards. Raiſe the ſong; ſend round the ſhell: and let joy be heard in my hall. When thou ſon of heaven, ſhalt fail! if thou ſhalt fail, thou mighty light! if thy brightneſs is for a ſeaſon, like Fingal; our fame ſhall ſurvive thy beams."

Such was the ſong of Fingal, in the day of his joy. His thouſand bards leaned forward from their ſeats, to hear the voice of the king. It was like the muſic of the harp on the gale of the ſpring. Lovely were thy thoughts, O Fingal! why had not Oſſian the ſtrength of thy ſoul? But thou ſtandeſt alone, my father; and who can equal the king of Morven?

The night paſſed away in ſong, and morning returned in joy; the mountains ſhewed their gray heads; and the blue face of ocean ſmiled. The white wave is ſeen tumbling round the diſtant rock; and the gray miſt riſes, ſlowly, from the lake. It came, in the figure of an aged man, along the ſilent

lent plain. Its large limbs did not move in steps; for a ghost supported it in mid air. It came towards Selma's hall, and dissolved in a shower of blood.

The king alone beheld the terrible sight, and he foresaw the death of the people. He came, in silence, to his hall; and took his father's spear. The mail rattled on his breast. The heroes rose around. They looked in silence on each other, marking the eyes of Fingal. They saw the battle in his face: the death of armies on his spear. A thousand shields, at once, are placed on their arms; and they drew a thousand swords. The hall of Selma brightened around. The clang of arms ascends. The gray dogs howl in their place. No word is among the mighty chiefs. Each marked the eyes of the king; and half assumed his spear.

"Sons of Morven," begun the king, "this is no time to fill the shell. The battle darkens near us; and death hovers over the land. Some ghost, the friend of Fingal, has forewarned us of the foe. The sons of the stranger come from the darkly rolling sea. For, from the water, came the sign of Morven's gloomy danger. Let each assume his heavy spear, and gird on his father's sword. Let the dark helmet rise on every head; and the mail pour its lightning from every side. The battle gathers like a tempeſt, and ſoon ſhall ye hear the roar of death."

The hero moved on before his hoſt, like a cloud before a ridge of heaven's fire; when it pours on the ſky of night, and mariners foreſee a ſtorm. On Cona's riſing heath they ſtood: the white boſomed maids beheld them above like a grove; they foreſaw the death of their youths, and looked towards the ſea with fear. The white wave deceived them for diſtant ſails, and the tear is on their cheek. The ſun roſe on the ſea, and we beheld a diſtant fleet. Like the miſt of ocean they came: and poured their youth upon the coaſt. The chief was among them, like the ſtag in the midſt of the herd. His ſhield is ſtudded with gold, and ſtately ſtrode the king of ſpears. He moved towards Selma; his thouſands moved behind.

"Go, with thy ſong of peace," ſaid Fingal; "go, Ullin, to the king of ſwords. Tell him that we are mighty in battle; and that the ghoſts of our foes are many. But renowned are they who have feaſted in my halls! they ſhew the arms [k] of my fathers in a foreign land: the ſons of the ſtrangers wonder, and bleſs the friend of Morven's race; for our names have been heard afar; the kings of the world ſhook in the midſt of their people."

Ullin

Ullin went with his song. Fingal rested on his spear: he saw the mighty foe in his armour: and he blest the stranger's son. "How stately art thou, son of the sea!" said the king of woody Morven. "Thy sword is a beam of might by thy side: thy spear is a fir that defies the storm. The varied face of the moon is not broader than thy shield. Ruddy is thy face of youth! soft the ringlets of thy hair! But this tree may fall; and his memory be forgot! The daughter of the stranger will be sad, and look to the rolling sea: the children will say, *We see a ship; perhaps it is the king of Balclutha.* The tear starts from their mother's eye. Her thoughts are of him that sleeps in Morven."

Such were the words of the king, when Ullin came to the mighty Carthon: he threw down the spear before him; and raised the song of peace. "Come to the feast of Fingal, Carthon, from the rolling sea! partake the feast of the king, or lift the spear of war. The ghosts of our foes are many: but renowned are the friends of Morven! Behold that field, O Carthon; many a green hill rises there, with mossy stones and rustling grass: these are the tombs of Fingal's foes, the sons of the rolling sea."

"Dost thou speak to the feeble in arms," said Carthon, "bard of the woody Morven? Is my face

face pale for fear, son of the peaceful song? Why, then, dost thou think to darken my soul with the tales of those who fell? My arm has fought in the battle; my renown is known afar. Go to the feeble in arms, and bid them yield to Fingal. Have not I seen the fallen Balclutha? And shall I feast with Comhal's son? Comhal! who threw his fire in the midst of my father's hall! I was young, and knew not the cause why the virgins wept. The columns of smoke pleased mine eye, when they rose above my walls; I often looked back, with gladness, when my friends fled along the hill. But when the years of my youth came on, I beheld the moss of my fallen walls: my sigh arose with the morning, and my tears descended with night. Shall I not fight, I said, to my soul, against the children of my foes? And I will fight, O bard; I feel the strength of my soul."

His people gathered around the hero, and drew, at once, their shining swords. He stands, in the midst, like a pillar of fire; the tear half-starting from his eye, for he thought of the fallen Balclutha, and the crowded pride of his soul arose. Sidelong he looked up to the hill, where our heroes shone in arms; the spear trembled in his hand: and, bending forward, he seemed to threaten the king.

"Shall

"Shall I," said Fingal to his soul, "meet, at once, the king: Shall I stop him, in the midst of his course, before his fame shall arise? But the bard, hereafter, may say, when he sees the tomb of Carthon; Fingal took his thousands, along with him, to battle, before the noble Carthon fell. No: bard of the times to come! thou shalt not lessen Fingal's fame. My heroes will fight the youth, and Fingal behold the battle. If he overcomes, I rush, in my strength, like the roaring stream of Cona. Who, of my heroes, will meet the son of the rolling sea? Many are his warriors on the coast: and strong is his ashen spear!"

Cathul[l] rose, in his strength, the son of the mighty Lormar: three hundred youths attend the chief, the race[m] of native streams. Feeble was his arm against Carthon, he fell; and his heroes fled. Connal[n] resumed the battle, but he broke his heavy spear: he lay bound on the field: and Carthon pursued his people. "Cleffammor!" said the king of Morven, "where is the spear of thy strength? Wilt thou behold Connal bound; thy friend, at the stream of Lora? Rise, in the light of thy steel, thou friend of Comhal. Let the youth of Balclutha feel the strength of Morven's race." He rose in the strength of his steel, shaking his grizzly locks.

He

He fitted the shield to his side; and rushed, in the pride of valour.

Carthon stood, on that heathy rock, and saw the hero's approach. He loved the terrible joy of his face: and his strength, in the locks of age. "Shall I lift that spear," he said, "that never strikes, but once, a foe? Or shall I, with the words of peace, preserve the warrior's life? Stately are his steps of age! lovely the remnant of his years. Perhaps it is the love of Moina; the father of Car-borne Carthon. Often have I heard, that he dwelt at the echoing stream of Lora."

Such were his words, when Clessammor came, and lifted high his spear. The youth received it on his shield, and spoke the words of peace: "Warrior of the aged locks! Is there no youth to lift the spear? Hast thou no son, to raise the shield before his father, and to meet the arm of youth? Is the spouse of thy love no more? or weeps she over the tombs of thy sons? Art thou of the kings of men? What will be the fame of my sword if thou shalt fall?"

It will be great, thou son of pride! begun the tall Clessammor, I have been renowned in battle; but I never told my name º to a foe. Yield to me, son of the wave, and then thou shalt know, that the mark of my sword is in many a field. "I

never

never yielded, king of spears!" replied the noble pride of Carthon: "I have also fought in battles; and I behold my future fame. Despise me not, thou chief of men; my arm, my spear is strong. Retire among thy friends, and let young heroes fight." "Why dost thou wound my soul," replied Clessammor with a tear? "Age does not tremble on my hand; I still can lift the sword. Shall I fly in Fingal's fight; in the fight of him I loved? Son of the sea! I never fled: exalt thy pointed spear."

They fought, like two contending winds, that strive to roll the wave. Carthon bade his spear to err; for he still thought that the foe was the spouse of Moina. He broke Clessammor's beamy spear in twain: and seized his shining sword. But as Carthon was binding the chief; the chief drew the dagger of his fathers. He saw the foe's uncovered side; and opened, there, a wound.

Fingal saw Clessammor low: he moved in the sound of his steel. The host stood silent, in his presence; they turned their eyes toward the hero. He came, like the sullen noise of a storm, before the winds arise: the hunter hears it in the vale, and retires to the cave of the rock. Carthon stood in his place: the blood is rushing down his side: he saw the coming down of the king; and his

VOL. I.   A a   hopes

hopes of fame arose [q]; but pale was his cheek: his hair flew loose, his helmet shook on high: the force of Carthon failed! but his soul was strong.

Fingal beheld the hero's blood; he stopt the uplifted spear. "Yield, king of swords!" said Comhal's son; "I behold thy blood. Thou hast been mighty in battle; and thy fame shall never fade." Art thou the king so far renowned," replied the car-borne Carthon? "Art thou that light of death, that frightens the kings of the world. But why should Carthon ask? for he is like the stream of his desart; strong as a river, in his course: swift as the eagle of the sky. O that I had fought with the king; that my fame might be great in the song! that the hunter, beholding my tomb, might say, he fought with the mighty Fingal. But Carthon dies unknown! he has poured out his force on the feeble."

"But thou shalt not die unknown," replied the king of woody Morven: "my bards are many, O 'Carthon, and their songs descend to future times. The children of the years to come shall hear the fame of Carthon; when they sit round the burning oak [r], and the night is spent in the songs of old. The hunter, sitting in the heath, shall hear the rustling blast; and, raising his eyes, behold the rock where Carthon fell. He shall

turn

turn to his son, and shew the place where the mighty fought; *There the king of Balclutha fought, like the strength of a thousand streams."*

Joy rose in Carthon's face: he lifted his heavy eyes. He gave his sword to Fingal, to lie within his hall, that the memory of Balclutha's king might remain on Morven. The battle ceased along the field, for the bard had sung the song of peace. The chiefs gathered round the falling Carthon, and heard his words, with sighs. Silent they leaned on their spears, while Balclutha's hero spoke. His hair sighed in the wind, and his words were feeble.

" King of Morven," Carthon said, " I fall in the midst of my course. A foreign tomb receives, in youth, the last of Reuthamir's race. Darkness dwells in Balclutha: and the shadows of grief in Crathmo. But raise my remembrance on the banks of Lora: where my fathers dwelt. Perhaps the husband of Moina will mourn over his fallen Carthon." His words reached the heart of Clessammor: he fell, in silence, on his son. The host stood darkened around: no voice is heard on the plains of Lora. Night came, and the moon, from the east, looked on the mournful field: but still they stood, like a silent grove that lifts its head on

Gormal, when the loud winds are laid, and dark autumn is on the plain.

Three days they mourned over Carthon; on the fourth his father died. In the narrow plain of the rock they lie; and a dim ghost defends their tomb. There lovely Moina is often seen; when the sun-beam darts on the rock, and all around is dark. There she is seen, Malvina, but not like the daughters of the hill. Her robes are from the strangers land; and she is still alone.

Fingal was sad for Carthon; he desired his bards to mark the day, when shadowy autumn returned. And often did they mark the day, and sing the hero's praise. "Who comes so dark from ocean's roar, like autumn's shadowy cloud? Death is trembling in his hand! his eyes are flames of fire! Who roars along dark Lora's heath? Who but Carthon king of swords? The people fall! see! how he strides, like the sullen ghost of Morven! But there he lies a goodly oak, which sudden blasts overturned! When shalt thou rise, Balclutha's joy! lovely car-borne Carthon? Who comes so dark from ocean's roar, like autumn's shadowy cloud?" Such were the words of the bards, in the day of their mourning: I have accompanied their voice; and added to their song. My soul has been mournful for Carthon; he fell in the days of his valour:

and

and thou, O Cleſſammor! where is thy dwelling in the air? Has the youth forgot his wound? And flies he, on the clouds, with thee? I feel the ſun, O Malvina, leave me to my reſt. Perhaps they may come to my dreams; I think I hear a feeble voice. The beam of heaven delights to ſhine on the grave of Carthon: I feel it warm around.

O thou that rolleſt above, round as the ſhield of my fathers! Whence are thy beams, O ſun! thy everlaſting light? Thou comeſt forth, in thy awful beauty, and the ſtars hide themſelves in the ſky; the moon, cold and pale, ſinks in the weſtern wave. But thou thyſelf moveſt alone: who can be a companion of thy courſe! The oaks of the mountains fall: the mountains themſelves decay with years; the ocean ſhrinks and grows again: the moon herſelf is loſt in heaven; but thou art for ever the ſame; rejoicing in the brightneſs of thy courſe. When the world is dark with tempeſts; when thunder rolls, and lightning flies; thou lookeſt in thy beauty, from the clouds, and laugheſt at the ſtorm. But to Oſſian, thou lookeſt in vain; for he beholds thy beams no more; whether thy yellow hair flows on the eaſtern clouds, or thou trembleſt at the gates of the weſt. But thou art perhaps, like me, for a ſeaſon, and thy years will have an end. Thou ſhalt ſleep in thy

clouds,

clouds, careless of the voice of the morning. Exult then, O sun, in the strength of thy youth! Age is dark and unlovely; it is like the glimmering light of the moon, when it shines through broken clouds, and the mist is on the hills: the blast of the north is on the plain, the traveller shrinks in the midst of his journey.

NOTES ON

CARTHON.

^a It was the opinion of the times, that deer saw the ghosts of the dead. To this day, when beasts suddenly start without any apparent cause, the vulgar think that they see the spirits of the deceased.

^b Fingal returns here, from an expedition against the Romans, which was celebrated by Ossian in a particular poem.

^c Probably wax-lights; which are often mentioned as carried, among other booty, from the Roman province.

^d Cleffamh-mor, *mighty deeds.*

^e Moina, *soft in temper and person.* We find the British names in this poem derived from the Galic, which is a proof that the ancient language of the whole island was one and the same.

^f Balclutha, i. e. *the town of Clyde,* probably the *Alcluth* of Bede.

^g Clutha, or Cluath, the Galic name of the river Clyde, the signification of the word is *bending,* in allusion to the winding

winding courſe of the river. From Clutha is derived its Latin name, Glotta.

ʰ The word in the original here rendered *reſtleſs wanderer*, is *Scuta*, which is the true origin of the *Scoti* of the Romans: an opprobrious name impoſed by the Britons, on the Caledonians, on account of the continual incurſions into their country.

ⁱ The title of this poem in the original, is *Duan na nlaoi*, i. e. *The Poem of Hymns*; probably on account of its many digreſſions from the ſubject, all which are in a lyric meaſure, as this ſong of Fingal. Fingal is celebrated by the Iriſh hiſtorians, for his wiſdom in making laws, his poetical genius, and his fore-knowledge of events. O'Flaherty goes ſo far as to ſay, that Fingal's laws were extant in his own time.

ᵏ It was a cuſtom among the ancient Scots, to exchange arms with their gueſts, and thoſe arms were preſerved long in the different families, as monuments of the friendſhip which ſubſiſted between their anceſtors.

ˡ Cath-'huil, *the eye of battle*.

ᵐ It appears, from this paſſage, that clanſhip was eſtabliſhed in the days of Fingal, though not on the ſame footing with the preſent tribes in the north of Scotland.

ⁿ This Connal is very much celebrated, in ancient poetry, for his wiſdom and valour: there is a ſmall tribe ſtill ſubſiſting, in the North, who pretend they are deſcended from him.

ᵒ Fingal did not then know that Carthon was the ſon of Cleſſammor.

ᵖ To tell one's name to an enemy was reckoned, in thoſe days of heroiſm, a manifeſt evaſion of fighting him; for, if it was once known, that friendſhip ſubſiſted, of old, between

the

the anceſtors of the combatants, the battle immediately ceaſed; and the ancient amity of their foreſathers was renewed. *A man who tells his name to his enemy,* was of old an ignominious term for a coward.

ᵠ This expreſſion admits of a double meaning, either that Carthon hoped to acquire glory by killing Fingal, or to be rendered famous by falling by his hand; the laſt is the moſt probable, as Carthon is already wounded.

ʳ In the north of Scotland, till very lately, they burnt a large trunk of an oak at their feſtivals; it was called *the trunk of the feaſt.* Time had ſo much conſecrated the cuſtom, that the vulgar thought it a kind of ſacrilege to diſuſe it.

THE
DEATH OF CUCHULLIN:
A POEM.

THE ARGUMENT.

Arth, the son of Cairbre, supreme king of Ireland, dying, was succeeded by his son Cormac, a minor. Cuchullin, the son of Semo, who had rendered himself famous by his great actions, and who resided, at the time, with Connal, the son of Caithbat, in Ulster, was elected regent. In the twenty-seventh year of Cuchullin's age, and the third of his administration, Torlath, the son of Cantela, one of the chiefs of that colony of Belgae, who were in possession of the south of Ireland, rebelled in Connaught, and advanced towards Temora, in order to dethrone Cormac, who, excepting Feradath, afterwards king of Ireland, was the only one of the Scottish race of kings existing in that country. Cuchullin marched against him, came up with him at the lake of Lego, and totally defeated his forces. Torlath fell in the battle by Cuchullin's hand; but as he himself pressed too eagerly on the flying enemy, he was mortally wounded by an arrow, and died the second day after. The good fortune of Cormac fell with Cuchullin: many set up for themselves, and anarchy and confusion reigned. At last Cormac was taken off; and Cairbar, lord of Atha, one of the competitors for the throne, having defeated all his rivals, became sole monarch of Ireland. The family of Fingal, who were in the interest of

cock's head is beneath his wing: the hind sleeps with the hart of the desart. They shall rise with the morning's light, and feed on the mossy stream. But my tears return with the sun, my sighs come on with the night. When wilt thou come in thine arms, O chief of mossy Tura?"

Pleasant is thy voice in Ossian's ear, daughter of car-borne Sorglan? But retire to the hall of shells; to the beam of the burning oak. Attend to the murmur of the sea: it rolls at Dunscaich's walls: let sleep descend on thy blue eyes, and the hero come to thy dreams.

Cuchullin sits at Lego's lake, at the dark rolling of waters. Night is around the hero; and his thousands spread on the heath: a hundred oaks burn in the midst, the feast of shells is smoking wide. Carril strikes the harp, beneath a tree; his gray locks glitter in the beam; the rustling blast of night is near, and lifts his aged hair. His song is of the Blue Togorma, and of its chief, Cuchullin's friend. "Why art thou absent, Connal, in the day of the gloomy storm? The chiefs of the south have convened against the car-borne Cormac: the winds detain thy sails, and thy blue waters roll around thee. But Cormac is not alone: the son of Semo fights his battles. Semo's son his battles fights! the terror of the stranger! he that is like the vapour of death, flowly borne by fultry winds. The fun reddens in its prefence, the people fall around."

Such was the fong of Carril, when a fon of the foe appeared; he threw down his pointlefs fpear, and fpoke the words of Torlath, Torlath the chief of heroes, from Lego's fable furge: he that led his thoufands to battle, againft car-borne Cormac, Cormac, who was diftant far, in Temora's [b] echoing halls: he learned to bend the bow of his fathers; and to lift the fpear. Nor long didft thou lift the fpear, mildly-fhining beam of youth! death ftands dim behind thee, like the darkened half of the moon behind its growing light. Cuchullin rofe before the bard,[c] that came from generous Torlath; he offered him the fhell of joy, and honoured the fon of fongs. "Sweet voice of Lego!" he faid, "what are the words of Torlath? Comes he to our feaft or battle, the car-borne fon of Cantela?"[d]

"He comes to thy battle," replied the bard, "to the founding ftrife of fpears. When morning is gray on Lego, Torlath will fight on the plain: and wilt thou meet him, in thine arms, king of the ifle of mift? Terrible is the fpear of Torlath! it is a meteor of night. He lifts it, and the people fall: death fits in the lightning of his fword. "Do I fear,"

fear," replied Cuchullin, "the spear of car-borne Torlath? He is brave as a thousand heroes; but my soul delights in war. The sword rests not by the side of Cuchullin, bard of the times of old! Morning shall meet me on the plain, and gleam on the blue arms of Semo's son. But sit thou, on the heath, O bard! and let us hear thy voice: partake of the joyful shell: and hear the songs of Temora."

"This is no time," replied the bard, "to hear the song of joy; when the mighty are to meet in battle like the strength of the waves of Lego. Why art thou so dark, Slimora!ᵉ with all thy silent woods? No green star trembles on thy top; no moon-beam on thy side. But the meteors of death are there, and the gray watry forms of ghosts. Why art thou dark, Slimora! with thy silent woods?" He retired, in the sound of his song; Carril accompanied his voice. The music was like the memory of joys that are past, pleasant and mournful to the soul. The ghosts of departed bards heard it from Slimora's side. Soft sounds spread along the wood, and the silent valleys of night rejoice. So, when he sits in the silence of noon, in the valley of his breeze, the humming of the mountain bee comes to Ossian's ear: the gale
drowns

drowns it often in its courfe; but the pleafant found returns again.

"Raife," faid Cuchullin, to his hundred bards, "the fong of the noble Fingal: that fong which he hears at night, when the dreams of his reft defcend: when the bards ftrike the diftant harp, and the faint light gleams on Selma's walls. Or let the grief of Lara rife, and the fighs of the mother of Calmar,[f] when he was fought, in vain, on his hills; and fhe beheld his bow in the hall. Carril, place the fhield of Caithbat on that branch; and let the fpear of Cuchullin be near; that the found of my battle may rife with the gray beam of the eaft." The hero leaned on his father's fhield: the fong of Lara rofe. The hundred bards were diftant far: Carril alone is near the chief. The words of the fong were his; and the found of his harp was mournful.

"Alcletha[g] with the aged locks! mother of car-borne Calmar! why doft thou look towards the defart, to behold the return of thy fon? Thefe are not his heroes, dark on the heath: nor is that the voice of Calmar: it is but the diftant grove, Alcletha! but the roar of the mountain-wind!" Who[h] bounds over Lara's ftream, fifter of the noble Calmar? Does not Alcletha behold his fpear?
But

But her eyes are dim! Is it not the ſon of Matha, daughter of my love?"

"It is but an aged oak, Alcletha!" replied the lovely weeping Alona. "It is but an oak, Alcletha, bent over Lara's ſtream. But who comes along the plain? ſorrow is in his ſpeed. He lifts high the ſpear of Calmar. Alcletha, it is covered with blood!" "But it is covered with the blood of foes, [k] ſiſter of car-borne Calmar! his ſpear never returned unſtained with blood, nor his bow from the ſtrife of the mighty. The battle is conſumed in his preſence: he is a flame of death, Alona! Youth! of the mournful ſpeed! where is the ſon of Alcletha? Does he return with his fame? in the midſt of his echoing ſhields? Thou art dark and ſilent! Calmar is then no more. Tell me not, warrior, *how he fell, for I cannot bear of his wound.*

Why doſt thou look towards the deſart, mother of car-borne Calmar?

Such was the ſong of Carril, when Cuchullin lay on his ſhield: the bards reſted on their harps, and ſleep fell ſoftly around. The ſon of Semo was awake alone; his ſoul was fixed on the war. The burning oaks began to decay; faint red light is ſpread around. A feeble voice is heard: the ghoſt of Calmar came. He ſtalked in the beam. Dark

THE DEATH OF CUCHULLIN.

is the wound in his fide. His hair is difordered and loofe. Joy fits darkly on his face: and he ſeems to invite Cuchullin to his cave.

"Son of the cloudy night!" faid the rifing chief of Errin; "Why doft thou bend thy dark eyes on me, ghoft of the car-borne Calmar? Wouldeft thou frighten me, O Matha's fon! from the battles of Cormac? Thy hand was not feeble in war; neither was thy voice ᵐ for peace. How art thou changed, chief of Lara! if thou now doft advife to fly! But, Calmar, I never fled. I never feared ⁿ the ghofts of the defart. Small is their knowledge, and weak their hands; their dwelling is in the wind. But my foul grows in danger, and rejoices in the noife of fteel. Retire thou to thy cave; thou art not Calmar's ghoft; he delighted in battle, and his arm was like the thunder of heaven."

He retired in his blaft with joy, for he had heard the voice of his praife. The faint beam of the morning rofe, and the found of Caithbat's buckler fpread. Gree Ullin's warriors convened, like the roar of many ftreams. The horn of war is heard over Lego; the mighty Torlath came.

"Why doft thou come with thy thoufands, Cuchullin," faid the chief of Lego. "I know the ftrength of thy arm, and thy foul is an unextin-
guifhed

guished fire. Why fight we not on the plain, and let our hosts behold our deeds? Let them behold us like roaring waves, that tumble round a rock: the mariners hasten away, and look on their strife with fear."

"Thou risest, like the sun, on my soul," replied the son of Semo. "Thine arm is mighty, O Torlath; and worthy of my wrath. Retire, ye men of Ullin, to Slimora's shady side; behold the chief of Erin, in the day of his fame. Carril; tell to mighty Connal, if Cuchullin must fall, tell him I accused the winds which roar on Togorma's waves. Never was he absent in battle, when the strife of my fame arose. Let this sword be before Cormac, like the beam of heaven: let his counsel sound in Temora in the day of danger."

He rushed, in the sound of his arms, like the terrible spirit of Loda,* when he comes in the roar of a thousand storms, and scatters battles from his eyes. He sits on a cloud over Lochlin's seas: his mighty hand is on his sword, and the winds lift his flaming locks. So terrible was Cuchullin in the day of his fame. Torlath fell by his hand, and Lego's heroes mourned. They gather around the chief like the clouds of the desart. A thousand swords rose at once; a thousand arrows flew; but he stood like a rock in the midst of a roaring sea.

They fell around; he strode in blood: dark Slimora echoed wide. The sons of Ullin came, and the battle spread over Lego. The chief of Erin overcame; he returned over the field with his fame. But pale he returned! The joy of his face was dark. He rolled his eyes in silence. The sword hung, unsheathed, in his hand, and his spear bent at every step.

"Carrill," said the king in secret, "the strength of Cuchullin fails. My days are with the years that are past: and no mourning of mine shall arise. They shall seek me at Temora, but I shall not be found. Cormac will weep in his hall, and say "Where is Tura's chief?" But my name is renowned! my fame in the song of bards. The youth will say in secret, "O let me die as Cuchullin died; renown clothed him like a robe; and the light of his fame is great." Draw the arrow from my side; and lay Cuchullin beneath that oak. Place the shield of Caithbat near, that they may behold me amidst the arms of my fathers."

"And is the son of Semo fallen?" said Carril with a sigh. "Mournful are Tura's walls; and sorrow dwells at Dunscaich. Thy spouse is left alone in her youth, the son ⁹ of thy love is alone. He shall come to Bragela, and ask her why she weeps. He shall lift his eyes to the wall, and see his

his father's sword. "Whose sword is that?" he will say: and the soul of his mother is sad. Who is that like the hart of the desart, in the murmur of his course: His eyes look wildly round in search of his friend. Connal, son of Colgar, where hast thou been, when the mighty fell? Did the seas of Togorma roll round thee? Was the wind of the south in thy sails? The mighty have fallen in battle, and thou wast not there. Let none tell it in Selma, nor in Morven's woody land; Fingal will be sad, and the sons of the desart mourn."

By the dark rolling waves of Lego they raised the hero's tomb. Luath, [4] at a distance, lies, the companion of Cuchullin, at the chase.

Blest [f] be thy soul, son of Semo; thou wert mighty in battle. Thy strength was like the strength of a stream: thy speed like the eagle's wing. Thy path in the battle was terrible: the steps of death were behind thy sword. Blest be thy soul, son of Semo; car-borne chief of Dunscaich! Thou hast not fallen by the sword of the mighty, neither was thy blood on the spear of the valiant. The arrow came, like the sting of death in a blast: nor did the feeble hand, which drew the bow, perceive it. Peace to thy soul, in thy cave, chief of the isle of mist!

"The

"The mighty are difperfed at Temora: there is none in Cormac's hall. The king mourns in his youth, for he does not behold thy coming. The found of thy fhield is ceafed: his foes are gathering round. Soft be thy reft in thy cave, chief of Erin's wars! Bragela will not hope thy return, or fee thy fails in ocean's foam. Her fteps are not on the fhore: nor her ear open to the voice of thy rowers. She fits in the hall of fhells, and fees the arms of him that is no more. Thine eyes are full of tears, daughter of car-borne Sorglan! Bleft be thy foul in death, O chief of fhady Cromla!"

NOTES ON

THE DEATH OF CUCHULLIN.

ᵃ Togorma, *i. e. the ifland of blue waves*, one of the Hebrides, was fubject to Connal, the fon of Caithbat, Cuchullin's friend. He is fometimes called the fon of Colgar, from one of that name who was the founder of the family. Connal, a few days before the news of Torlath's revolt came to Temora, had failed to Togorma, his native ifle; where he was detained by contrary winds during the war in which Cuchullin was killed.

ᵇ The royal palace of the Irifh kings; Teambrath according to fome of the bards.

ᶜ The bards were the heralds of ancient times; and their perfons were facred on account of their office. In later

times

NOTES ON THE DEATH OF CUCHULLIN.

times they abused that privilege; and as their persons were inviolable, they satyrised and lampooned so freely those who were not liked by their patrons, that they became a public nuisance. Screened under the character of heralds, they grosly abused the enemy when he would not accept the terms they offered.

^d Cean-teola', *head of a family.*

^e Slia'-mor, *great hill.*

^f Calmar the son of Matha. His death is related at large, in the third book of Fingal. He was the only son of Matha; and the family was extinct in him. The seat of the family was on the banks of the river Lara, in the neighbourhood of Lego, and probably near the place where Cuchullin lay; which circumstance suggested to him, the lamentation of Alcletha over her son.

^g Alcl-cla'tha, *decaying beauty;* probably a poetical name given the mother of Calmar, by the bard himself.

^h Alcletha speaks. Calmar had promised to return, by a certain day, and his mother and his sister Alona are represented by the bard as looking, with impatience, towards that quarter where they expected Calmar would make his first appearance.

ⁱ Alulne, *exquisitely beautiful.*

^k Alcletha speaks.

^l She addresses herself to Larnir, Calmar's friend, who had returned with the news of his death.

^m See Calmar's speech, in the first book of Fingal.

ⁿ See Cuchullin's reply to Connal, concerning Crugal's ghost. *Fing.* B. II.

^o Loda, in the third book of Fingal, is mentioned as a place of worship in Scandinavia; by the *spirit of Loda,* the poet

poet probably means Odin, the great deity of the northern nations.

*Conloch, who was afterwards very famous for his great exploits in Ireland. He was so remarkable for his dexterity in handling the javelin, that when a good markſman is deſcribed, it has paſſed into a proverb, in the north of Scotland, *He is unerring as the arm of Conloch.*

¶ It was of old, the cuſtom to bury the favourite dog near the maſter. This was not peculiar to the ancient Scots, for we find it practiſed by many other nations in their ages of heroiſm. There is a ſtone ſhewn ſtill at Dunſcaich, in the iſle of Sky, to which Cuchullin commonly bound in his dog Luath. The ſtone goes by his name to this day.

ᶠ This is the ſong of the bards over Cuchullin's tomb. Every ſtanza cloſes with ſome remarkable title of the hero, which was always the cuſtom in funeral elegies. The verſe of the ſong is a lyric meaſure, and it was of old ſung to the harp.

DAR-THULA:

DAR-THULA:

A POEM.

THE ARGUMENT.

It may not be improper here, to give the story which is the foundation of this poem, as it is handed down by tradition. Usnoth, lord of Etha, which is probably that part of Argyleshire which is near Loch Eta, an arm of the sea in Lorn, had three sons, Nathos, Althos, and Ardan, by Slissama, the daughter of Semo, and sister to the celebrated Cuchullin. The three brothers, when very young, were sent over to Ireland, by their father, to learn the use of arms, under their uncle Cuchullin, who made a great figure in that kingdom. They were just landed in Ulster when the news of Cuchullin's death arrived. Nathos, though very young, took the command of Cuchullin's army, made head against Cairbar the usurper, and defeated him in several battles. Cairbar at last having found means to murder Cormac the lawful king, the army of Nathos shifted sides, and he himself was obliged to return into Ulster, in order to pass over into Scotland. Dar-thula, the daughter of Colla, with whom Cairbar was in love, resided, at that time, in Selama, a castle in Ulster; she saw, fell in love, and fled with Nathos; but a storm rising at sea, they were unfortunately driven back on that part of the coast of Ulster, where Cairbar was encamped with his army, waiting for Fingal, who meditated an expedition into Ireland, to re-establish the Scottish race of kings on the throne of that kingdom. The
three

three brothers, after having defended themselves, for some time, with great bravery, were overpowered and slain, and the unfortunate Dar-thula killed herself upon the body of her beloved Nathos.

Ossian opens the poem, on the night preceding the death of the sons of Usnoth, and brings in, by way of episode, what passed before. He relates the death of Dar-thula differently from the common tradition; his account is the most probable, as suicide seems to have been unknown in those early times: for no traces of it are found in the old poetry.

DAUGHTER of heaven,² fair art thou! the silence of thy face is pleasant. Thou comest forth in loveliness: the stars attend thy blue steps in the east. The clouds rejoice in thy presence, O moon, and brighten their dark-brown sides. Who is like thee in heaven, daughter of the night? The stars are ashamed in thy presence, and turn aside their green, sparkling eyes. Whither dost thou retire from thy course, when the darkness of thy countenance grows? Hast thou thy hall like Ossian? Dwellest thou in the shadow of grief? Have thy sisters fallen from heaven? Are they who rejoiced with thee, at night, no more? Yes! they have fallen, fair light! and thou dost often retire to mourn. But thou thyself shalt fail, one night; and leave thy blue path in heaven. The stars will then lift their green heads: they who were ashamed

in

in thy presence, will rejoice. Thou art now clothed with thy brightness: look from thy gates in the sky. Burst the cloud, O wind, that the daughter of night may look forth, that the shaggy mountains may brighten, and the ocean roll its blue waves in light.

Nathos [c] is on the deep, and Althos that beam of youth, Arden is near his brothers; they move in the gloom of their course. The sons of Usnoth move in darkness, from the wrath of car-borne Cairbar [d]. Who is that dim, by their side? the night has covered her beauty. Her hair sighs on the ocean's wind; her robe streams in dusky wreaths. She is like the fair spirit of heaven, in the midst of his shadowy mist. Who is it but Dar-thula [e], the first of Erin's maids? She has fled from the love of Cairbar, with the car-borne Nathos. But the winds deceive thee, O Dar-thula; and deny the woody Etha to thy sails. These are not thy mountains, Nathos, nor is that the roar of thy climbing waves. The halls of Cairbar are near; and the towers of the foe lift their heads. Ullin stretches its green head into the sea; and Tura's bay receives the ship. Where have ye been, ye southern winds! when the sons of my love were deceived? But ye have been sporting on plains, and pursuing the thistle's beard. O that ye had been

been ruſtling in the ſails of Nathos, till the hills of Etha roſe! till they roſe in their clouds, and ſaw their coming chief! Long haſt thou been abſent, Nathos! and the day of thy return is paſt.

But the land of ſtrangers ſaw thee, lovely: thou waſt lovely in the eyes of Dar-thula. Thy face was like the light of the morning, thy hair like the raven's wing. Thy ſoul was generous and mild, like the hour of the ſetting ſun. Thy words were the gale of the reeds, or the gliding ſtream of Lora. But, when the rage of battle roſe, thou waſt like a ſea in a ſtorm; the clang of arms was terrible: the hoſt vaniſhed at the ſound of thy courſe. It was then Dar-thula beheld thee, from the top of her moſſy tower: from the tower of Selama [f], where her fathers dwelt.

"Lovely art thou, O ſtranger!" ſhe ſaid, for her trembling ſoul aroſe. "Fair art thou in thy battles, friend of the fallen Cormac! [g] Why doſt thou ruſh on, in thy valour, youth of the ruddy look? Few are thy hands, in battle, againſt the car-borne Cairbar! O that I might be freed of his love! [h] that I might rejoice in the preſence of Nathos! Bleſt are the rocks of Etha; they will behold his ſteps at the chaſe! they will ſee his white boſom, when the winds lift his raven hair!"

Such

Such were thy words, Dar-thula, in Selama's mossy towers. But, now, the night is round thee: and the winds have deceived thy sails. The winds have deceived thy sails, Dar-thula: their blustering sound is high. Cease a little while, O north wind, and let me hear the voice of the lovely. Thy voice is lovely, Dar-thula, between the rustling blasts.

"Are these the rocks of Nathos, and the roar of his mountain streams? Comes that beam of light from Usnoth's nightly hall? The mist rolls around, and the beam is feeble: but the light of Dar-thula's soul is the car-borne chief of Etha! Son of the generous Usnoth, why that broken sigh? Are we not in the land of strangers, chief of echoing Etha?"

"These are not the rocks of Nathos," he replied, "nor the roar of his streams. No light comes from Etha's halls, for they are distant far. We are in the land of strangers, in the land of car-borne Cairbar. The winds have deceived us, Dar-thula. Ullin here lifts her green hills. Go towards the north, Althos; be thy steps, Ardan, along the coast; that the foe may not come in darkness, and our hopes of Etha fail. I will go towards that mossy tower, and see who dwells about the beam. Rest, Dar-thula, on the shore! rest in peace, thou beam of light! the fword of Nathos is around thee, like the lightning of heaven."

He went. She fat alone and heard the rolling of the wave. The big tear is in her eye; and fhe looks for the car-borne Nathos. Her foul trembles at the blaft. And fhe turns her ear towards the tread of his feet. The tread of his feet is not heard. "Where art thou, fon of my love! The roar of the blaft is around me. Dark is the cloudy night. But Nathos does not return. What detains thee, chief of Etha? Have the foes met the hero in the ftrife of the night!"

He returned, but his face was dark: he had feen his departed friend. It was the wall of Tura, and the ghoft of Cuchullin ftalked there. The fighing of his breaft was frequent; and the decayed flame of his eyes terrible. His fpear was a column of mift: the ftars looked dim through his form. His voice was like hollow wind in a cave: and he told the tale of grief. The foul of Nathos was fad, like the fun in the day of mift, when his face is watry and dim.

Why art thou fad, O Nathos?" faid the lovely daughter of Colla. "Thou art a pillar of light to Dar-thula: the joy of her eyes is in Etha's chief. Where is my friend, but Nathos? My father refts in the tomb. Silence dwells on Selama: fadnefs

fpreads

spreads on the blue streams of my land. My friends have fallen, with Cormac. The mighty were slain in the battle of Ullin.

"Evening darkened on the plain. The blue streams failed before mine eyes. The unfrequent blast came rustling in the tops of Selama's groves. My seat was beneath a tree on the walls of my fathers. Truthil past before my soul; the brother of my love; he that was absent ¹ in the battle against the car-borne Cairbar. Bending on his spear, the gray-haired Colla came: his downcast face is dark, and sorrow dwells in his soul. His sword is on the side of the hero: the helmet of his fathers on his head. The battle grows in his breast. He strives to hide the tear.

"Dar-thula," he sighing said, "thou art the last of Colla's race. Truthil is fallen in battle. The king ᵏ of Selama is no more. Cairbar comes, with his thousands, towards Selama's walls. Colla will meet his pride, and revenge his son. But where shall I find thy safety, Dar-thula with the dark-brown hair! thou art lovely as the sun-beam of heaven, and thy friends are low! " And is the sun of battle fallen?" I said with a bursting sigh. " Ceased the generous soul of Truthil to lighten through the field? My safety, Colla, is in that bow; I have learned to pierce the deer. Is not

Cairbar

Cairbar like the hart of the defart, father of fallen Truthil?"

¹ The face of age brightened with joy: and the crowded tears of his eyes poured down. The lips of Colla trembled. His gray beard whiftled in the blaft. "Thou art the fifter of Truthil," he faid; "thou burneft in the fire of his foul. Take Dar-thula, take that fpear, that brazen fhield, that bur-nifhed helmet: they are the fpoils of a warrior: a fon¹ of early youth. When the light rifes on Se-lama, we go to meet the car-borne Cairbar. But keep thou near the arm of Colla; beneath the fhadow of my fhield. Thy father, Dar-thula, could once defend thee, but age is trembling on his hand. The ftrength of his arm has failed, and his foul is darkened with grief."

"We paffed the night in forrow. The light of morning rofe. I fhone in the arms of battle. The gray haired hero moved before. The fons of Se-lama convened around the founding fhield of Co-la. But few were they in the plain, and their locks were gray. The youths had fallen with Truthil, in the battle of car-borne Cormac.

"Companions of my youth!" faid Colla, "it was not thus you have feen me in arms. It was not thus I ftrode to battle, when the great Confa-dan fell. But ye are laden with grief. The darknefs

of

of age comes like the mist of the desart. My shield is worn with years; my sword is fixed ᵐ in its place. I said to my soul, thy evening shall be calm, and thy departure like a fading light. But the storm has returned; I bend like an aged oak. My boughs are fallen on Selama, and I tremble in my place. Where art thou, with thy fallen heroes, O my beloved Truthil! Thou answerest not from thy rushing blast; and the soul of thy father is sad. But I will be sad no more, Cairbar or Colla must fall. I feel the returning strength of my arm. My heart leaps at the sound of battle."

"The hero drew his sword. The gleaming blades of his people rose. They moved along the plain. Their gray hair streamed in the wind. Cairbar sat, at the feast, in the silent plain of Lona ⁿ. He saw the coming of the heroes, and he called his chiefs to battle. Why ᵒ should I tell to Nathos, how the strife of battle grew! I have seen thee, in the midst of thousands, like the beam of heaven's fire: it is beautiful, but terrible; the people fall in its red course. The spear of Colla flew, for he remembered the battles of his youth. An arrow came with its sound, and pierced the hero's side. He fell on his echoing shield. My soul started with fear; I stretched my buckler over him; but my heaving breast was seen. Cairbar came,
with

with his spear, and he beheld Selama's maid: joy rose on his dark-brown face: he stayed the lifted steel. He raised the tomb of Colla; and brought me weeping to Selama. He spoke the words of love, but my soul was sad. I saw the shields of my fathers, and the sword of car-borne Truthil. I saw the arms of the dead, and the tear was on my cheek.

Then thou didst come, O Nathos: and gloomy Cairbar fled. He fled like the ghost of the desart before the morning's beam. His hosts were not near: and feeble was his arm against thy steel. "Why part thou sad, O Nathos?" said the lovely maid of Colla.

"I have met," replied the hero, "the battle in my youth. My arm could not lift the spear, when first the danger rose; but my soul brightened before the war, as the green narrow vale, when the sun pours his streamy beams, before he hides his head in a storm. My soul brightened in danger before I saw Selama's fair; before I saw thee, like a star, that shines on the hill, at night; the cloud slowly comes, and threatens the lovely light. We are in the land of the foe, and the winds have deceived us, Dar-thula! the strength of our friends is not near, nor the mountains of Etha. Where shall I find thy peace, daughter of mighty Colla!

The brothers of Nathos are brave: and his own sword has shone in war. But what are the sons of Usnoth to the host of car-borne Cairbar! O that the winds had brought thy sails, Oscar, king of men! thou didst promise to come to the battles of fallen Cormac. Then would my hand be strong as the flaming arm of death. Cairbar would tremble in his halls, and peace dwell round the lovely Dar-thula. But why dost thou fall, my soul? The sons of Usnoth may prevail."

"And they will prevail, O Nathos," said the rising soul of the maid: "never shall Dar-thula behold the halls of gloomy Cairbar. Give me those arms of brass, that glitter to that passing meteor; I see them in the dark-bosomed ship. Dar-thula will enter the battle of steel. Ghost of the noble Colla! do I behold thee on that cloud? who is that dim beside thee? It is the car-borne Truthil. Shall I behold the halls of him that slew Selama's chief! - No: I will not behold them, spirits of my love!"

Joy rose in the face of Nathos when he heard the white-bosomed maid. "Daughter of Selama! thou shinest on my soul. Come, with thy thousands, Cairbar! the strength of Nathos is returned. And thou, O aged Usnoth, shalt not hear that thy son has fled. I remember thy words on Etha; when my sails begun to rise: when I spread them

Vol. I.   E e   towards

towards Ullin, towards the mossy walls of Tura. "Thou goest," he said, "O Nathos, to the king of shields; to Cuchullin chief of men who never fled from danger. Let not thine arm be feeble: neither be thy thoughts of flight; lest the son of Semo say that Etha's race are weak. His words may come to Usnoth, and sadden his soul in the hall." The tear was on his cheek. He gave this shining sword.

"I came to Tura's bay: but the halls of Tura were silent. I looked round, and there was none to tell of the chief of Dunscaich. I went to the hall of his shells, where the arms of his fathers hung. But the arms were gone, and aged Lamhor sat in tears. "Whence are the arms of steel," said the rising Lamhor? "The light of the spear has long been absent from Tura's dusky walls. Come ye from the rolling sea? Or from the mournful halls of Temora?"

"We come from the sea," I said, "from Usnoth's rising towers. We are the sons of Slissama, the daughter of car-borne Semo. Where is Tura's chief, son of the silent hall? But why should Nathos ask? for I behold thy tears. How did the mighty fall, son of the lonely Tura?"

"He fell not," Lamhor replied, "like the silent star of night, when it shoots through darkness and is is no more. But he was like a meteor that falls in a diſtant land; death attends its red courſe, and itſelf is the ſign of wars. Mournful are the banks of Lego, and the roar of ſtreamy Lara! There the hero fell, ſon of the noble Uſnoth."

"The hero fell in the midſt of ſlaughter," I ſaid with a burſting ſigh. "His hand was ſtrong in battle; and death was behind his ſword."

"We came to Lego's mournful banks. We found his riſing tomb. His companions in battle are there? his bards of many ſongs. Three days we mourned over the hero: on the fourth, I ſtruck the ſhield of Caithbat. The heroes gathered around with joy, and ſhook their beamy ſpears. Corlath was near with his hoſt, the friend of carborne Cairbar. We came like a ſtream by night, and his heroes fell. When the people of the valley roſe, they ſaw their blood with morning's light. But we rolled away, like wreaths of miſt, to Cormac's echoing hall. Our ſwords roſe to defend the king. But Temora's halls were empty. Cormac had fallen in his youth. The king of Erin was no more.

"Sadneſs ſeized the ſons of Ullin, they ſlowly, gloomily retired: like clouds that, long having threatened rain, retire behind the hills. The ſons of Uſnoth moved, in their grief, towards Tura's ſounding founding bay. We paffed by Selama, and Cairbar retired like Lano's mift, when it is driven by the winds of the defart.

"It was then I beheld thee, O maid, like the light of Etha's fun. *Lovely is that beam*, I faid, and the crowded figh of my bofom rofe. Thou cameft in thy beauty, Dar-thula, to Etha's mournful chief. But the winds have deceived us, daughter of Colla, and the foe is near."

"Yes! the foe is near," faid the ruftling ftrength of Althos. "I heard their clanging arms on the coaft, and faw the dark wreaths of Erin's ftandard. Diftinct is the voice of Cairbar, and loud as Cromla's falling ftream. He had feen the dark fhip on the fea, before the dufky night came down. His people watch on Lena's plain, and lift ten thoufand fwords." "And let them lift ten thoufand fwords," faid Nathos with a fmile. "The fons of car-borne Ufnoth will never tremble in danger. Why doft thou roll with all thy foam, thou roaring fea of Ullin! Why do ye ruftle, on your dark wings, ye whiftling tempefts of the fky? Do ye think, ye ftorms, that ye keep Nathos on the coaft? No: his foul detains him, children of the night! Althos! bring my father's arms: thou feeft them beaming to the ftars. Bring the fpear of Semo, it ftands in the dark-bofomed fhip."

He

He brought the arms. Nathos clothed his limbs in all their shining steel. The stride of the chief is lovely: the joy of his eyes terrible. He looks towards the coming of Cairbar. The wind is rustling in his hair. Dar-thula is silent at his side: her look is fixed on the chief. She strives to hide the rising sigh, and two tears swell in her eyes.

"Althos!" said the chief of Etha, "I see a cave in that rock. Place Dar-thula there: and let thy arm be strong. Ardan! we meet the foe, and call to battle gloomy Cairbar. O that he came in his founding steel, to meet the son of Usnoth! Dar-thula! if thou shalt escape, look not on the falling Nathos. Lift thy sails, O Althos, towards the echoing groves of Etha.

"Tell to the chief," that his son fell with fame; that my sword did not shun the battle. Tell him I fell in the midst of thousands, and let the joy of his grief be great. Daughter of Colla! call the maids to Etha's echoing hall. Let their songs arise from Nathos, when shadowy autumn returns. O that the voice of Cona* might be heard in my praise! then would my spirit rejoice in the midst of my mountain winds." And my voice shall praise thee, Nathos chief of the woody Etha! The voice of Ossian shall rise in thy praise, son of the generous Usnoth! Why was I not on Lena, when the

battle

battle rose? Then would the sword of Ossian have defended thee, or himself have fallen low.

We sat, that night, in Selma round the strength of the shell. The wind was abroad, in the oaks; the spirit of the mountain[b] shrieked. The blast came rustling through the hall, and gently touched my harp. The sound was mournful and low, like the song of the tomb. Fingal heard it first, and the crowded sighs of his bosom rose. "Some of my heroes are low," said the gray haired king of Morven. "I hear the sound of death on the harp of my son. Ossian, touch the sounding string; bid the sorrow rise; that their spirits may fly with joy to Morven's woody hills." I touched the harp before the king, the sound was mournful and low. "Bend forward from your clouds," I said, "ghosts of my fathers! bend; lay by the red terror of your course, and receive the falling chief; whether he comes from a distant land or rises from the rolling sea. Let his robe of mist be near; his spear that is formed of a cloud. Place an half-extinguished meteor by his side, in the form of the hero's sword. And, oh! let his countenance be lovely, that his friends may delight in his presence. Bend from your clouds," I said, "ghosts of my fathers! bend."

Such was my song, in Selma, to the lightly-trembling harp. But Nathos was on Ullin's shore,
surrounded

surrounded by the night; he heard the voice of the foe amidſt the roar of tumbling waves. Silent he heard their voice, and reſted on his ſpear. Morning roſe, with its beams: the ſons of Erin appear; like gray rocks, with all their trees, they ſpread along the coaſt. Cairbar ſtood, in the midſt, and grimly ſmiled when he ſaw the foe. Nathos ruſhed forward, in his ſtrength; nor could Dar-thula ſtay behind. She came with the hero, lifting her ſhining ſpear. And who are theſe, in their armour, in the pride of youth? Who but the ſons of Uſnoth, Althos, and dark haired Ardan.

"Come," ſaid Nathos, "come! chief of the high Temora! Let our battle be on the coaſt for the white-boſomed maid. His people are not with Nathos; they are behind that rolling ſea. Why doſt thou bring thy thouſands againſt the chief of Etha? Thou didſt fly c from him, in battle, when his friends were around him." "Youth of the heart of pride, ſhall Erin's king fight with thee? Thy fathers were not among the renowned, nor of the kings of men. Are the arms of foes in their halls? Or the ſhields of other times? Cairbar is renowned in Temora, nor does he fight with little men."

The tear ſtarts from car-borne Nathos; he turned his eyes to his brothers. Their ſpears flew, at
once,

once, and three heroes lay on earth. Then the light of their swords gleamed on high: the ranks of Erin yield; as a ridge of dark clouds before a blast of wind. Then Cairbar ordered his people; and they drew a thousand bows. A thousand arrows flew; the sons of Usnoth fell. They fell like three young oaks which stood alone on the hill; the traveller saw the lovely trees, and wondered how they grew so lonely: the blast of the desart came, by night, and laid their green heads low; next day he returned, but they were withered, and the heath was bare.

Dar-thula stood in silent grief, and beheld their fall; no tear is in her eye: but her look is wildly sad. Pale was her cheek; her trembling lips broke short an half-formed word. Her dark hair flew on the wind. But gloomy Cairbar came. "Where is thy lover now? the car-borne chief of Etha? Hast thou beheld the halls of Usnoth? Or the dark-brown hills of Fingal? My battle had roared on Morven, did not the winds meet Dar-thula. Fingal himself would have been low, and sorrow dwelling in Selma." Her shield fell from Dar-thula's arm, her breast of snow appeared. It appeared, but it was stained with blood, for an arrow was fixed in her side. She fell on the fallen
Nathos;

Nathos, like a wreath of snow. Her dark hair spreads on his face, and their blood is mixing round.

"Daughter of Colla thou art low!" said Cairbar's hundred bards; "silence is at the blue streams of Selama, for Truthil's ᶜ race have failed. When wilt thou rise in thy beauty, first of Erin's maids? Thy sleep is long in the tomb, and the morning distant far. The sun shall not come to thy bed, and say, "Awake Dar-thula! awake, thou first of women! the wind of spring is abroad. The flowers shake their heads on the green hills, the woods wave their growing leaves." Retire, O sun, the daughter of Colla is asleep. She will not come forth in her beauty: she will not move, in the steps of her loveliness."

Such was the song of the bards, when they raised the tomb. I sung, afterwards, over the grave, when the king of Morven came; when he came to green Ullin to fight with car-borne Cairbar.

NOTES ON

DAR-THULA:

ᵃ The address to the moon is very beautiful in the original. It is in a lyric measure, and appears to have been sung to the harp.

ᵇ The

NOTES ON DAR-THULA.

^b The poet means the moon in her wane.

^c Nathos fignifies *youthful;* Ailthos, *exquifite beauty;* Arden, *pride.*

^d Cairbar, who murdered Cormac king of Ireland, and ufurped the throne. He was afterwards killed by Ofcar the fon of Offian in a fingle combat. The poet, upon other occafions, gives him the epithet of red-haired.

^e Dar-thula, or Dart-'huile, *a woman with fine eyes.* She was the moft famous beauty of antiquity. To this day, when a woman is praifed for her beauty, the common phrafe is, that *fhe is as lovely as Dar-thula.*

^f The poet does not mean that Selama, which is mentioned as the feat of Tofcar in Ulfter, in the poem of Conlath and Cuthona. The word in the original fignifies either *beautiful to behold,* or a place *with a pleafant or wide profpect.* In thofe times, they built their houfes upon eminences, to command a view of the country, and to prevent their being furprifed; many of them on that account, were called Selama. The famous Selma of Fingal is derived from the fame root.

^g Cormac the young king of Ireland, who was murdered by Cairbar.

^h That is, of the love of Cairbar.

ⁱ The family of Colla preferved their loyalty to Cormac long after the death of Cuchullin.

^k It is very common, in Offian's poetry, to give the title of king to every chief that was remarkable for his valour.

^l The poet, to make the ftory of Dar-thula's arming herfelf for battle, more probable, makes her armour to be that of a very young man, otherwife it would fhock all belief,

'lief, that she, who was very young, should be able to carry it.

ᵐ It was the custom of those times, that every warrior at a certain age, or when he became unfit for the field, fixed his arms in the great hall, where the tribe feasted upon joyful occasions. He was afterwards never to appear in battle; and this stage of life was called the *time of fixing of the arms*.

ⁿ Lona, *a marshy plain*. It was the custom, in the days of Ossian, to feast after a victory. Cairbar had just provided an entertainment for his army, upon the defeat of Truthil the son of Colla, and the rest of the party of Cormac, when Colla and his aged warriors arrived to give him battle.

º The poet avoids the description of the battle of Lona, as it would be improper in the mouth of a woman, and could have nothing new, after the numerous descriptions, of that kind, in his other poems. He, at the same time, gives an opportunity to Dar-thula to pass a fine compliment on her lover.

ᵖ It is usual with Ossian, to repeat, at the end of the episodes, the sentence which introduced them. It brings back the mind of the reader to the main story of the poem.

ᑫ Oscar, the son of Ossian, had long resolved on the expedition, into Ireland, against Cairbar, who had assassinated his friend Cathol, the son of Moran, an Irishman of noble extraction, and in the interest of the family of Cormac.

ʳ Lamh-mhor, *a mighty hand*.

ˢ Temora was the royal palace of the supreme kings of Ireland. It is here called mournful, on account of the death of Cormac, who was murdered there by Cairbar who usurped his throne.

NOTES ON DAR-THULA.

t Slis-feamha, *soft bosom*. She was the wife of Usnoth, and daughter of Semo, the chief of the *isle of mist*.

u Althos had just returned from viewing the coast of Lena, whither he had been sent by Nathos, the beginning of the night.

x Cairbar had gathered an army, to the coast of Ulster, in order to oppose Fingal, who prepared for an expedition into Ireland, to re-establish the house of Cormac on the throne, which Cairbar had usurped. Between the wings of Cairbar's army was the bay of Tura, into which the ship of the sons of Usnoth was driven; so that there was no possibility of their escaping.

y Semo was grandfather to Nathos by the mother's side. The spear mentioned here was given to Usnoth on his marriage, it being the custom then for the father of the lady to give his arms to his son-in-law. The ceremony used upon these occasions is mentioned in other poems.

z Usnoth.

a Ossian, the son of Fingal, is, often, poetically called the voice of Cona.

b By the spirit of the mountain is meant that deep and melancholy sound which precedes a storm; well known to those who live in a high country.

c He alludes to the flight of Cairbar from Selama.

d Truthil was the founder of Dar-thula's family.

CARRIC-THURA.

CARRIC-THURA.

And shall the sons of the Wind frighten the King of Morven.

CARRIC-THURA:

A POEM.

THE ARGUMENT.

Fingal returning from an expedition which he had made into the Roman province, resolved to visit Cathulla king of Inistore, and brother to Comala, whose story is related, at large, in the dramatic poem published in this collection. Upon his coming in sight of Carric-thura, the palace of Cathulla, he observed a flame on its top, which, in those days, was a signal of distress. The wind drove him into a bay, at some distance from Carric-thura, and he was obliged to pass the night on the shore. Next day he attacked the army of Frothal king of Sora, who had besieged Cathulla in his palace of Carric-thura, and took Frothal himself prisoner, after he had engaged him in a single combat. The deliverance of Carric-thura is the subject of the poem, but several other episodes are interwoven with it. It appears from tradition, that this poem was addressed to a Culdee, or one of the first Christian missionaries, and that the story of the *Spirit of Loda*, supposed to be the ancient Odin of Scandinavia, was introduced by Ossian in opposition to the Culdee's doctrine. Be this as it will, it lets us into Ossian's notions of a superior being; and shews that he was not addicted to the superstition which prevailed all the world over, before the introduction of Christianity.

HAST [a] thou left thy blue course in heaven, golden-haired son of the sky! The west has
opened

opened its gates; the bed of thy repose is there. The waves come to behold thy beauty: they lift their trembling heads: they see thee lovely in thy sleep; but they shrink away with fear. Rest, in thy shadowy cave, O sun! and let thy return be in joy. But let a thousand lights arise to the sound of the harps of Selma: let the beam spread in the hall, the king of shells is returned! The strife of Crona [b] is past, like sounds that are no more: raise the song, O bards, the king is returned with his fame.

Such was the song of Ullin, when Fingal returned from battle: when he returned in the fair blushing of youth; with all his heavy locks. His blue arms were on the hero; like a gray cloud on the sun, when he moves in his robes of mist, and shews but half his beams. His heroes follow the king: the feast of shells is spread. Fingal turns to his bards, and bids the song to rise.

Voices of echoing Cona! he said, O bards of other times! Ye, on whose souls the blue hosts of our fathers rise! strike the harp in my hall; and let Fingal hear the song. Pleasant is the joy of grief! it is like the shower of spring, when it softens the branch of the oak, and the young leaf lifts its green head. Sing on, O bards, to-morrow we lift the sail. My blue course is through the ocean, to

Carric-

Carric-thura's walls; the mossy walls of Sarno, where Comala dwelt. There the noble Cathulla spreads the feast of shells. The boars of his woods are many, and the sound of the chase shall arise.

Cronnan^c, son of song! said Ullin, Minona, graceful at the harp: raise the song of Shilric, to please the king of Morven. Let Vinvela come in her beauty, like the showery bow, when it shews its lovely head on the lake, and the setting sun is bright. And she comes, O Fingal! her voice is soft but sad.

Vinvela. My love is a son of the hill. He pursues the flying deer. His gray dogs are panting around him; his bow-string sounds in the wind. Dost thou rest by the fount of the rock, or by the noise of the mountain stream? the rushes are nodding with the wind, the mist is flying over the hill. I will approach my love unperceived, and see him from the rock. Lovely I saw thee first by the aged oak of Branno^d; thou wert returning tall from the chase; the fairest among thy friends.

Shilric. What voice is that I hear? that voice like the summer wind. I sit not by the nodding rushes; I hear not the fount of the rock. Afar, Vinvela^e, afar I go to the wars of Fingal. My dogs attend me no more. No more I tread the hill. No more from on high I see thee, fair-moving

ving by the stream of the plain; bright as the bow of heaven; as the moon on the western wave.

Vinvela. Then thou art gone, O Shilric! and I am alone on the hill. The deer are seen on the brow; void of fear they graze along. No more they dread the wind: no more the rustling tree. The hunter is far removed; he is in the field of graves. Strangers, sons of the waves! spare my lovely Shilric.

Shilric. If fall I must in the field, raise high my grave, Vinvela. Gray stones and heaped-up earth, shall mark me to future times. When the hunter shall sit by the mound, and produce his food at noon, "Some warrior rests here," he will say; and my fame shall live in his praise. Remember me, Vinvela, when low on earth I lie!

Vinvela. Yes! I will remember thee; indeed my Shilric will fall. What shall I do, my love! when thou art gone for ever? Through these hills I will go at noon: I will go through the silent heath. There I will see the place of thy rest, returning from the chase. Indeed my Shilric will fall; but I will remember him.

And I remember the chief, said the king of woody Morven; he consumed the battle in his rage. But now my eyes behold him not. I met him, one day, on the hill; his cheek was pale;
his

his brow was dark. The sigh was frequent in his breast: his steps were towards the desart. But now he is not in the crowd of my chiefs, when the sounds of my shields arise. Dwells he in the narrow house, ' the chief of high Carmora ? '

Cronnan! said Ullin of other times, raise the song of Shilric; when he returned to his hills, and Vinvela was no more. He leaned on her gray mossy stone; he thought Vinvela lived. He saw her fair-moving * on the plain: but the bright form lasted not: the sun-beam fled from the field, and she was seen no more. Hear the song of Shilric, it is soft but sad.

I sit by the mossy fountain; on the top of the hill of winds. One tree is rustling above me. Dark waves roll over the heath. The lake is troubled below. The deer descend from the hill: No hunter at a distance is seen; no whistling cow-herd is nigh. It is mid-day: but all is silent. Sad are my thoughts alone. Didst thou but appear, O my love, a wanderer on the heath! thy hair floating on the wind behind thee; thy bosom heaving on the sight; thine eyes full of tears for thy friends, whom the mist of the hill had concealed! Thee I would comfort, my love, and bring thee to thy father's house.

But it is she that there appears, like a beam of light on the heath? bright as the moon in autumn, as the sun in a summer-storm, comest thou, lovely maid, over rocks, over mountains to me? She speaks: but how weak her voice, like the breeze in the reeds of the pool.

"Returnest thou safe from the war? Where are thy friends, my love? I heard of thy death on the hill; I heard and mourned thee, Shilric!" Yes, my fair, I return; but I alone of my race. Thou shalt see them no more: their graves I raised on the plain. But why art thou on the desart hill? Why on the heath, alone?

"Alone I am, O Shilric! alone in the winter-house. With grief for thee I expired. Shilric, I am pale in the tomb."

She fleets, she sails away; as gray mist before the wind! and, wilt thou not stay, my love? Stay and behold my tears? fair thou appearest, Vinvela! fair thou wast, when alive!

By the mossy fountain I will sit; on the top of the hill of winds. When mid-day is silent around, converse, O my love, with me! come on the wings of the gale! on the blast, of the mountain, come! Let me hear thy voice, as thou passest, when mid-day is silent around.

Such

Such was the song of Cronnan, on the night of Selma's joy. But morning rose in the east; the blue waters rolled in light. Fingal bade his sails to rise, and the winds came rustling from their hills. Inistore rose to sight, and Carric-thura's mossy towers. But the sign of distress was on their top: the green flame edged with smoke. The king of Morven struck his breast: he assumed, at once, his spear. His darkened brow bends forward to the coast: he looks back to the lagging winds. His hair is disordered on his back. The silence of the king is terrible.

Night came down on the sea: Rotha's bay received the ship. A rock bends along the coast with all its echoing wood. On the top is the circle¹ of Loda, and the mossy stone of power. A narrow plain spreads beneath, covered with grass and aged trees, which the midnight winds, in their wrath, had torn from the shaggy rock. The blue course of a stream is there: and the lonely blast of ocean pursues the thistle's beard. The flame of three oaks arose: the feast is spread around: but the soul of the king is sad, for Carric-thura's battling chief.

The wan, cold moon rose, in the east. Sleep descended on the youths: Their blue helmets glitter to the beam; the fading fire decays. But sleep did not rest on the king: he rose in the midst of his arms, and slowly ascended the hill to behold the flame of Sarno's tower.

The flame was dim and distant; the moon hid her red face in the east. A blast came from the mountain, and bore, on its wings, the spirit of Loda. He came to his place in his terrors, [k] and he shook his dusky spear. His eyes appear like flames in his dark face; and his voice is like distant thunder. Fingal advanced with the spear of his strength, and raised his voice on high.

Son of night, retire: call thy winds and fly: Why dost thou come to my presence, with thy shadowy arms? Do I fear thy gloomy form, dismal spirit of Loda? Weak is thy shield of clouds: feeble is that meteor, thy sword. The blast rolls them together; and thou thyself dost vanish. Fly from my presence son of night! call thy winds and fly!

Dost thou force me from my place, replied the hollow voice? The people bend before me. I turn the battle in the field of the valiant. I look on the nations and they vanish: my nostrils pour the blast of death. I come abroad on the winds: the tempests are before my face. But my dwelling is calm, above the clouds, the fields of my rest are pleasant.

Dwell then in my calm field, said Fingal, and let Comhal's son be forgot. Do my steps ascend, from my hills, into thy peaceful plains? Do I meet thee,

thee, with a spear, on thy cloud, spirit of dismal
Loda? Why then dost thou frown on Fingal? or
shake thine airy spear? But thou frownest in vain:
I never fled from mighty men. And shall the sons
of the wind frighten the king of Morven! No: he
knows the weakness of their arms.

Fly to thy land, replied the form: receive the
wind and fly. The blasts are in the hollow of my
hand: the course of the storm is mine. The king
of Sora is my son, he bends at the stone of my
power. His battle is around Carric-thura; and he
will prevail. Fly to thy land, son of Comhal, or
feel my flaming wrath.

He lifted high his shadowy spear; and bent forward his terrible height. But the king, advancing, drew his sword; the blade of dark brown Luno. The gleaming path of the steel winds through the gloomy ghost. The form fell shapeless into air, like a column of smoke, which the staff of the boy disturbs, as it rises from the half-extinguished furnace.

The spirit of Loda shrieked, as, rolled into himself, he rose on the wind. Inistore shook at the sound. The waves heard it on the deep: they stopped, in their course with fear: the companions of Fingal started, at once; and took their heavy spears.

spears. They missed the king: they rose with rage; all their arms resound.

The moon came forth in the east. The king returned in the gleam of his arms. The joy of his youths was great; their souls settled, as a sea from a storm. Ullin raised the song of gladness. The hills of Iniftore rejoiced. The flame of the oak arose; and the tales of heroes are told.

But Frothal, Sora's battling king, sits in sadness beneath a tree. The host spreads around Carric-thura. He looks towards the walls with rage. He longs for the blood of Cathulla, who, once, overcame the king in war. When Annir reigned [n] in Sora, the father of car-borne Frothal, a blast rose on the sea, and carried Frothal to Iniftore. Three days he feasted in Sarno's halls, and saw the slow rolling eyes of Comala. He loved her, in the rage of youth, and rushed to seize the white-armed maid. Cathulla met the chief. The gloomy battle rose. Frothal is bound in the hall: three days he pined alone. On the fourth, Sarno sent him to his ship, and he returned to his land. But wrath darkened in his soul against the noble Cathulla. When Annir's stone [o] of fame arose, Frothal came in his strength. The battle burned round Carric-thura, and Sarno's mossy walls.

Morning

Morning rose on Iniſtore. Frothal ſtruck his dark-brown ſhield. His chiefs ſtarted at the ſound; they ſtood, but their eyes were turned to the ſea. They ſaw Fingal coming in his ſtrength; and firſt the noble Thubar ſpoke.

" Who comes like the ſtag of the mountain, with all his herd behind him? Frothal, it is a foe; I ſee his forward ſpear. Perhaps it is the king of Morven, Fingal the firſt of men. His actions are well known on Gormal; the blood of his foes is in Sarno's halls. Shall I aſk the peace* of kings? He is like the thunder of heaven."

Son of the feeble hand, ſaid Frothal, ſhall my days begin in darkneſs? Shall I yield before I have conquered in battle, chief of ſtreamy Tora? The people would ſay in Sora, Frothal flew forth like a meteor; but the dark cloud met it, and it is no more. No: Thubar, I will never yield; my fame ſhall ſurround me like light. No: I will never yield, king of ſtreamy Tora.

He went forth with the ſtream of his people, but they met a rock: Fingal ſtood unmoved, broken they rolled back from his ſide. Nor did they roll in ſafety; the ſpear of the king purſued their flight. The field is covered with heroes. A riſing hill preſerved the flying hoſt.

Frothal

Frothal saw their flight. The rage of his bosom rose. He bent his eyes to the ground, and called the noble Thubar. "Thubar! my people fled. My fame has ceased to rise. I will fight the king; I feel my burning soul. Send a bard to demand the combat. Speak not against Frothal's words. But, Thubar! I love a maid; she dwells by Thano's stream, the white-bosomed daughter of Herman, Utha with the softly-rolling eyes. She feared the daughter [P] of Iniftore, and her soft sighs rose, at my departure. Tell to Utha that I am low; but that my soul delighted in her."

Such were his words, resolved to fight. But the soft sigh of Utha was near. She had followed her hero over the sea, in the armour of a man. She rolled her eye on the youth, in secret, from beneath a glittering helmet. But now she saw the bard as he went, and the spear fell thrice from her hand. Her loose hair flew on the wind. Her white breast rose, with sighs. She lifted up her eyes to the king; she would speak, but thrice she failed.

Fingal heard the words of the bard; he came in the strength of steel. They mixed their deathful spears, and raised the gleam of their swords. But the steel of Fingal descended and cut Frothal's shield in twain. His fair side is exposed; half bent he foresees his death.

Darkness

Darkness gathered on Utha's soul. The tear rolled down her cheek. She rushed to cover the chief with her shield; but a fallen oak met her steps. She fell on her arm of snow; her shield, her helmet flew wide. Her white bosom heaved to the sight; her dark-brown hair is spread on earth.

Fingal pitied the white-armed maid: he stayed the uplifted sword. The tear was in the eye of the king, as, bending forward he spoke. "King of streamy Sora! fear not the sword of Fingal. It was never stained with the blood of the vanquished; it never pierced a fallen foe. Let thy people rejoice along the blue waters of Tora: let the maids of thy love be glad: Why shouldest thou fall in thy youth, king of streamy Sora?"

Frothal heard the words of Fingal, and saw the rising maid: they stood in silence, in their beauty: like two young trees of the plain, when the shower of spring is on their leaves, and the loud winds are laid.

"Daughter of Herman," said Frothal, "didst thou come from Tora's streams; didst thou come, in thy beauty, to behold thy warrior low? But he was low before the mighty, maid of the slow-rolling eye! The feeble did not overcome the son of car-borne Annir. Terrible art thou, O king of Morven!

Morven! in battles of the spear. But, in peace, thou art like the sun, when he looks through a silent shower: the flowers lift their fair heads before him; and the gales shake their wings. O that thou wert in Sora! that my feast were spread! The future kings of Sora would see thy arms and rejoice. They would rejoice at the fame of their fathers, who beheld the mighty Fingal.

"Son of Annir," replied the king, "the fame of Sora's race shall be heard. When chiefs are strong in battle, then does the song arise! But if their swords are stretched over the feeble: if the blood of the weak has stained their arms; the bard shall forget them in the song, and their tombs shall not be known. The stranger shall come and build there, and remove the heaped-up earth. An half-worn sword shall rise before him; and bending above it, he will say, "These are the arms of chiefs of old, but their names are not in song. Come thou, O Frothal, to the feast of Iniftore; let the maid of thy love be there: and our faces will brighten with joy."

Fingal took his spear, moving in the steps of his might. The gates of Carric-thura are opened. The feast of shells is spread. The voice of music arose. Gladness brightened in the hall. The voice of Ullin was heard: the harp of Selma was strung.

Utha

Utha rejoiced in his prefence, and demanded the fong of grief; the big tear hung in her eye, when the foft ‘ Crimora fpoke. Crimora the daughter of Rinval, who dwelt at Lotha's ‘ mighty ſtream. The tale was long, but lovely; and pleafed the blufhing maid of Tora.

Crimora. ‘ Who cometh from the hill, like a cloud tinged with the beam of the weſt? Whofe voice is that, loud as the wind, but pleafant as the harp of Carril!" It is my love in the light of ſteel; but fad is his darkened brow. Live the mighty race of Fingal? or what difturbs my Connal?'

Connal. They live. I faw them return from the chafe, like a ſtream of light. The fun was on their fhields. Like a ridge of fire they defcended the hill. Loud is the voice of the youth; the war, my love, is near. To-morrow the terrible Dargo comes to try the force of our race. The race of Fingal he defies; the race of battle and wounds.

Crimora. Connal, I faw his fails like gray miſt on the fable wave. They ſlowly came to land. Connal, many are the warriors of Dargo!

Connal. Bring me thy father's fhield; the boffy, iron fhield of Rinval; that fhield like the full moon when it moves darkened through heaven.

Crimora. That fhield I bring, O Connal; but it did not defend my father. By the fpear of Gormar he fell. Thou may'ſt fall, O Connal!

Connal.

Connal. Fall indeed I may: But raise my tomb, Crimora. Gray stones, a mound of earth, shall keep my memory. Bend thy red eye over my tomb, and beat thy mournful heaving breast. Though fair thou art, my love, as the light; more pleasant than the gale of the hill; yet I will not stay. Raise my tomb, Crimora.

Crimora. Then give me those arms of light; that sword, and that spear of steel. I shall meet Dargo with thee, and aid my lovely Connal. Farewell, ye rocks of Ardven! ye deer! and ye streams of the hill! We shall return no more. Our tombs are distant far.

"And did they return no more?" said Utha's bursting sigh. "Fell the mighty in battle, and did Crimora live? Her steps were lonely, and her soul was sad for Connal. Was he not young and lovely; like the beam of the setting sun?" Ullin saw the virgin's tear, and took the softly-trembling harp: the song was lovely, but sad, and silence was in Carric-thura.

Autumn is dark on the mountains; gray mist rests on the hills. The whirlwind is heard on the heath. Dark rolls the river through the narrow plain. A tree stands alone on the hill, and marks the slumbering Connal. The leaves whirl round with the wind, and strew the grave of the dead. At

At times are seen here the ghosts of the deceased, when the musing hunter alone stalks slowly over the heath.

Who can reach the source of thy race, O Connal? and who recount thy fathers? Thy family grew like an oak on the mountain, which meeteth the wind with its lofty head. But now it is torn from the earth. Who shall supply the place of Connal? Here was the din of arms? and here the groans of the dying. Bloody are the wars of Fingal! O Connal! it was here thou didst fall. Thine arm was like a storm; thy sword a beam of the sky; thy height, a rock on the plain; thine eyes, a furnace of fire. Louder than a storm was thy voice, in the battles of thy steel. Warriors fell by thy sword, as the thistle by the staff of a boy. Dargo the mighty came on, like a cloud of thunder. His brows were contracted and dark. His eyes like two caves in a rock. Bright rose their swords on each side; dire was the clang of their steel.

The daughter of Rinval was near; Crimora bright in the armour of man; her yellow hair is loose behind, her bow is in her hand. She followed the youth to the war, Connal her much-beloved. She drew the string on Dargo; but erring pierced her Connal. He falls like an oak on the

plain

plain; like a rock from the shaggy hill. What shall she do, hapless maid? He bleeds; her Connal dies. All the night long she cries, and all the day, "O Connal, my love, and my friend?" With grief the sad mourner dies. Earth here incloses the lovelieſt pair on the hill. The graſs grows between the ſtones of the tomb; I often ſit in the mournful ſhade. The winds ſigh through the graſs; their memory ruſhes on my mind. Undiſturbed you now ſleep together; in the tomb of the mountain you reſt alone.

"And ſoft be your reſt," ſaid Utha, "children of ſtreamy Lotha. I will remember you with tears, and my ſecret ſong ſhall riſe; when the wind is in the groves of Tora, and the ſtream is roaring near. Then ſhall ye come on my ſoul, with all your lovely grief."

Three days feaſted the kings: on the fourth their white ſails aroſe. The winds of the north carry the ſhip of Fingal to Morven's woody land. But the ſpirit of Loda ſat, in his cloud, behind the ſhips of Frothal. He hung forward with all his blaſts, and ſpread the white-boſomed ſails. The wounds of his form were not forgot; he ſtill feared [r] the hand of the king.

NOTES

NOTES ON
CARRIC-THURA.

^a The song of Ullin, with which the poem opens, is in a lyric measure. It was usual with Fingal, when he returned from his expeditions, to send his bards singing before him. This species of triumph is called, by Ossian, *the song of victory*.

^b Ossian has celebrated the *strife of Crona*, in a particular poem. This poem is connected with it, but it was impossible for the translator to procure that part which relates to Crona, with any degree of purity.

^c One should think that the parts of Shilric and Vinvela were represented by Cronnan and Minona, whose very names denote that they were singers, who performed in public. Cronnan signifies *a mournful sound*; Minona, or Min-onn, *soft air*. All the dramatic poems of Ossian appear to have been presented before Fingal, upon solemn occasions.

^d Bran, or Branno, signifies *a mountain stream*; it is here some river known by that name, in the days of Ossian. There are several small rivers in the north of Scotland, still retaining the name of Bran; in particular one which falls into the Tay, at Dunkeld.

^e Bhin bheul, *a woman with a melodious voice*. Bh in the Gallic Language has the same sound with the *v* in English.

^f The grave.

^g Carn-mor, *high rocky hill*.

ᵏ The distinction, which the ancient Scots made between good and bad spirits, was, that the former appeared sometimes in the day time in lonely unfrequented places; but the latter seldom but by night, and always in a dismal gloomy scene.

ˡ *The circle of Loda* is supposed to be a place of worship among the Scandinavians, as the spirit of Loda is thought to be the same with their god Odin.

ᵏ He is described, in a simile, in the poem concerning the death of Cuchullin.

ˡ The famous sword of Fingal, made by Lun, or Luno, a smith of Lochlin.

ᵐ Annir was also the father of Erragon, who was killed after the death of his brother Frothal. The death of Erragon is the subject of *the battle of Lora*, a poem in this collection.

ⁿ That is, after the death of Annir. To erect the stone of one's fame, was, in other words, to say that the person was dead.

º Honourable terms of peace.

ᵖ By the daughter of Iniftore, Frothal means Comala, of whose death Utha probably had not heard; consequently she feared that the former passion of Frothal for Comala might return.

ᵠ Frothal and Utha.

ʳ There is a propriety in introducing this episode, as the situation of Crimora and Utha were so similar.

ˢ Lotha was the ancient name of one of the great rivers in the north of Scotland. The only one of them that still retains a name of a like sound is Lochy, in Invernessshire; but whether it is the river mentioned here, the translator will not pretend to say.

ᵗ Cri-

ᵗ *Cri-mora, a woman of a great soul.*

ᵘ Perhaps the Carril mentioned here is the same with Carril the son of Kinfena, Cuchullin's bard. The name itself is proper to any bard, as it signifies *a sprightly and harmonious sound.*

ˣ Connal, the son of Diaran, was one of the most famous heroes of Fingal; he was slain in a battle against Dargo, a Briton; but whether by the hand of the enemy, or that of his mistress, tradition does not determine.

ʸ The story of Fingal, and the spirit of Loda, supposed to be the famous Odin, is the most extravagant fiction in all Ossian's poems. It is not, however, without precedents in the best poets; and it must be said for Ossian, that he says nothing but what perfectly agreed with the notions of the times, concerning ghosts. They thought the souls of the dead were material, and consequently susceptible of pain. Whether a proof could be drawn from this passage, that Ossian had no notion of a divinity, I shall leave to others to determine: it appears, however, that he was of opinion, that superior beings ought to take no notice of what passed among men.

THE
SONGS OF SELMA.

THE ARGUMENT.

This poem fixes the antiquity of a custom, which is well known to have prevailed afterwards, in the north of Scotland, and in Ireland. The bards, at an annual feast, provided by the king or chief, repeated their poems, and such of them as were thought, by him, worthy of being preserved, were carefully taught to their children, in order to have them transmitted to posterity. It was one of those occasions that afforded the subject of the present poem to Ossian. It is called in the original, The Songs of Selma, which title it was thought proper to adopt in the translation.

The poem is entirely lyric, and has great variety of versification. The address to the evening star, with which it opens, has, in the original, all the harmony that numbers could give it; flowing down with all that tranquillity and softness, which the scene described naturally inspires.

STAR of the descending night! fair is thy light in the west! thou liftest thy unshorn head from thy cloud: thy steps are stately on thy hill. What dost thou behold in the plain? The stormy winds are laid. The murmur of the torrent comes from afar. Roaring waves climb the distant rock. The flies of evening are on their feeble wings, and

the

the hum of their courſe is on the field. What doſt thou behold, fair light? But thou doſt ſmile and depart. The waves come with joy around thee, and bathe thy lovely hair. Farewel, thou ſilent beam! Let the light of Oſſian's ſoul ariſe.

And it does ariſe in its ſtrength! I behold my departed friends. Their gathering is on Lora, as in the days that are paſt. Fingal comes like a watry column of miſt: his heroes are around. And ſee the bards of the ſong, gray-haired Ullin; ſtately Ryno; Alpin,[a] with the tuneful voice, and the ſoft complaint of Minona! How are ye changed, my friends, ſince the days of Selma's feaſt! when we contended, like the gales of the ſpring, that, flying over the hill, by turns bend the feebly whiſtling graſs.

Minona then came forth in her beauty; with down-caſt look and tearful eye; her hair flew ſlowly on the blaſt that ruſhed unfrequent from the hill. The ſouls of the heroes were ſad when ſhe raiſed the tuneful voice; for often had they ſeen the grave of Salgar,[b] and the dark dwelling of white-boſomed Colma.[c] Colma left alone on the hill, with all her voice of muſic! Salgar promiſed to come: but the night deſcended round. Hear the voice of Colma, when ſhe ſat alone on the hill!

THE SONGS OF SELMA.

Colma. It is night; I am alone, forlorn on the hill of storms. The wind is heard in the mountain. The torrent shrieks down the rock. No hut receives me from the rain; forlorn on the hill of winds.

Rise, moon! from behind thy clouds; stars of the night appear! Lead me, some light, to the place where my love rests from the toil of the chase! his bow near him, unstrung; his dogs panting around him. But here I must sit alone, by the rock of the mossy stream. The stream and the wind roar; nor can I hear the voice of my love. Why delays my Salgar, why the son of the hill, his promise? Here is the rock, and the tree; and here the roaring stream. Thou didst promise with night to be here. Ah! whither is my Salgar gone? With thee would I fly, my father; with thee, my brother of pride. Our race have long been foes; but we are not foes, O Salgar!

Cease a little while, O wind! stream, be thou silent a while! let my voice be heard over the heath; let my wanderer hear me. Salgar! it is I who call. Here is the tree, and the rock. Salgar, my love! I am here. Why delayest thou thy coming? Lo! the moon appeareth. The flood is bright in the vale. The rocks are gray on the face of the hill. But I see him not on the brow;

his dogs before him tell not that he is coming. Here I must sit alone.

But who are these that lie beyond me on the heath? Are they my love and my brother? Speak to me, O my friends! they answer not. My soul is tormented with fears. Ah! they are dead. Their swords are red from the fight. O my brother! my brother! why hast thou slain my Salgar? why, O Salgar! hast thou slain my brother? Dear were ye both to me! what shall I say in your praise? Thou wert fair on the hill among thousands; he was terrible in fight. Speak to me; hear my voice, sons of my love! But alas! they are silent; silent forever! Cold are their breasts of clay! Oh! from the rock of the hill: from the top of the windy mountain, speak ye ghosts of the dead! speak, I will not be afraid. Whither are ye gone to rest? In what cave of the hill shall I find you? No feeble voice is on the wind: no answer half-drowned in the storms of the hill.

I sit in my grief. I wait for morning in my tears. Rear the tomb, ye friends of the dead; but close it not till Colma come. My life flies away like a dream: why should I stay behind? Here shall I rest with my friends, by the stream of the sounding rock. When night comes on the hill; when the wind is on the heath; my ghost shall stand in the

the wind, and mourn the death of my friends. The hunter shall hear from his booth. He shall fear but love my voice. For sweet shall my voice be for my friends; for pleasant were they both to me.

Such was thy song, Minona softly-blushing maid of Torman. Our tears descended for Colma, and our souls were sad. Ullin came with the harp, and gave the song of Alpin. The voice of Alpin was pleasant: the soul of Ryno was a beam of fire. But they had rested in the narrow house: and their voice was not heard in Selma. Ullin had returned one day from the chase, before the heroes fell. He heard their strife on the hill; their song was soft but sad. They mourned the fall of Morar, first of mortal men. His soul was like the soul of Fingal; his sword like the sword of Oscar. But he fell, and his father mourned: his sister's eyes were full of tears. Minona's eyes were full of tears, the sister of car-borne Morar. She retired from the song of Ullin, like the moon in the west, when she foresees the shower, and hides her fair head in a cloud. I touched the harp, with Ullin; the song of mourning rose.

Ryno. The wind and the rain are over: calm is the noon of day. The clouds are divided in heaven. Over the green hills flies the inconstant sun. Red through the stony vale comes down the stream of of the hill. Sweet are thy murmurs, O stream! but more sweet is the voice I hear. It is the voice of Alpin, the son of song, mourning for the dead. Bent is the head of age, and red his tearful eye. Alpin, thou son of song, why alone on the silent hill? why complainest thou, as a blast in the wood; as a wave on the lonely shore!

Alpin. My tears, O Ryno! are for the dead; my voice, for the inhabitants of the grave. Tall thou art on the hill; fair among the sons of the plain. But thou shalt fall like Morar;[d] and the mourner shall sit on thy tomb. The hills shall know thee no more; thy bow shall lie in the hall, unstrung.

Thou wert swift, O Morar! as a roe on the hill; terrible as a meteor of fire. Thy wrath was as the storm. Thy sword in battle, as lightning in the field. Thy voice was like a stream after rain; like thunder on distant hills. Many fell by thy arm; they were consumed in the flames of thy wrath. But when thou didst return from war, how peaceful was thy brow? Thy face was like the sun after rain; like the moon in the silence of night; calm as the breast of the lake when the loud wind is laid.

Narrow is thy dwelling now; dark the place of thine abode. With three steps I compass thy grave, O thou who wast so great before! Four stones,
with

with their heads of mofs, are the only memorial of thee. A tree with fcarce a leaf, long grafs which whiftles in the wind, mark to the hunter's eye the grave of the mighty Morar. Morar! thou art low indeed. Thou haft no mother to mourn thee; no maid with her tears of love. Dead is fhe that brought thee forth. Fallen is the daughter of Morglan

Who on his ftaff is this? who is this, whofe head is white with age, whofe eyes are red with tears, who quakes at every ftep. It is thy father, O Morar! the father of no fon but thee. He heard of thy fame in battle; he heard of foes difperfed. He heard of Morar's fame; why did he not hear of his wound? Weep, thou father of Morar; weep; but thy fon heareth thee not. Deep is the fleep of the dead; low their pillow of duft. No more fhall he hear thy voice; no more fhall he awake at thy call. When fhall it be morn in the grave, to bid the flumberer awake? Farewel, thou braveft of men! thou conqueror in the field! but the field fhall fee thee no more: nor the dark wood be lightened with the fplendor of thy fteel. Thou haft left no fon. But the fong fhall preferve thy name. Future times fhall hear of thee; they fhall hear of the fallen Morar.

The grief of all arose, but most the bursting sigh of Armin. ' He remembers the death of his son, who fell in the days of his youth. Carmor ⁵ was near the hero, the chief of the echoing Galmal. Why bursts the sigh of Armin, he said? Is there a cause to mourn? The song comes, with its music, to melt and please the soul. It is like soft mist, that, rising from a lake, pours on the silent vale; the green flowers are filled with dew, but the sun returns in his strength, and the mist is gone. Why art thou sad, O Armin, chief of sea-surrounded Gorma?

Sad! I am indeed: nor small my cause of woe! Carmor, thou hast lost no son; thou hast lost no daughter of beauty. Colgar the valiant lives; and Annira fairest maid. The boughs of thy family flourish, O Carmor! but Armin is the last of his race. Dark is thy bed, O Daura! and deep thy sleep in the tomb. When shalt thou awake with thy songs? with all thy voice of music?

Arise, winds of autumn, arise; blow upon the dark heath! streams of the mountains, roar! howl, ye tempests, in the top of the oak! walk through broken clouds, O moon! show by intervals thy pale face! bring to my mind that sad night, when all my children fell; when Arindal the mighty fell; when Daura the lovely failed. Daura, my daughter!

Vol. I.   K k   thou

thou wert fair; fair as the moon on the hills of Fura;[b] white as the driven snow; sweet as the breathing gale. Arindal, thy bow was strong, thy spear was swift in the field: thy look was like mist on the wave; thy shield, a red cloud in a storm. Armar, renowned in war, came, and sought Daura's love; he was not long denied; fair was the hope of their friends.

Erath, son of Odgal, repined; for his brother was slain by Armar. He came disguised like a son of the sea: fair was his skiff on the wave; white his locks of age; calm his serious brow. Fairest of women, he said, lovely daughter of Armin! a rock not distant in the sea, bears a tree on its side; red shines the fruit afar. There Armar waits for Daura. I came to carry his love along the rolling sea. She went; and she called on Armar. Nought answered, but the son[1] of the rock. Armar, my love! my love! why tormentest thou me with fear? hear, son of Ardnart, hear: it is Daura who calleth thee! Erath the traitor fled laughing to the land. She lifted up her voice, and cried for her brother and her father. Arindal! Armin! none to relieve your Daura.

Her voice came over the sea. Arindal my son descended from the hill: rough in the spoils of the chase. His arrows rattled by his side; his bow was

was in his hand: five dark gray dogs attended his
steps. He saw fierce Erath on the shore: he seized
and bound him to an oak. Thick bend the thongs
of the hide around his limbs; he loads the wind
with his groans. Arindal ascends the wave in his
boat, to bring Daura to land. Armar came in his
wrath, and let fly the gray-feathered shaft. It
sunk; it sunk in thy heart. O Arindal my son!
for Erath the traitor thou diedst. The oar is stopped at once; he panted on the rock and expired.
What is thy grief, O Daura, when round thy feet
is poured thy brother's blood. The boat is broken
in twain by the waves. Armar plunges into the
sea, to rescue his Daura, or die. Sudden a blast
from the hill comes over the waves. He sunk,
and he rose no more.

Alone, on the sea-beat rock, my daughter was
heard to complain. Frequent and loud were her
cries; nor could her father relieve her. All night
I stood on the shore. I saw her by the faint beam
of the moon. All night I heard her cries. Loud
was the wind; and the rain beat hard on the side
of the mountain. Before morning appeared, her
voice was weak. It died away, like the evening-
breeze among the grass of the rocks. Spent with
grief she expired. And left thee Armin alone,
gone is my strength in the war, and fallen my pride

among women. When the storms of the mountain come; when the north lifts the waves on high; I sit by the sounding shore, and look on the fatal rock. Often by the setting moon I see the ghosts of my children. Half-viewless, they walk in mournful conference together. Will none of you speak in pity? They do not regard their father. I am sad, O Carmor, nor small is my cause of woe!

Such were the words of the bards in the days of song; when the king heard the music of harps, and the tales of other times. The chiefs gathered from all their hills, and heard the lovely sound. They praised the voice¹ of Cona! the first among a thousand bards. But age is now on my tongue; and my soul has failed. I hear, sometimes, the ghosts of bards, and learn their pleasant song. But memory fails in my mind; I hear the call of years. They say, as they pass along, why does Ossian sing? Soon shall he lie in the narrow house, and no bard shall raise his fame. Roll on, ye dark-brown years, for you bring no joy on your course. Let the tomb open to Ossian, for his strength has failed. The sons of song are gone to rest: my voice remains, like a blast, that roars, lonely, on a sea-surrounded rock, after the winds are laid. The dark moss whistles there, and the distant mariner sees the waving trees.

NOTES

NOTES ON
THE SONGS OF SELMA.

ª Alpin is from the same root with Albion, or rather Albin, the ancient name of Britain; Alp, *high* in *land*, or *country*. The present name of our island has its origin in the Celtic tongue; so that those who derived it from any other, betrayed their ignorance of the ancient language of our country. *Britain* comes from *Breac't in, variegated island,* so called from the face of the country, from the natives painting themselves, or from their party-coloured clothes.

ᵇ Sealg-'er, *a hunter.*

ᶜ Cul-math, *a woman with fine hair.*

ᵈ Mor-er, *great men.*

ᵉ Torman, the son of Carthul, lord of I-mora, one of the western isles.

ᶠ Armin, *a hero.* He was chief, or petty king of Gorma, i. e. *the blue island;* supposed to be one of the Hebrides.

ᵍ Cear-mor, *a tall dark-complexioned man.*

ʰ Fuar-a, *cold island.*

ⁱ By *the son of the rock,* the poet means the echoing back of the human voice from a rock. The vulgar were of opinion, that this repetition of sound was made by a spirit within the rock; and they, on that account, called it *mac-talla; the son who dwells in the rock.*

ᵏ The poet here only means that Erath was bound with leathern thongs.

ˡ Ossian is sometimes poetically called *the voice of Cona.*

CALTHON

CALTHON AND COLMAL:

A POEM.

THE ARGUMENT.

This piece, as many more of Ossian's compositions, is addressed to one of the first Christian missionaries. The story of the poem is handed down, by tradition, thus: In the country of the Britons between the walls, two chiefs lived in the days of Fingal, Dunthalmo, lord of Teutha, supposed to be the Tweed; and Rathmor, who dwelt at Clutha, well known to be the river Clyde. Rathmor was not more renowned for his generosity and hospitality, than Dunthalmo was infamous for his cruelty and ambition. Dunthalmo, through envy, or on account of some private feuds, which subsisted between the families, murdered Rathmor at a feast; but being afterwards touched with remorse, he educated the two sons of Rathmor, Calthon and Colmar, in his own house. They growing up to man's estate, dropped some hints that they intended to revenge the death of their father, upon which Dunthalmo shut them up in two caves on the banks of Teutha, intending to take them off privately. Colmal, the daughter of Dunthalmo, who was secretly in love with Calthon, helped him to make his escape from prison, and fled with him to Fingal, disguised in the habit of a young warrior, and implored his aid against Dunthalmo. Fingal sent Ossian with three hundred men, to Colmar's relief. Dunthalmo having previously murdered Colmar, came to a battle with Ossian; but he was killed by that hero, and his army totally defeated.

Calthon

Calthon married Colmal, his deliverer; and Ossian returned to Morven.

PLEASANT is the voice of thy song, thou lonely dweller of the rock. It comes on the sound of the stream, along the narrow vale. My soul awakes, O stranger! in the midst of my hall. I stretch my hand to the spear, as in the days of other years. I stretch my hand, but it is feeble; and the sigh of my bosom grows. Wilt thou not listen, son of the rock, to the song of Ossian? My soul is full of other times; the joy of my youth returns. Thus the sun appears in the west, after the steps of his brightness have moved behind a storm; the green hills lift their dewy heads: the blue streams rejoice in the vale. The aged hero comes forth on his staff, and his gray hair glitters in the beam. Dost thou not behold, son of the rock, a shield in Ossian's hall? It is marked with the strokes of battle; and the brightness of its bosses has failed. That shield the great Dunthalmo bore, the chief of streamy Teutha. Dunthalmo bore it in battle, before he fell by Ossian's spear. Listen son of the rock, to the tale of other years.

Rathmor was a chief of Clutha. The feeble dwelt in his hall. The gates of Rathmor were never closed; his feast was always spread. The sons of the stranger came, and blessed the generous chief of of Clutha. Bards raised the song, and touched the harp: and joy brightened on the face of the mournful. Dunthalmo came, in his pride, and rushed into the combat of Rathmor. The chief of Clutha overcame; the rage of Dunthalmo rose. He came, by night, with his warriors; and the mighty Rathmor fell. He fell in his halls, where his feast was often spread for strangers.

Colmar and Calthon were young, the sons of car-borne Rathmor. They came, in the joy of youth, into their father's hall. They behold him in his blood, and their bursting tears descend. The soul of Dunthalmo melted, when he saw the children of youth; he brought them to Alteutha's [1] walls; they grew in the house of their foe. They bent the bow in his presence; and came forth to his battles. They saw the fallen walls of their fathers; they saw the green thorn in the hall. Their tears descended in secret; and, at times, their faces were mournful. Dunthalmo beheld their grief: his darkening soul designed their death. He closed them in two caves, on the echoing banks of Teutha. The sun did not come there with his beams; nor the moon of heaven by night. The sons of Rathmor remained in darkness, and foresaw their death.

The daughter of Dunthalmo wept in silence, the fair-haired, blue-eyed Colmal. [b] Her eye had rolled

in

in secret on Calthon; his loveliness swelled in her soul. She trembled for her warrior; but what could Colmal do? Her arm could not lift the spear; nor was the sword formed for her side. Her white breast never rose beneath a mail. Neither was her eye the terror of heroes. What canst thou do, O Colmal! for the falling chief? Her steps are unequal; her hair is loose: her eye looks wildly through her tears. She came, by night, to the hall [c]; and armed her lovely form in steel; the steel of a young warrior, who fell in the first of his battles. She came to the cave of Calthon, and loosed the thong from his hands.

"Arise, son of Rathmor," she said, "arise, the night is dark. Let us fly to the king of Selma [d], chief of fallen Clutha! I am the son of Lamgal, who dwelt in thy father's hall. I heard of thy dark dwelling in the cave, and my soul arose. Arise, son of Rathmor, for the night is dark." "Blest voice!" replied the chief, "comest thou from the darkly-rolling clouds? for often the ghosts of his fathers descended to Calthon's dreams, since the sun has retired from his eyes, and darkness has dwelt around him. Or art thou the son of Lamgal, the chief I often saw in Clutha? But shall I fly to Fingal and Colmar my brother low? shall I fly to Morven, and the hero closed in night?

No: give me that spear, son of Lamgal, Calthon will defend his brother."

"A thousand warriors," replied the maid, "stretch their spears round car-borne Colmar. What can Calthon do against a host so great? Let us fly to the king of Morven, he will come with battle. His arm is stretched forth to the unhappy; the lightning of his sword is round the weak. Arise, thou son of Rathmor; the shades of night will fly away. Dunthalma will behold thy steps on the field, and thou must fall in thy youth."

The sighing hero rose; his tears descend for car-borne Colmar. He came with the maid to Selma's hall; but he knew not that it was Colmal. The helmet covered her lovely face; and her breast rose beneath the steel. Fingal returned from the chase, and found the lovely strangers. They were like two beams of light, in the midst of the hall. The king heard the tale of grief; and turned his eyes around. A thousand heroes half-rose before him; claiming the war of Teutha. I came with my spear from the hill, and the joy of battle rose in my breast: for the king spoke to Ossian in the midst of the people.

"Son of my strength," he said, "take the spear of Fingal; go to Teutha's mighty stream, and save the car-borne Colmar. Let thy fame return before

fore thee like a pleasant gale; that my soul may rejoice over my son, who renews the renown of our fathers. Ossian! be thou a storm in battle; but mild when the foes are low! It was thus my fame arose, O my son; and be thou like Selma's chief. When the haughty come to my halls, my eyes behold them not. But my arm is stretched forth to the unhappy. My sword defends the weak."

I rejoiced in the words of the king: and took my rattling arms. Diaran rose at my side, and Dargo king of spears. Three hundred youths followed our steps: the lovely strangers were at my side. Dunthalmo heard the sound of our approach; he gathered the strength of Teutha. He stood on a hill with his host; they were like rocks broken with thunder, when their bent trees are singed and bare, and the streams of their chinks have failed.

The stream of Teutha rolled, in its pride, before the gloomy foe. I sent a bard to Dunthalmo, to offer the combat on the plain; but he smiled in the darkness of his pride. His unsettled host moved on the hill; like the mountain cloud, when the blast has entered its womb, and scatters the curling gloom on every side.

They brought Colmar to Teutha's bank, bound with a thousand thongs. The chief is sad, but

lovely,

lovely, and his eye is on his friends; for we ſtood, in our arms, on the oppoſite bank of Teutha. Dunthalmo came with his ſpear, and pierced the hero's ſide: he rolled on the bank in his blood, and we heard his broken ſighs.

Calthon ruſhed into the ſtream: I bounded forward on my ſpear. Teutha's race fell before us. Night came rolling down. Dunthalmo reſted on a rock, amidſt an aged wood. The rage of his boſom burned againſt the car-borne Calthon. But Calthon ſtood in his grief; he mourned the fallen Colmar; Colmar ſlain in youth, before his fame aroſe.

I bade the ſong of woe to riſe, to ſoothe the mournful chief; but he ſtood beneath a tree, and often threw his ſpear on the earth. The humid eye of Colmal rolled near in a ſecret tear: ſhe foreſaw the fall of Dunthalmo, or of Clutha's battling chief.

Now half the night had paſſed away. Silence and darkneſs were on the field; ſleep reſted on the eyes of the heroes: Calthon's ſettling ſoul was ſtill. His eyes were half-cloſed; but the murmur of Teutha had not yet failed in his ear. Pale, and ſhewing his wounds, the ghoſt of Colmar came: he bended his head over the hero, and raiſed his feeble voice.

"Sleeps

"Sleeps the son of Rathmor in his might, and his brother low? Did we not rise to the chase together, and pursue the dark-brown hinds? Colmar was not forgot till he fell; till death had blasted his youth. I lie pale beneath the rock of Lona. O let Calthon rise! the morning comes with its beams; and Dunthalmo will dishonour the fallen." He passed away in his blast. The rising Calthon saw the steps of his departure. He rushed in the sound of his steel; and unhappy Colmal rose. She followed her hero through night, and dragged her spear behind. But when Calthon came to Lona's rock, he found his fallen brother. The rage of his bosom rose, and he rushed among the foe. The groans of death ascend. They close around the chief. He is bound in the midst, and brought to gloomy Dunthalmo. The shout of joy arose; and the hills of night replied.

I started at the sound: and took my father's spear. Diaran rose at my side; and the youthful strength of Dargo. We missed the chief of Clutha, and our souls were sad. I dreaded the departure of my fame; the pride of my valour rose. "Sons of Morven," I said, "it is not thus our fathers fought. They rested not on the field of strangers, when the foe did not fall before them. Their strength was like the eagles of heaven; their

renown

renown is in the song. But our people fall by degrees, and our fame begins to depart. What shall the king of Morven say, if Ossian conquers not at Teutha? Rise in your steel, ye warriors, and follow the sound of Ossian's course. He will not return, but renowned, to the echoing walls of Selma."

Morning rose on the blue waters of Teutha; Colmal stood before me in tears. She told of the chief of Clutha: and thrice the spear fell from her hand. My wrath turned against the stranger; for my soul trembled for Calthon. "Son of the feeble hand," I said, "do Teutha's warriors fight with tears! The battle is not won with grief; nor dwells the sigh in the soul of war. Go to the deer of Carmun, or the lowing herds of Teutha. But leave these arms, thou son of fear: a warriour may lift them in battle."

I tore the mail from her shoulders. Her snow breast appeared. She bent her red face to the ground. I looked in silence to the chiefs. The spear fell from my hand; and the sigh of my bosom rose. But when I heard the name of the maid, my crowding tears descended. I blessed the lovely beam of youth, and bade the battle move.

Why, son of the rock, should Ossian tell how Teutha's warriors died? They are now forgot in their

their land; and their tombs are now found on the heath. Years came on with their tempests; and the green mounds mouldered away. Scarce is the grave of Dunthalmo seen, or the place where he fell by the spear of Ossian. Some gray warrior, half blind with age, sitting by night at the flaming oak of the hall, tells now my actions to his sons, and the fall of the dark Dunthalmo. The faces of youth bend sidelong towards his voice; surprise and joy burn in their eyes.

I found the son [a] of Rathmor bound to an oak; my sword cut the thongs from his hands. And I gave him the white-bosomed Colmal. They dwelt in the halls of Teutha; and Ossian returned to Selma.

NOTES ON

CALTHON AND COLMAL.

[a] Al-teutha, or rather Balteutha, *the town of Tweed*, the name of Dunthalmo's seat. It is observable, that all the names in this poem, are derived from the Gallic language; which, as I have remarked in a preceding note, is a proof that it was once the universal language of the whole island.

[b] Cœl-

b Caol-mhal, *a woman with small eye-brows;* small eye-brows were a distinguishing part of beauty in Ossian's time: and he seldom fails to give them to the fine women of his poems.

c That is, the hall where the arms taken from enemies were hung up as trophies. Ossian is very careful to make his stories probable; for he makes Colmal put on the arms of a youth killed in his first battle, as more proper for a young woman, who cannot be supposed strong enough to carry the armour of a full grown warrior.

d Fingal.

e Diaran, father of that Connal who was unfortunately killed by Crimora, his mistress.

f Dargo, the son of Collath, is celebrated in other poems by Ossian. He is said to have been killed by a boar at a hunting party. The lamentation of his mistress, or wife, Mingala, over his body, is extant; but whether it is of Ossian's composition, I cannot determine. It is generally ascribed to him, and has much of his manner; but some traditions mention it as an imitation by some later bard. As it has some poetical merit, I have subjoined it.

"THE spouse of Dargo came in tears: for Dargo was no more! The heroes sigh over Lartho's chief: and what shall sad Mingala do? The dark soul vanished like morning mist, before the king of spears: but the generous glowed in his presence like the morning star.

Who was the fairest and most lovely? who but Collath's stately son? Who sat in the midst of the wife, but Dargo of the mighty deeds?

Thy hand touched the trembling harp: Thy voice was soft as summer winds. Ah me! what shall the heroes say?

for

for Dargo fell before a boar Pale is the lovely cheek; the look of which was firm in danger! Why haft thou failed on our hills, thou fairer than the beams of the fun?

The daughter of Adonfion was lovely in the eyes of the valiant; fhe was lovely in their eyes, but fhe chofe to be the fpoufe of Dargo.

But thou art alone, Mingala! the night is coming with its clouds; where is the bed of thy repofe? Where but in the tomb of Dargo!

Why doft thou lift the ftone, O bard! why doft thou fhut the narrow houfe? Mingala's eyes are heavy, bard! She muft fleep with Dargo.

Laft night I heard the fong of joy in Lartho's lofty hall. But filence now dwells around my bed. Mingala refts with Dargo.

Calthon.

LATHMON:
A POEM.

THE ARGUMENT.

Lathmon, a British prince, taking advantage of Fingal's absence in Ireland, made a defcent on Morven, and advanced within fight of Selma the royal palace. Fingal arrived
in the mean time, and Lathmor retreated to a hill, where
his army was furprifed by night, and himfelf taken pri-
foner by Offian and Gaul the fon of Morni. This exploit
of Gaul and Offian bears a near refemblance to the beautiful epifode of Nifus and Euryalus in Virgil's ninth Æneid.
The poem opens, with the firft appearance of Fingal on
the coaft of Morven, and ends, it may be fuppofed, a-
bout noon the next day.

SELMA, thy halls are filent. There is no found
in the woods of Morven. The wave tumbles
alone on the coaft. The filent beam of the fun is
on the field. The daughters of Morven come
forth, like the bow of the fhower; they look towards green Ullin for the white fails of the king.
He had promifed to return, but the winds of the
north arofe.

Who pours from the eaftern hill, like a ftream
of darknefs? It is the hoft of Lathmon. He has
heard of the abfence of Fingal. He trufts in the
wind

wind of the north. His foul brightens with joy. Why doft thou come, Lathmon ? The mighty are not in Selma. Why comeft thou with thy forward fpear ? Will the daughters of Morven fight ? But ftop, O mighty ftream, in thy courfe! Does not Lathmon behold thefe fails ? Why doft thou vanifh, Lathmon, like the mift of the lake? But the fqually ftorm is behind thee; Fingal purfues thy fteps!

The king of Morven ftarted from fleep, as we rolled on the dark-blue wave. He ftretched his hand to his fpear, and his heroes rofe around. We knew that he had feen his fathers, for they often defcended to his dreams, when the fword of the foe rofe over the land; and the battle darkened before us. "Whither haft thou fled, O wind," faid the king of Morven ? "Doft thou rufile in the chambers of the fouth, and purfue the fhower in other lands? Why doft thou not come to my fails? to the blue face of my feas? The foe is in the land of Morven, and the king is abfent. But let each bind on his mail, and each affume his fhield. Stretch every fpear over the wave; let every fword be unfheathed. Lathmon[a] is before us with his hoft: he that fled[b] from Fingal on the plains of Lona. But he returns, like a collected ftream, and his roar is between our hills."

Such were the words of Fingal. We rushed into Carmona's bay. Ossian ascended the hill; and thrice struck his bossy shield. The rock of Morven replied; and the bounding roes came forth. The foes were troubled in my presence: and collected their darkened host; for I stood, like a cloud on the hill, rejoicing in the arms of my youth.

Morni [c] sat beneath a tree, at the roaring waters of Strumon: [d] his locks of age are gray: he leans forward on his staff; young Gaul is near the hero, hearing the battles of his youth. Often did he rise, in the fire of his soul, at the mighty deeds of Morni. The aged heard the sound of Ossian's shield: he knew the sign of battle. He started at once from his place. His gray hair parted on his back. He remembers the actions of other years."

"My son," he said to fair-haired Gaul, "I hear the sound of battle. The king of Morven is returned, the sign of war is heard. Go to the halls of Strumon, and bring his arms to Morni. Bring the arms which my father wore in his age, for my arm begins to fail. Take thou thy armour, O Gaul; and rush to the first of thy battles. Let thine arm reach to the renown of thy fathers. Be thy course in the field, like the eagle's wing. Why shouldst thou fear death, my son! the valiant fall with fame; their shields turn the dark stream of

danger

danger away, and renown dwells on their gray hairs. Doſt thou not ſee, O Gaul, how the ſteps of my age are honoured? Morni moves forth, and the young meet him, with reverence, and turn their eyes, with ſilent joy, on his courſe. But I never fled from danger, my ſon! my ſword lightened through the darkneſs of battle. The ſtranger melted before me; the mighty were blaſted in my preſence."

Gaul brought the arms to Morni: the aged warrior covered himſelf with ſteel. He took the ſpear in his hand, which was often ſtained with the blood of the valiant. He came towards Fingal, his ſon attended his ſteps. The ſon of Comhal rejoiced over the warrior, when he came in the locks of his age.

"King of the roaring Strumon!" ſaid the riſing joy of Fingal; "do I behold thee in arms, after thy ſtrength has failed? Often has Morni ſhone in battles, like the beam of the riſing ſun; when he diſperſes the ſtorms of the hill, and brings peace to the glittering fields. But why didſt thou not reſt in thine age? Thy renown is in the ſong. The people behold thee, and bleſs the departure of mighty Morni. Why didſt thou not reſt in thine age? For the foe will vaniſh before Fingal."

"Son

"Son of Comhal," replied the chief, "the strength of Morni's arm has failed. I attempt to draw the sword of my youth, but it remains in its place. I throw the spear, but it falls short of the mark; and I feel the weight of my shield. We decay like the grass of the mountain, and our strength returns no more. I have a son, O Fingal, his soul has delighted in the actions of Morni's youth; but his sword has not been lifted against the foe, neither has his fame begun. I come with him to battle; to direct his arm. His renown will be a sun to my soul, in the dark hour of my departure. O that the name of Morni were forgot among the people! that the heroes would only say, *Behold the father of Gaul.*"

"King of Strumon," Fingal replied, "Gaul shall lift the sword in battle. But he shall lift it before Fingal; my arm shall defend his youth. But rest thou in the halls of Selma; and hear of our renown. Bid the harp be strung; and the voice of the bard arise, that those who fall may rejoice in their fame; and the soul of Morni brighten with gladness. Ossian! thou hast fought in battles: the blood of strangers is on thy spear: let thy course be with Gaul in the strife; but depart not from the side of Fingal; lest the foe find you alone; and your fame fail at once."

I saw

I sawᵉ Gaul in his arms, and my foul was mixed with his: for the fire of the battle was in his eyes! he looked to the foe with joy. We spoke the words of friendship in secret; and the lightning of our swords poured together; for we drew them behind the wood, and tried the strength of our arms on the empty air. *

Night came down on Morven. Fingal sat at the beam of the oak. Morni sat by his side with all his gray waving locks. Their discourse is of other times, and the actions of their fathers. Three bards, at times, touched the harp; and Ullin was near with his song. He sung of the mighty Comhal; but darkness gathered ᶠ on Morni's brow. He rolled his red eye on Ullin; and the song of the bard ceased. Fingal observed the aged hero, and he mildly spoke.

"Chief of Strumon, why that darkness? Let the days of other years be forgot. Our father's contended in battle; but we meet together, at the feast. Our swords are turned on the foes, and they melt before us on the field. Let the days of our fathers be forgot, king of mossy Strumon."

"King of Morven," replied the chief, I remember thy father with joy. He was terrible in battle; the rage of the chief was deadly. My eyes were full of tears, when the king of heroes fell. The
                                                          valiant

valiant fall, O Fingal, and the feeble remain on the hills. How many heroes have passed away, in the days of Morni! And I did not shun the battle; neither did I fly from the strife of the valiant. Now let the friends of Fingal rest; for night is around; that they may rise, with strength, to battle against car-borne Lathmon. I hear the sound of his host, like thunder heard on a distant heath. Ossian! and fair-haired Gaul! ye are swift in the race. Observe the foes of Fingal from that woody hill. But approach them not, your fathers are not near to shield you. Let not your fame fall at once. The valour of youth may fail."

We heard the words of the chief with joy, and moved in the clang of our arms. Our steps are on the woody hill. Heaven burns with all its stars. The meteors of death fly over the field. The distant noise of the foe reached our ears. It was then Gaul spoke, in his valour; his hand half-unsheathed the sword.

"Son of Fingal," he said, "why burns the soul of Gaul? my heart beats high. My steps are disordered; and my hand trembles on my sword. When I look towards the foe, my soul lightens before me, and I see their sleeping host. Tremble thus the souls of the valiant in battles of the spear? How would the soul of Morni rise if we should rush on the foe! Our renown would grow in the fong; and our fteps be ftately in the eyes of the brave."

"Son of Morni," I replied, "my foul delights in battle. I delight to fhine in battle alone, and to give my name to the bards. But what if the foe fhould prevail; fhall I behold the eyes of the king? They are terrible in his difpleafure, and like the flames of death. But I will not behold them in his wrath. Offian fhall prevail or fall. But fhall the fame of the vanquifhed rife? They pafs away like a fhadow. But the fame of Offian fhall rife. His deeds fhall be like his fathers. Let us rufh in our arms; fon of Morni, let us rufh to battle. Gaul! if thou fhalt return, go to Selma's lofty wall. Tell to Everallin that I fell with fame; carry this fword to Branno's daughter. Let her give it to Ofcar, when the years of his youth fhall arife."

"Son of Fingal," Gaul replied with a figh; "fhall I return after Offian is low! What would my father fay, and Fingal king of men? The feeble would turn their eyes and fay, *Behold the mighty Gaul who left his friend in his blood!*" Ye fhall not behold me, ye feeble, but in the midft of my renown. Offian! I have heard from my father the mighty deeds of heroes; their mighty deeds when alone; for the foul increafes in danger."

"Son of Morni," I replied and strode before him on the heath, "our fathers shall praise our valour, when they mourn our fall. A beam of gladness shall rise on their souls, when their eyes are full of tears. They will say, *Our sons have not fallen like the grass of the field, for they spread death around them.* But why should we think of the narrow house? The sword defends the valiant. But death pursues the flight of the feeble; and their renown is not heard."

We rushed forward through night; and came to the roar of a stream which bent its blue course round the foe, through trees that echoed to its noise; we came to the bank of the stream, and saw the sleeping host. Their fires were decayed on the plain: and the lonely steps of their scouts were distant far. I stretched my spear before me to support my steps over the stream. But Gaul took my hand, and spoke the words of the valiant.

"Shall the son of Fingal rush on a sleeping foe? Shall he come like a blast by night when it overturns the young trees in secret? Fingal did not thus receive his fame, nor dwells renown on the gray hairs of Morni, for actions like these. Strike, Ossian, strike the shield of battle, and let their thousands rise. Let them meet Gaul in his first battle, that he may try the strength of his arm."

My

My soul rejoiced over the warrior, and my bursting tears descended. "And the foe shall meet Gaul," I said: " the same of Morni's son shall arise. But rush not too far, my hero: let the gleam of thy steel be near to Ossian. Let our hands join in slaughter. Gaul! dost thou not behold that rock? Its gray side dimly gleams to the stars. If the foe shall prevail, let our back be towards the rock. Then shall they fear to approach our spears; for death is in our hands."

I struck thrice my echoing shield. The starting foe arose. We rushed on in the sound of our arms. Their crowded steps fly over the heath; for they thought that the mighty Fingal came; and the strength of their arms withered away. The sound of their flight was like that of flame, when it rushes through the blasted groves. It was then the spear of Gaul flew in his strength: it was then his sword arose. Cremor fell; and mighty Leth. Dunthormo struggled in his blood. The steel rushed through Crotha's side, as bent, he rose on his spear; the black stream poured from the wound, and hissed on the half extinguished oak. Cathmin saw the steps of the hero behind him, and ascended a blasted tree; but the spear pierced him from behind. Shrieking, panting, he fell; moss and withered

withered branches purfue his fall, and ftrew the blue arms of Gaul.

Such were thy deeds, fon of Morni, in the firft day of thy battles. Nor flept the fword by thy fide, thou laft of Fingal's race! Offian rufhed forward in his ftrength, and the people fell before him; as the grafs by the ftaff of the boy, when he whiftles along the field, and the gray beard of the thiftle falls. But carelefs the youth moves on; his fteps are towards the defart.

Gray morning rofe before us, the winding ftreams are bright along the heath. The foe gathered on a hill; and the rage of Lathmon rofe. He bent the red eye of his wrath: he is filent in his rifing grief. He often ftruck his boffy fhield; and his fteps are unequal on the heath. I faw the diftant darknefs of the hero, and I fpoke to Morni's fon.

" Car-borne [c] chief of Strumon, doft thou behold the foe? They gather on the hill in their wrath. Let our fteps be towards the king [h]. He fhall rife in his ftrength, and the hoft of Lathmon vanifh. Our fame is around us, warrior, the eyes of the aged [i] will rejoice. But let us fly, fon of Morni, Lathmon defcends the hill." " Then let our fteps be flow," replied the fair-haired Gaul; " let the foe fay with a fmile, Behold the *warriors*

of

of night, they are, like ghosts, terrible in darkness, but they melt away before the beam of the east. Ossian, take the shield of Gormar who fell beneath thy spear, that the aged heroes may rejoice, when they shall behold the actions of their sons."

Such were our words on the plain, when Sulmath * came to car-borne Lathmon: Sulmath chief of Dutha at the dark-rolling stream of Duvranna¹. " Why dost thou not rush, son of Nuath, with a thousand of thy heroes? Why dost thou not descend with thy host, before the warriors fly? their blue arms are beaming to the rising light, and their steps are before us on the heath."

" Son of the feeble hand," said Lathmon, " shall my host descend! They are but two, son of Dutha, and shall a thousand lift their steel? Nuath would mourn, in his hall, for the departure of his fame. His eyes would turn from Lathmon, when the tread of his feet approached. Go thou to the heroes, chief of Dutha, for I behold the stately steps of Ossian. His fame is worthy of my steel; let him fight with Lathmon."

The noble Sulmath came. I rejoiced in the words of the king. I raised the shield on my arm; and Gaul placed in my hand the sword of Morni. We returned to the murmuring stream; Lathmon came in his strength. His dark host rolled, like

the

the clouds, behind him: but the son of Nuath was bright in his steel.

"Son of Fingal," said the hero, "thy fame has grown on our fall. How many lie there of my people by thy hand, thou king of men! Lift now thy spear against Lathmon; and lay the son of Nuath low. Lay him low among his people, or thou thyself must fall. It shall never be told in my halls that my warriors fell in my presence; that they fell in the presence of Lathmon when his sword rested by his side: the black eyes of Cutha [m] would roll in tears, and her steps be lonely in the vales of Dunlathmon.

"Neither shall it be told," I replied, "that the son of Fingal fled. Were his steps covered with darkness, yet would not Ossian fly; his soul would meet him and say, *Does the bard of Selma fear the foe?* No: he does not fear the foe. His joy is in the midst of battle."

Lathmon came on with his spear, and pierced the shield of Ossian. I felt the cold steel at my side; and drew the sword of Morni: I cut the spear in twain; the bright point fell glittering on the ground. The son of Nuath burnt in his wrath, and lifted high his sounding shield. His dark eyes rolled above it, as bending forward, it shone like a gate of brass. But Ossian's spear pierced the

brightness

brightness of its bosses, and sunk in a tree that rose behind. The shield hung on the quivering lance! but Lathmon still advanced. Gaul foresaw the fall of the chief, and stretched his buckler before my sword; when it descended, in a stream of light over the king of Dunlathmon.

Lathmon beheld the son of Morni, and the tear started from his eye. He threw the sword of his fathers on the ground, and spoke the words of the valiant. " Why should Lathmon fight against the first of mortal men? Your souls are beams from heaven; your swords the flames of death. Who can equal the renown of the heroes, whose actions are so great in youth? O that ye were in the halls of Nuath, in the green dwelling of Lathmon! then would my father say, that his son did not yield to the feeble. But who comes, a mighty stream, along the echoing heath? the little hills are troubled before him, and a thousand spirits are on the beams of his steel; the spirits of those who are to fall by the arm of the king of resounding Morven. Happy art thou, O Fingal, thy sons shall fight thy battles; they go forth before thee; and they return with the steps of renown."

Fingal came, in his mildness, rejoicing in secret over the actions of his son. Morni's face brightened with gladness, and his aged eyes looked faintly

through

through the tears of joy. We came to the halls of Selma, and sat round the feast of shells. The maids of the song came into our presence, and the mildly blushing Everallin. Her dark hair spread on her neck of snow, her eye rolled in secret on Ossian; she touched the harp of music, and we blessed the daughter of Branno.

Fingal rose in his place, and spoke to Dunlathmon's battling king. The sword of Trenmor trembled by his side, as he lifted up his mighty arm. "Son of Nuath," he said, "why dost thou search for fame in Morven? We are not of the race of the feeble; nor do our swords gleam over the weak. When did we come to Dunlathmon, with the sound of war? Fingal does not delight in battle, though his arm is strong. My renown grows on the fall of the haughty. The lightning of my steel pours on the proud in arms. The battle comes; and the tombs of the valiant rise; the tombs of my people rise, O my fathers! and I at last must remain alone. But I will remain renowned, and the departure of my soul shall be one stream of light. Lathmon! retire to thy place. Turn thy battles to other lands. The race of Morven are renowned, and their foes are the sons of the unhappy."

NOTES

NOTES ON LATHMON.

ᵃ It is said, by tradition, that it was the intelligence of Lathmon's invasion, that occasioned Fingal's return from Ireland; though Ossian more poetically, ascribes the cause of Fingal's knowledge to his dream.

ᵇ He alludes to a battle wherein Fingal had defeated Lathmon. The occasion of this first war, between those heroes, is told by Ossian in another poem, which the translator has seen.

ᶜ Morni was chief of a numerous tribe, in the days of Fingal, and his father Comhal. The last mentioned hero was killed in battle against Morni's tribe; but the valour and conduct of Fingal reduced them, at last, to obedience. We find the two heroes perfectly reconciled in this poem.

ᵈ Stru'mone, *stream of the hill.* Here the proper name of a rivulet in the neighbourhood of Selma.

ᵉ Ossian speaks. The contrast between the old and young heroes is strongly marked. The circumstance of the latter's drawing their swords is well imagined, and agrees with the impatience of young soldiers, just entered upon action.

ᶠ Ullin had chosen ill the subject of his song. *The darkness which gathered on Morni's brow,* did not proceed from any dislike he had to Comhal's name, though they were foes, but from his fear that the song would awaken Fingal to remembrance of the feuds which had subsisted of old between the families. Fingal's speech on this occasion abounds with generosity and good sense.

g Car-borne is a title of honour beftowed, by Offian, indifcriminately on every hero; as every chief, in his time, kept a chariot or litter by way of ftate.

h Fingal.

i Fingal and Morni.

k Suil-mhath, *a man of good eye-fight.*

l Dubh-bhranna, *dark mountain-ftream.* What river went by this name, in the days of Offian, is not eafily afcertained, at this diftance of time. A river in Scotland, which falls into the fea at Banff, ftill retains the name of Duvran. If that is meant, by Offian, in this paffage, Lathmon muft have been a prince of the Pictifh nation, or thofe Caledonians who inhabited of old the eaftern coaft of Scotland.

m Cutha appears to have been Lathmon's wife or miftrefs.

n It was thought, in Offian's time, that each perfon had his attending fpirit. The traditions concerning this opinion are dark and unfatisfactory.

OITHONA;

OITHONA:

A POEM.

THE ARGUMENT.

Gaul, the son of Morni, attended Lathmon into his own country, after his being defeated in Morven, as related in the preceding poem. He was kindly entertained by Nuath the father of Lathmon, and fell in love with his daughter Oithona. The lady was no less enamoured of Gaul, and a day was fixed for their marriage. In the mean time Fingal, preparing for an expedition into the country of the Britons, sent for Gaul. He obeyed, and went; but not without promising to Oithona to return, if he survived the war, by a certain day. Lathmon too was obliged to attend his father Nuath in his wars, and Oithona was left alone at Dunlathmon, the seat of the family. Dunrommath, lord of Uthal, supposed to be one of the Orkneys, taking advantage of the absence of her friends, came and carried off, by force, Oithona, who had formerly rejected his love, into Tromathon, a desart island, where he concealed her in a cave.

Gaul on the day appointed; heard of the rape, and sailed to Tromathon, to revenge himself on Dunrommath. When he landed, he found Oithona disconsolate, and resolved not to survive the loss of her honour. She told him the story of her misfortunes, and she scarce ended, when Dunrommath with his followers appeared at the further end of the island. Gaul prepared to attack him,

recommending

recommending to Oithona to retire, till the battle was over. She seemingly obeyed; but she secretly armed herself, rushed into the thickest of the battle, and was mortally wounded. Gaul pursuing the flying enemy, found her just expiring on the field; he mourned over her, raised her tomb, and returned to Morven. Thus is the story handed down by tradition; nor is it given with any material difference in the poem, which opens with Gaul's return to Dunlathmon, after the rape of Oithona.

DARKNESS dwells around Dunlathmon, though the moon shews half her face on the hill. The daughter of night turns her eyes away; for she beholds the grief that is coming. The son of Morni is on the plain; but there is no sound in the hall. No long-streaming beam of light comes trembling through the gloom. The voice of Oithona is not heard amidst the noise of the streams of Duvranna " Whither art thou gone in thy beauty, dark-haired daughter of Nuath? Lathmon is in the field of the valiant, but thou didst promise to remain in the hall; thou didst promise to remain in the hall till the son of Morni returned. Till he returned from Strumon, to the maid of his love. The tear was on thy cheek at his departure; the sigh rose in secret in thy breast. But thou dost not come to meet him, with songs, with the lightly-trembling sound of the harp."

Such

OITHONA.

OITHONA.

The Son of Morni stood in their path by the Rock: the Warriors of Duuronimo bled.

Such were the words of Gaul, when he came to Dunlathmon's towers. The gates were open and dark. The winds were blustering in the hall. The trees strowed the threshold with leaves; and the murmur of night was abroad. Sad and silent, at a rock, the son of Morni sat: his soul trembled for the maid; but he knew not whither to turn his course. The son [b] of Leth stood at a distance, and heard the winds in his bushy hair. But he did not raise his voice, for he saw the sorrow of Gaul.

Sleep descended on the heroes. The visions of night arose. Oithona stood in a dream, before the eyes of Morni's son. Her dark hair was loose and disordered: her lovely eye rolled in tears. Blood stained her snowy arm. The robe half hid the wound of her breast. She stood over the chief, and her voice was heard.

"Sleeps the son of Morni, he that was lovely in the eyes of Oithona? Sleeps Gaul at the distant rock, and the daughter of Nuath low? The sea rolls round the dark isle of Tromathon; I sit in my tears in the cave. Nor do I sit alone, O Gaul, the dark chief of Cuthal is there. He is there in the rage of his love. And what can Oithona do?"

A rougher blast rushed through the oak. The dream of night departed. Gaul took his aspen spear;

spear; he stood in the rage of wrath. Often did his eyes turn to the east, and accuse the lagging light. At length the morning came forth. The hero lifted up the sail. The winds came rustling from the hill; and he bounded on the waves of the deep. On the third day arose Tromathon ᶜ, like a blue shield in the midst of the sea. The white wave roared against its rocks; sad Oithona sat on the coast. She looked on the rolling waters, and her tears descend. But when she saw Gaul in his arms, she started and turned her eyes away. Her lovely cheek is bent and red; her white arm trembles by her side. Thrice she strove to fly from his presence; but her steps failed her as she went.

"Daughter of Nuath," said the hero, "why dost thou fly from Gaul? Do my eyes send forth the flame of death? Or darkens hatred in my soul? Thou art to me the beam of the east rising in a land unknown. But thou coverest thy face with sadness, daughter of high Dunlathmon? Is the foe of Oithona near? My soul burns to meet him in battle. The sword trembles on the side of Gaul, and longs to glitter in his hand. Speak, daughter of Nuath, dost thou not behold my tears?"

"Car-borne chief of Strumon," replied the sighing maid, "why comest thou over the dark-blue wave

wave to Nuath's mournful daughter? Why did I not pass away in secret, like the flower of the rock, that lifts its fair head unseen, and strows its withered leaves on the blast? Why didst thou come, O Gaul, to hear my departing sigh? I pass away in my youth; and my name shall not be heard. Or it will be heard with sorrow, and the tears of Nuath will fall. Thou wilt be sad, son of Morni, for the fallen fame of Oithona. But she shall sleep in the narrow tomb, far from the voice of the mourner. Why didst thou come, chief of Strumon, to the sea-beat rocks of Tromathon?"

"I came to meet thy foes, daughter of car-borne Nuath! the death of Cuthal's chief darkens before me; or Morni's son shall fall. Oithona! when Gaul is low, raise my tomb on that oozy rock; and when the dark-bounding ship shall pass, call the sons of the sea; call them, and give this sword that they may carry it to Morni's hall; that the gray-haired hero may cease to look towards the desart for the return of his son."

" And shall the daughter of Nuath live," she replied with a bursting sigh? " Shall I live in Tromathon, and the son of Morni low? My heart is not of that rock; nor my soul careless as that sea, which lifts its blue waves to every wind, and rolls beneath the storm. The blast which shall lay thee low,

low, fhall fpread the branches of Oithona on earth. We fhall wither together, fon of car-borne Morni! The narrow houfe is pleafant to me, and the gray ftone of the dead: for never more will I leave thy rocks, fea-furrounded Tromathon! Night ^d came on with her clouds, after the departure of Lathmon, when he went to the wars of his fathers, to the mofs-covered rock of Duthormoth; night came on, and I fat in the hall, at the beam of the oak. The wind was abroad in the trees. I heard the found of arms. Joy rofe in my face; for. I thought of thy return. It was the chief of Cuthal, the red-haired ftrength of Dunrommath. His eyes rolled in fire: the blood of my people was on his fword. They who defended Oithona fell by the gloomy chief. What could I do? My arm was weak; it could not lift the fpear. He took me in my grief, amidft my tears he raifed the fail. He feared the returning ftrength of Lathmon, the brother of unhappy Oithona. But behold, he comes with his people! the dark wave is divided before him! Whither wilt thou turn thy fteps, fon of Morni? Many are the warriors of Dunrommath!"

"My fteps never turned from battle," replied the hero as he unfheathed his fword; "and fhall I begin to fear, Oithona, when thy foes are near? Go to thy cave, daughter of Nuath, till our battle ceafe.

ceafe. Son of Leth, bring the bow of our fathers; and the founding quiver of Morni. Let our three warriors bend the yew. Ourſelves will lift the ſpear. They are an hoſt on the rock; but our ſouls are ſtrong."

The daughter of Nuath went to the cave: a troubled joy roſe on her mind, like the red path of the lightening on a ſtormy cloud. Her ſoul was reſolved, and the tear was dried from her wildly-looking eye. Dunrommath ſlowly approached; for he ſaw the ſon of Morni. Contempt contract-ed his face, a ſmile is on his dark-brown cheek; his red eye rolled, half-concealed, beneath his ſhaggy brows.

" Whence are the ſons of the ſea," begun the gloomy chief? " Have the winds driven you to the rocks of Tromathon? Or come you in ſearch of the white-handed daughter of Nuath? The ſons of the unhappy, ye feeble men, come to the hand of Dunromunath. His eyes ſpares not the weak, and he delights in the blood of ſtrangers. Oithona is a beam of light, and the chief of Cuthal enjoys it in ſecret; would thou come on its lovelineſs like a cloud, ſon of the feeble hand! Thou mayeſt come, but ſhalt thou return to the halls of thy fathers?"

" Doſt thou not know me," ſaid Gaul, " red-haired chief of Cuthal? Thy feet were ſwift on the heath,

heath, in the battle of car-borne Lathmon; when the sword of Morni's son pursued his host, in Morven's woody land. Dunrommath! thy words are mighty, for thy warriors gather behind thee. But do I fear them, son of pride? I am not of the race of the feeble."

Gaul advanced in his arms; Dunrommath shrunk behind his people. But the spear of Gaul pierced the gloomy chief, and his sword lopped off his head, as it bended in death. The son of Morni shook it thrice by the lock; the warriors of Dunrommath fled. The arrows of Morven pursued them: ten fell on the mossy rocks. The rest lift the sounding sail, and bound on the echoing deep. Gaul advanced towards the cave of Oithona. He beheld a youth leaning against a rock. An arrow had pierced his side: and his eye rolled faintly beneath his helmet. The soul of Morni's son is sad, he came and spoke the words of peace.

"Can the hand of Gaul heal thee, youth of the mournful brow? I have searched for the herbs of the mountains; I have gathered them on the secret banks of their streams. My hand has closed the wound of the valiant, and their eyes have blessed the son of Morni. Where dwelt thy fathers, warrior? Were they of the sons of the mighty?

Sadness

Sadness shall come, like night, on thy native streams; for thou art fallen in thy youth."

"My fathers," replied the stranger, "were of the race of the mighty; but they shall not be sad; for my fame is departed like morning mist. High walls rise on the banks of Duvranna; and see their mossy towers in the stream; a rock ascends behind them with its bending firs. Thou mayest behold it far distant. There my brother dwells. He is renowned in battle: give him this glittering helmet."

The helmet fell from the hand of Gaul; for it was the wounded Oithona. She had armed herself in the cave, and came in search of death. Her heavy eyes are half-closed; the blood pours from her side. "Son of Morni," she said, "prepare the narrow tomb. Sleep comes, like a cloud, on my soul. The eyes of Oithona are dim. O had I dwelt at Duvranna, in the bright beam of my fame! then had my years come on with joy; and the virgins would bless my steps. But I fall in youth, son of Morni, and my father shall blush in his hall."

She fell pale on the rock of Tromathon. The mournful hero raised her tomb. He came to Morven; but we saw the darkness of his soul. Ossian took the harp in the praise of Oithona. The brightness brightnefs of the face of Gaul returned. But his figh rofe, at times, in the midft of his friends, like blafts that fhake their unfrequent wings, after the ftormy winds are laid.

NOTES ON
OITHONA.

[a] Oi-thona, *the virgin of the wave*.

[b] Morlo, the fon of Leth, is one of Fingal's moft famous heroes. He and three other men attended Gaul on his expedition to Tromathon.

[c] Trom-thon, *heavy or deep founding wave*.

[d] Oithona relates how fhe was carried away by Dunrommath.

CROMA;

A POEM.

THE ARGUMENT.

Malvina the daughter of Toscar is overheard by Ossian lamenting the death of Oscar her lover. Ossian, to divert her grief, relates his own actions in an expedition which he undertook, at Fingal's command, to aid Crothar the petty king of Croma, a country in Ireland; against Rothmar who invaded his dominions. The story is delivered down thus, in tradition. Crothar king of Croma being blind with age, and his son too young for the field, Rothmar the chief of Tromlo resolved to avail himself of the opportunity offered of annexing the dominions of Crothar to his own. He accordingly marched into the country subject to Crothar, but which he held of Arth or Artho, who was at the time, supreme king of Ireland.

Crothar being, on account of his age and blindness, unfit for action, sent for aid to Fingal king of Scotland; who ordered his son Ossian to the relief of Crothar. But before his arrival, Fovar-gormo, the son of Crothar, attacking Rothmar, was slain himself, and his forces totally defeated. Ossian renewed the war; came to battle, killed Rothmar, and routed his army. Croma being thus delivered of its enemies, Ossian returned to Scotland.

" IT was the voice of my love! few are his visits to the dreams of Malvina! Open your airy halls, ye fathers of mighty Toscar. Unfold the gates

gates of your clouds; the steps of Malvina's departure are near. I have heard a voice in my dream. I feel the fluttering of my soul. Why didst thou come, O blast, from the dark-rolling of the lake? Thy rustling wing was in the trees, the dream of Malvina departed. But she beheld her love, when his robe of mist flew on the wind; the beam of the sun was on his skirts, they glittered like the gold of the stranger. It was the voice of my love! few are his visits to my dreams!

"But thou dwellest in the soul of Malvina, son of mighty Ossian. My sighs arise with the beam of the east; my tears descend with the drops of night. I was a lovely tree, in thy presence, Oscar, with all my branches round me; but thy death came like a blast from the desart, and laid my green head low; the spring returned with its flowers, but no leaf of mine arose. The virgins saw me silent in the hall, and they touched the harp of joy. The tear was on the cheek of Malvina: the virgins beheld me in my grief. Why art thou sad, they said; thou first of the maids of Lutha? Was he lovely as the beam of the morning, and stately in thy sight?"

Pleasant is thy song in Ossian's ear, daughter of streamy Lutha! Thou hast heard the music of departed bards in the dream of thy rest, when sleep
fell

fell on thine eyes, at the murmur of Moruth. [a] When thou didst return from the chase, in the day of the sun, thou hast heard the music of the bards, and thy song is lovely. It is lovely, O Malvina, but it melts the soul. There is a joy in grief when peace dwells in the breast of the sad. But sorrow wastes the mournful, O daughter of Toscar, and their days are few. They fall away, like the flower on which the sun looks in his strength after the mildew has passed over it, and its head is heavy with the drops of night. Attend to the tale of Ossian, O maid; he remembers the days of his youth.

The king commanded; I raised my sails, and rushed into the bay of Croma: into Croma's sounding bay in lovely Innis-fail. [b] High on the coast arose the towers of Crothar king of spears; Crothar renowned in the battles of his youth; but age dwelt then around the chief. Rothmar raised the sword against the hero; and the wrath of Fingal burned. He sent Ossian to meet Rothmar in battle, for the chief of Croma was the companion of his youth. I sent the bard before me with songs; I came into the hall of Crothar. There sat the hero amidst the arms of his fathers, but his eyes had failed. His gray locks waved around a staff, on which the warrior leaned. He hummed the

song

song of other times, when the sound of our arms reached his ears. Crothar rose, stretched his aged hand, and blessed the son of Fingal.

"Ossian," said the hero, "the strength of Crothar's arm has failed. O could I lift the sword, as on the day that Fingal fought at Strutha! He was the first of mortal men; but Crothar had also his fame. The king of Morven praised me, and he placed on my arm the bossy shield of Calthar, whom the hero had slain in war. Dost thou not behold it on the wall, for Crothar's eyes have failed? Is thy strength, like thy father's, Ossian? let the aged feel thine arm."

I gave my arm to the king; he feels it with his aged hands. The sigh rose in his breast, and his tears descended. "Thou art strong, my son," he said, " but not like the king of Morven. But who is like that hero among the mighty in war? Let the feast of my halls be spread; and let my bards raise the song. Great is he that is within my walls, sons of echoing Croma!" The feast is spread. The harp is heard; and joy is in the hall. But it was joy covering a sigh, that darkly dwelt in every breast. It was like the faint beam of the moon spread on a cloud in heaven. At length the music ceased, and the aged king of Croma
spoke;

spoke; he spoke without a tear, but the sigh swelled in the midst of his voice.

"Son of Fingal! dost thou not behold the darkness of Crothar's hall of shells? My soul was not dark at the feast, when my people lived. I rejoiced in the presence of strangers, when my son shone in the hall. But, Ossian, he is a beam that is departed, and left no streak of light behind. He is fallen, son of Fingal, in the battles of his father. Rothmar the chief of grassy Tromlo heard that my eyes had failed; he heard that my arms were fixed in the hall, and the pride of his soul arose. He came towards Croma; my people fell before him. I took my arms in the hall, but what could sightless Crothar do? My steps were unequal; my grief was great. I wished for the days that were past. Days! wherein I fought; and conquered in the field of blood. My son returned from the chase; the fair-haired Fovar-gormo[c]. He had not lifted his sword in battle, for his arm was young. But the soul of the youth was great; the fire of valour burnt in his eyes. He saw the disordered steps of his father, and his sigh arose. "King of Croma," he said, "is it because thou hast no son; is it for the weakness of Fovar-gormo's arm that thy sighs arise? I begin, my father, to feel the strength of my arm; I have drawn the sword of my youth; and I have bent the bow. Let me meet this Rothmar, with the youths of Croma; let me meet him, O my father; for I feel my burning soul."

"And thou shalt meet him," I said, "son of sightless Crothar! But let others advance before thee, that I may hear the tread of thy feet at thy return; for my eyes behold thee not, fair-haired Fovar-gormo! He wept, he met the foe; he fell. The foe advances towards Croma. He who slew my son is near, with all his pointed spears."

It is not time to fill the shell, I replied, and took my spear. My people saw the fire of my eyes, and they rose around. All night we strode along the heath. Gray morning rose in the east. A green narrow vale appeared before us; nor did it want its blue stream. The dark host of Rathmor are on its banks, with all their glittering arms. We fought along the vale; they fled; Rothmar sunk beneath my sword. Day had not descended in the west when I brought his arms to Crothar. The aged hero felt them with his hands; and joy brightened in his soul.

The people gather to the hall; the sound of the shells is heard. Ten harps are strung; five bards advance, and sing, by turns [d], the praise of Ossian; they poured forth their burning souls, and the

harp

harp anfwered to their voice. The joy of Croma was great; for peace returned to the land. The night came on with filence, and the morning returned with joy. No foe came in darknefs, with his glittering fpear. The joy of Croma was great; for the gloomy Rothmar was fallen.

I raifed my voice for Fovar-gormo, when they laid the chief in earth. The aged Crothar was there, but his figh was not heard. He fearched, for the wound of his fon, and found it in his breaft. Joy rofe in the face of the aged. He came and fpoke to Offian.

"King of fpears!" he faid, "my fon has not fallen without his fame. The young warrior did not fly; but met death as he went forward in his ftrength. Happy are they who die in youth, when their renown is heard! The feeble will not behold them in the hall; or fmile at their trembling hands. Their memory fhall be honoured in the fong; the young tear of the virgin falls. But the aged wither away, by degrees, and the fame of their youth begins to be forgot. They fall in fecret; the figh of their fon is not heard. Joy is around their tomb; and the ftone of their fame is placed without a tear. Happy are they who die in youth, when their renown is around them!"

NOTES ON CROMA:

^a Mor'-ruth, *great stream*.

^b *Innis-fail*, one of the ancient names of Ireland.

^c Faobhar-gorm, *the blue point of steel*.

^d Those extempore compositions were in great repute among succeeding bards. The pieces extant of that kind shew more of the good ear, than of the poetical genius of their authors. The translator has only met with one poem of this sort, which he thinks worthy of being preserved. It is a thousand years later than Ossian, but the authors seem to have observed his manner, and adopted some of his expressions. The story of it is this. Five bards, passing the night in the house of a chief, who was a poet himself, went severally to make their observations on, and returned with an extempore description of, night. The night happened to be one in October, as appears from the poem; and in the north of Scotland, it has all that variety which the bards ascribe to it, in their descriptions.

FIRST BARD.

NIGHT is dull and dark. The clouds rest on the hills. No star with green trembling beam; no moon looks from the sky. I hear the blast in the wood; but I hear it distant far. The stream of the valley murmurs; but its murmur is sullen and sad. From the tree at the grave of the dead the long-howling owl is heard. I see a dim form on the plain! It is a ghost! it fades—it flies. Some funeral shall pass this way: the meteor marks the path.

The diſtant dog is howling from the hut of the hill. The ſtag lies on the mountain moſs: the hind is at his ſide. She hears the wind in his branchy horns. She ſtarts, but lies again.

The roe is in the cleft of the rock; the heath-cock's head is beneath his wing. No beaſt, no bird is abroad, but the owl and the howling fox. She on a leafleſs tree: he in a cloud on the hill.

Dark, panting, trembling, ſad, the traveller has loſt his way. Through ſhrubs, through thorns, he goes, along the gurgling rill. He fears the rock and the fen. He fears the ghoſt of night. The old tree groans to the blaſt; the falling branch reſounds. The wind drives the withered burs, clung together, along the graſs. It is the light tread of a ghoſt! He trembles amidſt the night.

Dark, duſky, howling is night, cloudy, windy, and full of ghoſts! The dead are abroad! my friends, receive me from the night.

SECOND BARD.

THE wind is up. The ſhower deſcends. The ſpirit of the mountain ſhrieks. Woods fall from high. Windows flap. The growing river roars. The traveller attempts the ford. Hark that ſhriek! he dies:—The ſtorm drives the horſe from the hill, the goat, the lowing cow. They tremble as drives the ſhower, beſide the mouldering bank.

The hunter ſtarts from ſleep, in his lonely hut; he wakes the fire decayed. His wet dogs ſmoke around him. He fills the chinks with heath. Loud roar two mountain ſtreams which meet beſide his booth.

Sad on the ſide of a hill the wandering ſhepherd ſits. The tree reſounds above him. The ſtream roars down the rock.

rock. He waits for the rifing moon to guide him to his home.

Ghosts ride on the storm to-night. Sweet is their voice between the squalls of wind. Their songs are of other worlds.

The rain is paſt. The dry wind blows. Streams roar, and windows flap. Cold drops fall from the roof. I fee the starry sky. But the shower gathers again. The west is gloomy and dark. Night is stormy and dismal; receive me, my friends, from night.

THIRD BARD.

The wind still sounds between the hills; and whistles through the grass of the rock. The firs fall from their place. The turfy hut is torn. The clouds, divided, fly over the sky, and shew the burning stars. The meteor, token of death! flies sparkling through the gloom. It rests on the hill. I see the withered fern, the dark-browed rock, the fallen oak. Who is that in his shroud beneath the tree, by the stream?

The waves dark-tumble on the lake, and lash its rocky sides. The boat is brimful in the cove; the oars on the rocking tide. A maid sits sad beside the rock, and eyes the rolling stream. Her lover promised to come. She saw his boat, when yet it was light, on the lake. Is this his broken boat on the shore? Are thefe his groans on the wind?

Hark! the hail rattles around. The flaky snow descends. The tops of the hills are white. The stormy winds abate. Various is the night and cold; receive me, my Friends, from night.

FOURTH

FOURTH BARD.

Night is calm and fair; blue, starry, settled is night. The winds, with the clouds, are gone. They sink behind the hill. The moon is up on the mountain. Trees glitter: streams shine on the rock. Bright rolls the settled lake; bright the stream of the vale.

I see trees overturned; the shocks of corn on the plain: The wakeful hind rebuilds the shocks, and whistles on the distant field.

Calm, settled, fair is night! Who comes from the place of the dead? That form with the robe of snow; white arms and dark-brown hair! It is the daughter of the chief of the people; she that lately fell! Come let us view thee, O maid! thou that hast been the delight of heroes! The blast drives the phantom away, white, without form, it ascends the hill. The breezes drive the blue mist, slowly over the narrow vale. It rises on the hill, and joins its head to heaven. Night is settled, calm, blue, starry, bright with the moon. Receive me not, my friends, for lovely is the night.

FIFTH BARD.

Night is calm, but dreary. The moon is in a cloud in the west. Slow moves that pale beam along the shaded hill. The distant wave is heard. The torrent murmurs on the rock. The cock is heard from the booth. More than half the night is past. The house-wife, groping in the gloom, rekindles the settled fire. The hunter thinks that day approaches, and calls his bounding dogs. He ascends the hill and whistles on his way. A blast removes the cloud. He sees the starry plough of the north. Much of the night is to pass. He nods by the mossy rock.

Hark!

Hark! the whirlwind is in the wood! A low murmur in the vale! It is the mighty army of the dead returning from the air.

The moon rests behind the hill. The beam is still on that lofty rock. Long are the shadows of the trees. Now it is dark over all. Night is dreary, silent, and dark; receive me, my friends, from night.

THE CHIEF.

Let clouds rest on the hills: spirits fly and travellers fear. Let the winds of the woods arise, the sounding storms descend. Roar streams and windows flap, and green winged meteors fly; rise the pale moon from behind her hills, or inclose her head in clouds; night is alike to me, blue, stormy, or gloomy the sky. Night flies before the beam, when it is poured on the hill. The young day returns from his clouds, but we return no more.

Where are our chiefs of old? Where our kings of mighty name? The fields of their battles are silent. Scarce their mossy tombs remain. We shall also be forgot. This lofty house shall fall. Our sons shall not behold the ruins in grass. They shall ask of the aged, "Where stood the walls of our fathers?"

Raise the song, and strike the harp; send round the shells of joy. Suspend a hundred tapers on high. Youths and maids begin the dance. Let some gray bard be near me to tell the deeds of other times; of kings renowned in our land, of chiefs we behold no more. Thus let the night pass until morning shall appear in our halls. Then let the bow be at hand, the dogs, the youths of the chase. We shall ascend the hill with day; and awake the deer.

BERRATHON.

BERRATHON:
A POEM.

THE ARGUMENT.

Fingal, in his voyage to Lochlin, whither he had been invited by Starno, the father of Agandecca, touched at Berrathon, an island of Scandinavia, where he was kindly entertained by Larthmor the petty king of the place, who was a vassal of the supreme kings of Lochlin. The hospitality of Larthmor gained him Fingal's friendship, which that hero manifested, after the imprisonment of Larthmor by his own son; by sending Ossian and Toscar, the father of Malvina, so often mentioned, to rescue Larthmor, and to punish the unnatural behaviour of Uthal. Uthal was handsome and much admired by the ladies. Nina-thoma the beautiful daughter of Torthoma, a neighbouring prince, fell in love and fled with him. He proved unconstant; for another lady, whose name is not mentioned, gaining his affections, he confined Nina-thoma to a desart island near the coast of Berrathon. She was relieved by Ossian, who, in company with Toscar, landing on Berrathon, defeated the forces of Uthal, and killed him in a single combat. Nina-thoma, whose love not all the bad behaviour of Uthal could erase, hearing of his death, died of grief. In the mean time Larthmor is restored, and Ossian and Toscar returned in triumph to Fingal. The present poem opens with an elegy on the death of Malvina, the daughter of Toscar, and closes with the presages of the poet's death.

BEND thy blue course, O stream, round the narrow plain of Lutha [a]. Let the green woods

woods hang over it from their mountains: and the sun look on it at noon. The thistle is there on its rock, and shakes its beard to the wind. The flower hangs its heavy head, waving, at times, to the gale. "Why dost thou awake me, O gale," it seems to say, "I am covered with the drops of heaven? The time of my fading is near, and the blast that shall scatter my leaves. To-morrow shall the traveller come, he that saw me in my beauty shall come; his eyes will search the field, but they will not find me! So shall they search in vain, for the voice of Cona, after it has failed in the field. The hunter shall come forth in the morning, and the voice of my harp shall not be heard. "Where is the son of car-borne Fingal?" The tear will be on his cheek. Then come thou, O Malvina [b], with all thy music, come; lay Ossian in the plain of Lutha: let his tomb rise in the lovely field.

Malvina! where art thou with thy songs: with the soft sound of thy steps? Son [c] of Alpin art thou near? where is the daughter of Toscar? "I passed, O son of Fingal, by Tarlutha's mossy walls. The smoke of the hall was ceased: silence was among the trees of the hill. The voice of the chase was over. I saw the daughters of the bow. I asked about Malvina, but they answered not. They turned their faces away: thin darkness covered their

their beauty. They were like stars, on a rainy hill, by night, each looking faintly through her mist."

Pleasant [d] be thy rest, O lovely beam! soon hast thou set on our hills! The steps of thy departure were stately, like the moon on the blue, trembling wave. But thou hast left us in darkness, first of the maids of Lutha! We sit, at the rock, and there is no voice; no light but the meteor of fire! Soon hast thou set, Malvina, daughter of generous Toscar! But thou risest like the beam of the east, among the spirits of thy friends, where they sit in their stormy halls, the chambers of the thunder. A cloud hovers over Cona: its blue curling sides are high. The winds are beneath it, with their wings; within it is the dwelling [e] of Fingal. There the hero sits in darkness; his airy spear is in his hand. His shield half covered with clouds, is like the darkened moon; when one half still remains in the wave, and the other looks sickly on the field.

His friends sit around the king, on mist; and hear the songs of Ullin: he strikes the half viewless harp; and raises the feeble voice. The lesser heroes, with a thousand meteors, light the airy hall. Malvina rises, in the midst; a blush is on her cheek. She beholds the unknown faces of her fathers, and turns aside her humid eyes. "Art thou come so soon," said Fingal, "daughter of generous Toscar?

Sadness dwells in the halls of Lutha. My aged son [f] is sad. I hear the breeze of Cona, that was wont to lift thy heavy locks. It comes to the hall, but thou art not there; its voice is mournful among the arms of thy fathers. Go with thy rustling wing, O breeze! and sigh on Malvina's tomb. It rises yonder beneath the rock, at the blue stream of Lutha. The maids [g] are departed to their place; and thou alone, O breeze, mournest there."

But who comes from the dusky west, supported on a cloud? A smile is on his gray, watery face; locks of mist fly on the wind: he bends forward on his airy spear: it is thy father, Malvina! "Why shinest thou, so soon, on our clouds," he says, "O lovely light of Lutha? But thou wert sad, my daughter, for thy friends were passed away. The sons of little men [h] were in the hall; and none remained of the heroes, but Ossian king of spears."

And dost thou remember Ossian, car-borne Toscar [i] son of Conloch? The battles of our youth were many; our swords went together to the field. They saw us coming like two falling rocks; and the sons of the stranger fled. "There come the warriors of Cona," they said; "their steps are in the paths of the vanquished." Draw near, son of Alpin, to the song of the aged. The actions of other times are in my soul: my memory beams on the

the days that are past. On the days of the mighty Toscar, when our path was in the deep. Draw near, son of Alpin, to the last sound of the voice of Cona.

The king of Morven commanded, and I raised my sails to the wind. Toscar chief of Lutha stood at my side, as I rose on the dark-blue wave. Our course was to sea-surrounded Berrathon,* the isle of many storms. There dwelt, with his locks of age, the stately strength of Larthmor. Larthmor who spread the feast of shells to Comhal's mighty son, when he went to Starno's halls, in the days of Agandecca. But when the chief was old, the pride of his son arose, the pride of fair-haired Uthal, the love of a thousand maids. He bound the aged Larthmor, and dwelt in his sounding halls.

Long pined the king in his cave, beside his rolling-sea. Morning did not come to his dwelling; nor the burning oak by night. But the wind of ocean was there, and the parting beam of the moon. The red star looked on the king, when it trembled on the western wave. Snitho came to Selma's hall: Snitho companion of Larthmor's youth. He told of the king of Berrathon: the wrath of Fingal rose. Thrice he assumed the spear, resolved to stretch his hand to Uthal. But the memory [1] of his actions rose before the king, and

he

he sent his son and Toscar. Our joy was great on the rolling sea; and we often half unsheathed our swords. For never before had we fought alone, in the battles of the spear.

Night came down on the ocean; the winds departed on their wings. Cold and pale is the moon. The red stars lift their heads. Our course is slow along the coast of Berrathon; the white waves tumble on the rocks. "What voice is that," said Toscar, "which comes between the sounds of the waves? It is soft but mournful, like the voice of departed bards. But I behold the maid, she sits on the rock alone. Her head bends on her arm of snow: her dark hair is in the wind. Hear, son of Fingal, her song, it is smooth as the gliding waters of Lavath." We came to the silent bay, and heard the maid of night.

"How long will ye roll around me, blue-tumbling waters of ocean? My dwelling was not always in caves, nor beneath the whistling tree. The feast was spread in Torthoma's hall; my father delighted in my voice. The youths beheld me in the steps of my loveliness, and they blessed the dark-haired Nina-thoma. It was then thou didst come, O Uthal! like the sun of heaven. The souls of the virgins are thine, son of generous Larthmor! But why dost thou leave me alone in the midst of roaring

roaring waters? Was my foul dark with thy death? Did my white hand lift the fword? Why then haft thou left me alone, king of high Finthormo?"*

The tear ftarted from my eye when I heard the voice of the maid. I ftood before her in my arms, and fpoke the words of peace. "Lovely dweller of the cave, what figh is in that breaft? Shall Offian lift his fword in thy prefence, the deftruction of thy foes? Daughter of Torthoma, rife, I have heard the words of thy grief. The race of Morven are around thee, who never injured the weak. Come to our dark-bofomed fhip, thou brighter than that fetting moon. Our courfe is to the rocky Berrathon, to the echoing walls of Finthormo." She came in her beauty, fhe came with all her lovely fteps. Silent joy brightened in her face, as when the fhadows fly from the field of fpring; the blue ftream is rolling in brightnefs, and the green bufh bends over its courfe.

The morning rofe with its beams. We came to Rothma's bay. A boar rufhed from the wood; my fpear pierced his fide. I rejoiced over the blood,° and forefaw my growing fame. But now the found of Uthal's train came from the high Finthormo; they fpread over the heath to the chafe of the boar. Himfelf comes flowly on, in the pride of his ftrength. He lifts his two pointed
fpears.

spears. On his side is the hero's sword. Three youths carry his polished bows: the bounding of five dogs is before him. His warriors move on, at a distance, admiring the steps of the king. Stately was the son of Larthmor! but his soul was dark. Dark as the troubled face of the moon, when it foretells the storms.

We rose on the heath before the king; he stopt in the midst of his course. His warriors gathered around, and a gray-haired bard advanced. "Whence are the sons of the strangers?" begun the bard. "The children of the unhappy come to Berrathon; to the sword of car-borne Uthal. He spreads no feast in his hall: the blood of strangers is on his streams. If from Selma's walls ye come, from the mossy walls of Fingal, chuse three youths to go to your king to tell of the fall of his people. Perhaps the hero may come and pour his blood on Uthal's sword; so shall the fame of Finthormo arise, like the growing tree of the vale."

"Never will it rise, O bard," I said in the pride of my wrath. "He would shrink in the presence of Fingal, whose eyes are the flames of death. The son of Comhal comes, and the kings vanish in his presence; they are rolled together, like mist, by the breath of his rage. Shall three tell to Fingal,

gal, that his people fell? Yes! they may tell it
bard? but his people shall fall with fame."

I stood in the darkness of my strength: Toscar
drew his sword at my side. The foe came on like
a stream: the mingled sound of death arose. Man
took man, shield met shield; steel mixed its beams
with steel. Darts hiss through air; spears ring on
mails; and swords on broken bucklers bound. As
the noise of an aged grove beneath the roaring
wind, when a thousand ghosts break the trees by
night, such was the din of arms. But Uthal fell
beneath my sword; and the sons of Berrathon fled.
It was then I saw him in his beauty, and the tear
hung in my eye. "Thou art fallen, young tree,"
I said, "with all thy beauty round thee. Thou
art fallen on thy plains, and the field is bare. The
winds come from the desart, and there is no sound
in thy leaves! Lovely art thou in death, son of
car-borne Larthmor."

Nina-thoma sat on the shore, and heard the
sound of battle. She turned her red eyes on Leth-
mal the gray-haired bard of Selma, for he had remained on the coast, with the daughter of Torthoma. "Son of the times of old!" she said, "I
hear the noise of death. Thy friends have met
with Uthal, and the chief is low! O that I had
remained on the rock, inclosed with the tumbling
waves!

waves! Then would my foul be fad, but his death would not reach my ear. Art thou fallen on thy heath, O fon of high Finthormo! thou didſt leave me on a rock, but my foul was full of thee. Son of high Finthormo! art thou fallen on thy heath?"

She roſe pale in her tears, and faw the bloody fhield of Uthal; fhe faw it in Offian's hand; her ſteps were diſtracted on the heath. She flew; fhe found him; fhe fell. Her foul came forth in a figh. Her hair is ſpread on his face. My burfting tears defcend. A tomb aroſe on the unhappy; and my fong was heard. "Reft, haplefs children of youth! at the noife of that moſſy ſtream. The virgins will fee your tomb, at the chafe, and turn away their weeping eyes. Your fame will be in the fong; the voice of the harp will be heard in your praiſe. The daughters of Selma fhall hear it; and your renown fhall be in other lands. Reft, children of youth, at the noife of the moſſy ſtream."

Two days we remained on the coaſt. The heroes of Berrathon convened. We brought Larthmor to his halls; the feaſt of fhells was ſpread. The joy of the aged was great; he looked to the arms of his fathers; the arms which he left in his hall, when the pride of Uthal aroſe. We were renowned before Larthmor, and he bleſſed the chiefs of Morven; but he knew not that his fon was

was low, the stately strength of Uthal. They had told that he had retired to the woods, with the tears of grief; they had told it, but he was silent in the tomb of Rothma's heath."

On the fourth day we raised our sails to the roar of the northern wind. Larthmor came to the coast, and his bards raised the song. The joy of the king was great, he looked to Rothma's gloomy heath; he saw the tomb of his son; and the memory of Uthal rose. "Who of my heroes," he said, " lies there? He seems to have been of the kings of spears? Was he renowned in my halls, before the pride of Uthal rose? Ye are silent, sons of Berrathon, is the king of heroes low? My heart melts for thee, O Uthal! though thy hand was against thy father! O that I had remained in the cave! that my son had dwelt in Finthormo! I might have heard the tread of his feet, when he went to the chase of the boar. I might have heard his voice on the blast of my cave. Then would my soul be glad: but now darkness dwells in my halls."

Such were my deeds, son of Alpin, when the arm of my youth was strong; such were ⁹ the actions of Toscar, the car-borne son of Conloch. But Toscar is on his flying cloud; and I am alone at Lutha: my voice is like the last sound of the wind, away to Fingal's airy hall. Bear it to Fingal's hall, that he may hear the voice of his son; the voice of him that praised the mighty.

The blast of the north opens thy gates, O king, and I behold thee sitting on mist, dimly gleaming in all thine arms. Thy form now is not the terror of the valiant: but like a watery cloud; when we see the stars behind it, with their weeping eyes. Thy shield is like the aged moon: thy sword a vapour half-kindled with fire. Dim and feeble is the chief, who travelled in brightness before. But thy steps' are on the winds of the desart, and the storms darken in thy hand. Thou takest the sun in thy wrath, and hidest him in thy clouds. The sons of little men are afraid; and a thousand showers descend. But when thou comest forth in thy mildness; the gale of the morning is near thy course. The sun laughs in his blue fields; and the gray stream winds in its valley. The bushes shake their green heads in the wind. The roes bound towards the desart.

But there is a murmur in the heath! the stormy winds abate! I hear the voice of Fingal. Long has it been absent from mine ear! "Come, Ossian, come away," he says: "Fingal has received his fame. We passed away, like flames that had shone for a season, our departure was in renown. Though the

the plains of our battles are dark and silent; our fame is in the four gray stones. The voice of Ossian has been heard; and the harp was strung in Selma. Come Ossian, come away," he says, " and fly with thy fathers on clouds."

And come I will, thou king of men! the life of Ossian fails. I begin to vanish on Cona; and my steps are not seen in Selma. Beside the stone of Mora I shall fall asleep. The winds whistling in my gray hair shall not waken me. Depart on thy wings, O wind: thou canst not disturb the rest of the bard. The night is long, but his eyes are heavy; depart thou rustling blast.

But why art thou sad, son of Fingal? Why grows the cloud of thy soul? The chiefs of other times are departed; they have gone without their fame. The sons of future years shall pass away; and another race arise. The people are like the waves of ocean: like the leaves of woody Morven, they pass away in the rustling blast, and other leaves lift their green heads. Did thy beauty last, O Ryno?' Stood the strength of car-borne Oscar? Fingal himself passed away; and the halls of his fathers forgot his steps. And shalt thou remain, aged bard! when the mighty have failed? But my fame shall remain, and grow like the oak of Morven; which lifts its broad head to the storm, and rejoices in the course of the wind.

NOTES

NOTES ON BERRATHON:

ª Lutha, *swift stream.*

ᵇ Mal-mhina, *soft or lovely brow. Mh* in the Gallic language has the same sound with *v* in English.

ᶜ Tradition has not handed down the name of this son of Alpin. His father was one of Fingal's principal bards, and he appears himself to have had a poetical genius.

ᵈ Ossian speaks. He calls Malvina a beam of light, and continues the metaphor throughout the paragraph.

ᵉ The description of this ideal palace of Fingal is very poetical, and agreeable to the notions of those times, concerning the state of the deceased, who were supposed to pursue, after death, the pleasures and employments of their former life. The situation of Ossian's heroes, in their separate state, if not entirely happy, is more agreeable, than the notions of the ancient Greeks concerning their departed heroes. See Hom. Odyss. l. 11.

ᶠ Ossian; who had a great friendship for Malvina, both on account of her love for his son Oscar, and her attention to his own poems.

ᵍ That is, the young virgins who sung the funeral elegy over her tomb.

ʰ Ossian, by way of disrespect, calls those who succeeded the heroes whose actions he celebrates, *the sons of little men.* Tradition is entirely silent concerning what passed in the north, immediately after the death of Fingal and all his heroes; but it appears from that term of ignominy just mentioned, that the actions of their successors were not to be compared to those of the renowned Fingalians.

To L.

ceased, who, it was supposed, had the command of the winds and storms, but in combat were not a match for valiant men.

* Ryno, the son of Fingal, who was killed in Ireland, in the war against Swaran, [Fing. B. V.] was remarkable for the beauty of his person, his swiftness and great exploits. Minvane, the daughter of Morni, and sister to Gaul, was in love with Ryno. The following is her lamentation over her lover.

She blushing said, from Morven's rocks, bends over the darkly-rolling sea. She saw the youths in all their arms. Where, Ryno, where art thou?

Our dark looks told that he was low! That pale the hero flew on clouds! That in the grass of Morven's hills, his feeble voice was heard in wind!

And is the son of Fingal fallen, on Ullin's mossy plains? Strong was the arm that conquered him! Ah me! I am alone!

Alone I will not be, ye winds! that lift my dark-brown hair. My sighs will not long mix with your stream; for I must sleep with Ryno.

I see thee not with beauty's steps returning from the chase. The night is round Minvane's love; and silence dwells with Ryno.

Where are thy dogs, and where thy bow? Thy shield that was so strong? Thy sword like heaven's descending fire? The bloody spear of Ryno.

I see them mixed in thy ship; I see them stained with blood. No arms are in thy narrow hall, O darkly-dwelling Ryno!

When will the morning come, and say, arise, thou king of spears! arise, the hunters are abroad. The hinds are near thee, Ryno!

Away, thou fair-haired morning, away! the slumbering king hears thee not! The hinds bound over his narrow tomb! for death dwells round young Ryno.

But I will tread softly, my king! and steal to the bed of thy repose. Minvane will lie in silence, near her slumbering Ryno.

The maids shall seek me; but they shall not find me; they shall follow my departure with songs. But I will not hear you, O maids; I sleep with fair-haired Ryno.

END OF VOLUME FIRST.

www.ingramcontent.com/pod-product-compliance
Lightning Source LLC
Chambersburg PA
CBHW032352230426
43672CB00007B/678

9783741139963